Bruce Dessau was the pop columnist of *The Listener* for three years. He writes regularly for the *Guardian* and *Time Out*. His favourite song by George Michael is 'Everything She Wants'.

Bruce Dessau

GEORGE MICHAEL
The Making of a Superstar

PAN BOOKS
London, Sydney and Auckland

First published 1989 by Sidgwick & Jackson Ltd
This revised edition with a new epilogue published 1991 by Pan Books Ltd
Cavaye Place, London SW10 9PG
9 8 7 6 5 4 3 2 1
© Bruce Dessau 1989
Epilogue © Bruce Dessau 1991
ISBN 0 330 31486 6

Typeset by Hewer Text Composition Services, Edinburgh
Printed in England by Clays Ltd, St Ives plc

For my Parents

Contents

*I would like to thank everyone who helped out
in the writing of this book.*

1

Everything But the Pool

George Michael and Andrew Ridgeley are preparing to perform together as Wham! for the last time. On an unusually flaming June afternoon, the temperature in North London has risen into the mid-90s. In the packed arena, perspiring fans of the band are doused by jets of water bestowed upon them by the cheerful security team.

Backstage George Michael is understandably nervous. This is the most important day in twenty-three years and five days of life. Four years of fame have been leading up to this day. Wham!'s final concert, the culmination of George's life so far, is about to get underway. More importantly still, he knows that from today he has to go it alone; no longer will Andrew Ridgeley be alongside him to draw off the most intense press attention. Furthermore, today is the day he bids a tearful farewell to teeny stardom; from here, if he is to survive where so many of his peers have failed, he has to shift up a gear and move into adult orbit. Moral support is offered by his family. His mother, Lesley, and his father, Jack, look on proudly as he sits in his dressing room while his sisters Melanie and Yioda tend to his hair and clothes.

As George collects his thoughts there is a disturbance outside. George's friend Elton John is making merry with his entourage outside his own mobile caravan. There is the

1

reassuring sound of pop chatter as the glitterati of the entertainment business, old and new, gather round the stocky
superstar. Rod Stewart drinks champagne with his col-
league Ronnie Lane, while Duran Duran's Simon Le Bon
and some refugees from Frankie Goes To Hollywood sway
in unison, suggesting that they have already enjoyed their
share of 'shampoo'. The Kemp brothers from Spandau
Ballet 'tut tut' at their friends' behaviour, but eventually
succumb to the lure of the liquor and totter away.

George Michael is trying to keep a clear head amid
the junket. Video games on the machines set up for the
occasion help a little, but the heat distracts his attention.
Instead he decides to watch support act Gary Glitter on one
of the video monitors. Chatting with Andrew, they agree
that the humidity is overwhelming and they just can't relax.
Fortunately Elton John has been around a bit; knowing
what the day would be like he seems to have thought of
everything. According to the *Sun*, he has brought his own
well-stocked bar along with his 60ft mobile caravan and,
most perspicaciously, a portable swimming pool. George
looks at Andrew. Andrew looks at George. The tension
of the occasion is too much. There is only one thing to
do. They strip down to swimming costumes and take a
plunge.

Revived by the cool, clear water they summon the waiter
and spend the run-up to their last hours as Wham! sipping
cocktails by the pool. His nerves steadied, George returns
to his dressing room so that his sister Melanie can fine-tune
his hair. Then he is ready to face his public. . . .

Reports of Wham!'s farewell concert made great capital
out of the bacchanalian revelries taking place backstage.
In particular the *Sun* delighted in describing the poolside
activities that were part of George Michael's build-up to
his performance as if they were a scene straight out of an
episode of *Dallas*, even calling the provider of the service
'Pool Party Elton' in their headline.

There was a pool backstage at Wembley Stadium that day. It was a children's paddling pool. About six feet long, four feet wide and six inches deep. The image doesn't seem quite the same now.

The story of George Michael is a story of illusion. But an illusion that eventually became a reality. It is the story of the unholy relationship that pop developed with the press in the 1980s, one of misinformation and manipulation: popaganda.

But popaganda involves more than this. In its hero, George Michael, it charts the rise of a new kind of pop star. One who fights fiercely to keep his private life private. One who controls his own destiny but tries to find time to ring his parents every day. One who wouldn't drive a Cadillac into a hotel swimming pool even if the damage was tax-deductible. Popaganda is the story of a revolt into style without the revolt.

'If you tell a lie, tell a big one. If you repeat it often enough people will believe it.'

Dr Joseph Goebbels

2

Childhood

George Michael's youth was singularly uneventful. His formative years gave no indication of a future different from any other child born into the English middle classes of the early 1960s. At school he excelled at neither studies nor sports. He was not particularly introverted, nor a charismatic extrovert. His most notable eccentricity was a certain fussiness about food, which saw him taking peanut butter and jam sandwiches to school rather than suffer the homogenous dining hall stodge.

The early education of Georgios Kyriacos Panayiotou, as he was known, was interrupted by his family's constant upward mobility. As his Greek-Cypriot restaurateur father prospered, they moved further and further north from their urban roots; Georgios' struggle to make lasting, character-forming relationships with his peers was continually thwarted by his parents' insistence on bettering themselves. By 1975 they seemed to have come to rest in the half rustic, half suburban surrounds of Radlett in Hertfordshire – though the grudging Georgios sometimes had other ideas. On winter mornings he would bury himself deep inside his coat and vow that if he ever made any money he would get out of England and find somewhere where the climate was more agreeable.

Georgios was born on 25 June 1963, a year that was becoming a watershed in British social history, Philip Larkin's *annus mirabilis*. In August there was an uproar when the BBC extended its broadcasting hours to midnight

rather than 11.15 p.m. There was less furore over the introduction of voluntary breath tests. Parental consent was still
required for anyone under the age of twenty-one wishing to
marry, while in Bradford the Marriage Guidance Council
appointed an officer called Mr Love. One of the classics of
British cinema that year was *Billy Liar*, starring a youthful
Tom Courtney as the humble undertaker's assistant who
dreamed of a great, ennobled future and a place in the
history books.

In politics, the Secretary of State for War, John Profumo,
resigned after sharing the bed of a call girl, Christine Keeler,
a breach of public morality and security that nearly brought
down the Conservative Government. In the event, thirteen
years of Tory rule were ended a year later as the new
premier, Harold Wilson, officially ushered in the Swinging
Sixties.

Of course, this epoch really began in 1963 with the emer-
gence of the Beatles as full-blown stars with a succession
of major hits kicked off by 'Please Please Me'. They had
paid their dues in the dives of Hamburg and the cellars
of the Cavern in Liverpool and were now reaping the
rewards. They were even preparing to conquer the States,
in those days something of a musical coals-to-Newcastle
job, welcomed amid the collective grief that followed the
assassination of President Kennedy that November.

Born in Margaret Thatcher's constituency of Finchley and
Friern Barnet, Georgios' earliest memories are as scattered
and as innocuous as any child's. His earliest recollection is
of seeing the goats at Whipsnade Zoo at the age of four.
At six he had his first crush on primary school teacher
Mrs Wilson; but then who didn't?

School was pleasant enough despite the lack of geographical stability, but Georgios' best memories are reserved for
regular holidays in Cyprus, where he stayed at his father's
home village near Famagusta. There he amused himself by
hunting down exotic pink lizards and newts. But he also
revealed a darker side. Escaping to the sun had its *longueur*,

and he relieved the boredom with occasional shoplifting sprees, nurturing a reputation as a mini-master criminal. He started with sweets and ice cream, then graduated to toy cars. When he was finally caught his father dealt out swift and severe punishment to the pint-sized car thief. It was the only time his father ever hit him, and it left an indelible impression on more than his backside.

Back in chilly England, Georgios' holidays consisted of trips to the Kent coast, to Birchington where he used to stay with friends of his mother and go on adventures to the funfair in Margate. It would not be unreasonable to suggest that Georgios' childhood was one of consummate suburban spoiling. As his parents' fortunes turned upwards, so Georgios reaped the material benefits. The boy was indulged by his mother to compensate for the frequent absences of his father, who was invariably out working his way up in the restaurant business. His parents were keen to save enough to move on from the cramped flat above a launderette at 73 Church Lane in Finchley that the baby Georgios was brought home to. By the late 1960s they were already on the move, first to the commuter suburb of Burnt Oak. With two sisters, Melanie (three years older) and Yioda (five years older), for close company at home, he soon got to know and understand women. As the only son, Georgios was rather indulged by his parents, and by his sisters who exercised their maternal instincts on the baby brother, and he soon developed a healthy respect for the opposite sex. The close but non-sexual presence of women was totally natural to the growing boy.

Surprisingly, Georgios' Greek-Cypriot culture played little part in his childhood. His father worked so hard that George heard little Greek in the house as he played with his English mother, Lesley. Occasionally, however, the large extended family would get together for a local wedding, and Georgios would find himself caught up in the ethnic enthusiasm of the occasion, proudly watching as his father danced effortlessly to traditional bouzouki music, glasses of retsina balanced precariously on his head.

As the Swinging Sixties fizzled into the sagging seventies, one of the evolving industries was gadgetry. The silicon chip was about to mark the dawn of computer culture, while cassette machines had already come onto the market to replace reel-to-reel tape recorders. They may have looked like some flotsam from an Apollo mission, but one of the big attractions was their portability. Another was the ease with which you could make your own recordings. Just set up the mike, shut out any extraneous noises and you, too, could be a recording star. Amid a fierce price war, mail-order ads sang the praises of the devices in the Sunday papers. Send off the princely sum of £13.99 (plus p&p), and in twenty-eight days one of the technological wonders would be yours.

If there was one significant event in Georgios' life before the age of ten, it was when he was presented with a portable cassette recorder by his parents on his seventh birthday. Georgios Panayiotou was transfixed by pop music and now he possessed the tools with which to entertain his fantasies of fame. He would pass the time recording his favourite songs from the radio. As with many of his contemporaries, top of the list were teen stars the Jackson Five and David Cassidy. One game was to record his own voice over the tracks and indulge in delusions of grandeur.

As Georgios grew up, he watched his father Kyriacos, 'Jack', repeat a process of assimilation and gentrification experienced many times before by other waves of immigrants. Having married a working-class Englishwoman, Lesley, they were part of the *nouveau riche* middle classes by the seventies. They were not the first generation to adopt this *modus vivendi*. Jewish refugees from the last war and beyond had settled in the East End of London, but as they worked hard and prospered they chose to ripple out to the leafier, more opulent enclaves of Golders Green and

Totteridge. Later on in the seventies and early eighties it would be Asians, many of whom had fled the barbarity of Idi Amin's despotic Ugandan regime, who undertook a diaspora into the surrounds of London.

A Greek population had existed in North London many years before Georgios' birth; the roots that had been put down by his antecedents could be observed by strolling down Green Lane in Haringey and seeing posters advertising traditional Greek music nights and the proliferation of kebab houses that had swept across England but seemed to be cloned from just one such emporium somewhere close to Finsbury Park.

Greek Cypriots had been arriving in larger numbers since the Turks invaded their island in 1974, but George's father had arrived as a young man with six brothers back in the 1950s and had set about the process of social advancement by working as a waiter. Georgios had the best of both cultures. He developed a strong-willed, typically Mediterranean, fearsome loyalty to his family whilst realizing that similar bonds could be formed with new acquaintances. Nevertheless, his father's continual absences led his natural empathies to lie with his indigenous environment; he found that he had more in common with his English friends than with his Greek cousins, and the anglicized name George caught on easily at school. With success came that march ever northwards – from Finchley to Burnt Oak and Edgware. The seventies signalled a boom time for the Panayiotous. Jack opened a succession of restaurants and the material rewards of his industry became self-evident. The decidedly upmarket Radlett marked their real entry into the *nouveau riche*, and Jack acquired a racehorse. The family house was extremely spacious and set in a nice quasi-rural area; when you went there you couldn't move for the displays of ostentatious affluence.

George's itinerant childhood had dogged his education, and after a year at Kingsbury High School, his family's final move to Radlett meant that he started a new year, aged twelve, at a new comprehensive establishment, Bushey Meads School, in September 1975. Placed in the top stream it was not long before he encountered Andrew Ridgeley. Born on 26 January 1963, Ridgeley was only five months older than George but already exhibited a world-weary nonchalance characteristic of the average sixteen-year-old. He too was a new arrival in Hertfordshire, with a similarly exotic background. Ridgeley had an assurance and *élan* that seemed destined to shunt him into the limelight, in contrast to the pop-obsessive George, whose disinclination to excel at any academic activity suggested to his franker teachers that he would not amount to much.

Born in Windlesham, Surrey, Andrew John Ridgeley had an English mother and an Egyptian father, who worked for the local camera firm. Where George's father had passed on a cheerful demeanour that seemed destined to result in fat, Andrew's Egyptian blood had presented him with sultry matinée idol looks, his dark brown eyes and matching hair conjuring up a prepubescent Rudolph Valentino. As is often the case with attractive children, he had developed a sharp sense of style in dress and an unhealthy air of cool. This, combined with his excellence at sports – particularly football – helped to make him one of the better-known boys of his year. His infamy also accounted for an endless list of nicknames that he was to acquire over the years, some more affectionate than others, some self-explanatory, others better left unexplained: Ab, Nodge, Ange, Frab, Normal, Pongo, Steamer, Gimpey and The Wally. Later on Rocky was added, inspired by Ridgeley's uncanny resemblance to Sylvester Stallone.

Symbolically, Ridgeley and Panayiotou's fateful, near mythical, meeting took place at play rather than in the classroom. During break, the ritualistic and typically lout-ish school game of 'King of the Wall' was in progress. It involved ascending the school wall and retaining your place there as 'king'. The cocksure Ridgeley had comfortably repelled all climbers when he taunted the new podgy boy into daring to usurp him. In this somewhat prophetic fable, Ridgeley soon found himself tumbling to the asphalt. George's puppy fat may have blighted his adolescence later on, but here it enabled him to hurl his hefty frame into the svelte champion and send him crashing.

Legend would have it that this moment sealed a friendship that would last – with certain adjustments in the power balance – to the present day. For the time being, the incident earned the new arrival some invaluable kudos since he had silenced the class loudmouth and taken him down a few pegs. Something in Ridgeley's adolescent psyche had made him aware that this ungainly duckling's brains could complement his own hollow brawn and they became firm friends, George acquiring the abridged nomenclature of Yog.

They soon discovered a shared compulsive interest in pop music. Seated next to each other in class they would scour the charts to follow the progress of their favourites. By now George had relinquished his love of teeny-pop; while the Top Twenty was clogged up with the crass glam-rock of Gary Glitter and tartan terrors the Bay City Rollers, his new heroes were the latest exponents of the classically well-crafted pop song, Elton John and Queen, also favoured by his nascent soul mate. Mini-seminars were held each week on the merits of the previous evening's edition of *Top of the Pops*, and Saturday afternoons would see them rushing out to buy their singles and LPs. When George did not have the money he would tape his friends' records and was not averse to stealing cassette covers from the local shop to make his versions seem authentic.

Although their friendship was a firm one, it had its moments of turbulence. Andrew considered George 'a bit of a wimp' and clearly felt superior to his new friend. George, meanwhile, hoped that some of Andrew's allure would rub off if he continued as his stout sidekick. But the friendship was no mere Don Quixote – Sancho Panza set-up. The twosome developed a hilarious rapport that swiftly got them known around school. Each had a profound influence on the other. As George later reflected in *Rolling Stone*: 'I suppose we spent all the time aspiring to be different parts of each other.' As their social lives enlarged, minor delinquency sealed their friendship – gatecrashing parties, getting drunk and trying to get off with girls. After each escapade George would look a mess, while Andrew always seemed to remain clean and cool.

In the Panayiotou household there was concern about their son's future. In an effort to push George into a pursuit that might settle him down his parents paid for violin lessons, though he was more interested in playing the drums he had been given for his twelfth birthday. Furthermore, his mother considered Andrew a disruptive influence and did not like him visiting the house. But as much as his parents tried to keep him on the straight and narrow, George was already deciding on a different direction.

The autumn of 1976 saw a new type of music emerge in London. Punk rock exploded onto the music scene, and the caustic cacophony of the Sex Pistols and their ilk was soon rippling out and being felt in the suburbs. George remained unmoved, finding his musical course a long way from the three-chord thrashes of the spiky-topped bands that were being formed all around by people little more than a handful of years older than him. Pricked by the first pangs of sexual desire, George felt that the punk ethos did not fit in with the way he wanted to live: 'It was a matter of sexuality as opposed to individuality. Punk was definitely not sexy. But I did understand at the same time that it was very healthy for the music scene.' His middle-class cosseting and relatively tolerant parents, combined with a burgeoning anti-intellectual soul-boy stance, left him with little time or sympathy for the New Wave: 'I had nothing to rebel against . . . I was far more interested in going out and strutting my funky stuff, seeing how many girls you

11

could pull. There were very few pretty punk girls. They were usually dead ugly.' Even at his most chubby, George had few of the adolescent insecurities that led so many of a similar age to find an affinity in the existential angst of punk.

There were also geographical factors. By the time punk reached Radlett via the charts and the media blitz of 1977, it had been reduced to little more than a symbolic sneer. It could hardly compete with the dance music that had dictated the styles of suburban youth since the sixties mod era, when scooters had given kids the mobility to frequent West End clubs and check out visiting R&B stars.

Andrew, however, latched more readily onto punk. He was an ardent supporter of the Jam, while one of the earliest melodies he picked out on his guitar was 'A Forest' by the Cure. Andrew always seemed to flit from phase to phase, whereas George was more purposeful and direct. For a while Andrew considered a career as a soccer star, but that was scuppered when he became a skateboard fanatic and suffered various injuries, including a broken nose, in typically irresponsible feats of derring-do.

Towards the end of 1977 George was making his initial tentative forays into full-blown teen romance. His first love was based, quite sensibly, on a mutual enthusiasm for discos. He later recalled the disingenuous genesis of their relationship: 'We got together after a bit of snogging at a party. I knew she had amorous designs on me because she kept crying on my shoulder.' He marked the landmark of the fourth week of their romance by buying her a copy of Chic's 'Dance Dance Dance', but a month later she had lost interest. There were also brief snogging dalliances with others – *de rigueur* within his age group. At this stage, however, sex and romance were not necessarily opposite sides of the same coin: George once claimed to having lost his virginity in unimaginably sordid style at the tender age of thirteen to an older woman. This is an incident he later drew a veil over, suggesting that his original boast was

no more than youthful braggadocio, falling in line with
Wham!'s early Don Juanish myth-manufacturing.

If punk had become part of the establishment by 1978,
it still had a long way to go before it overhauled disco
and soul in terms of sales. Punk was sold on the basis of
rebellion, which tends to be a passing phase, while disco
was marketed as a vinyl supplement to sex, which remains
pretty constant among the record-buying public. And in
John Travolta the disco brigade found a role model who
was infinitely more appealing to their romantic sensibilities
than Johnny Rotten. Travolta combined the smouldering
looks of James Dean, the moves of the Temptations, and
the peacock strut that every narcissistic soul-boy aspired
to.

Saturday Night Fever may have been located in New
York, but it helped to spawn a thriving suburban disco
scene in England, as clubs opened up around the metropolis
to meet the demands of a dance-crazed generation of
soul-boys. Ridgeley deserted punk in favour of this new,
more comfortable cult while George divided his nights
between the clubs and retaining his links with the Greek
Cypriot community. Taking advantage of his precocious
size and premature stubble, George joined Andrew in
serving their social apprenticeship on the local disco circuit
where they devised dance routines which would later stand
them in considerable stead.

By now George's association with the suave Ridgeley
was beginning to bring his own physical shortcomings
into sharp relief. Stricken with myopia and partial colour-
blindness (which thwarted his early ambitions to become a
pilot), he had to wear glasses that cruelly resembled milk-
bottle bottoms. Demands were made on his doting parents
to buy him contact lenses, which the family optician,
although advising against them for someone as young as
fifteen, finally acceded to. But the removal of the spectacles
only revealed another of George's ego-shaking adolescent
hang-ups – a huge pair of bushy seagull wings attempting

to pass muster as eyebrows. On the advice of his sisters, and with their expert tutelage, he mastered the use of tweezers.

Like David Bowie, whose 1973 album *Aladdin Sane* he particularly cherished, George knew that changing his appearance would alter not just how he was perceived by others, but his self-perception too. Spots remained a handicap. Creams and lotions were applied to keep the worst outbursts at bay, but even in the early days of Wham! friends recall him suffering sporadically from serious attacks of acne. The only compensation was his Greek ancestry: he sprouted facial hair in his early teens which helped to conceal most epidermal blemishes. In later years he would maintain that the only Greek thing about him was his hirsuteness.

Gradually, George Michael was evolving. Fate and lucky timing played their part in the transformation. When Liverpool and England footballer Kevin Keegan – another figure whose success owed as much to effort and graft as it did to talent – opted for a curly perm in the mid-seventies, he set a trend in men's hair fashions which George was able to embrace inconspicuously. The untameable frizzy mop of dark hair that had haunted him became his crowning glory overnight. With an outward appearance concomitant with a new inner confidence, he broadened his horizons, increasing the number of trips he made with Andrew to the clubs of nearby Watford and Harrow.

As if by magic, George started to get invited to teenage parties and could retire from the gatecrashing fraternity. Romances blossomed with increasing regularity. Hardly the classic adolescent Adonis, however, one school contemporary remembers him as 'just really nice and friendly', unlike Andrew, whose youthful arrogance, it appears, made him as many enemies as pals.

George still lived in the shadow of Ridgeley's swaggering proto-manhood. One night, on their way home from a particularly disastrous party in the summer of 1979, a disconsolate, drunken, sixteen-year-old George spilled out his insecurities to his best friend, before proceeding to spill the alcoholic contents of his stomach over his garish green trousers. It was the first time he had ever got really drunk, and as he squatted on the grass he started to cry. No one had commented on his new trousers! No one fancied him! He was much too ugly! So passionate was the outburst that he managed to burst a blood vessel in one of his eyes. There was still some way to go before the transformation was complete.

Andrew was only human, too. At a different party he expressed more than a twinge of insecurity when George told him, *in vino veritas*, that his mum didn't like him and didn't want him round any more. In a scene of heartstring-tugging humility, Andrew followed George round the party crying, 'Yog, you're my best mate, you mustn't let your mother split us up like this.' These semi-sober emotional outbursts helped to strengthen the duo's resolve to stick together through thick and thin.

While George got to grips with the painful processes of academic life at Bushey Meads, Andrew deserted the regimentation of school after O levels in 1979 to move to Cassio College to take his A levels part-time. George's parents, like any self-respecting upwardly mobile couple, put pressure on their increasingly wayward son to continue at school. They were still convinced, not incorrectly, that Ridgeley was leading him astray, particularly when they heard George talk of forming a band with his friend. George's sixth form studies were also becoming increasingly part-time as he started to spend more and more of his days lounging around at Andrew's house in Chiltern Avenue plotting their future.

Towards the end of the seventies, music was changing again. George's beloved soul was evolving into jazz-funk, a more obtuse, more thought-through development in dance music, the equivalent of rock and roll ten years earlier when it was turning into meandering, introspective progressive rock. Jazz-funk now ruled the dance floors, but it was less spontaneous than soul, rendering pure pop-disco redundant and making a virtue of complex instrumental breaks. In England, bands like Level 42 and Shakatak excelled at this kind of technically proficient but uninspired sound, a style that became the preserve of a unique soul-boy sub-culture, of people who tended to drive customized Ford Cortinas with a pair of furry dice hanging in front of the windscreen. These were marginally less adventurous, older soul fans, perhaps on the verge of settling down, and they came from a tangibly more working-class background than George and Andrew who were still young and energetic enough to demand some-thing with more spirit. They found it in ska, as Coventry band the Specials triggered off the 2 Tone/ska revival with the single 'Gangsters' in the summer of 1979.

That summer, with O levels behind them, the duo had a stay of execution from parental demands of aca-demic excellence and were able to work off their excess adrenalin in a never-ending series of parties. With 2 Tone resuscitating the punk ethic of simplicity, the duo latched onto the idea that anyone could be in a band. Amid the latest scenes of pop dementia, talk turned to reality as the friends decided that they too could get a recording contract and become stars overnight. Hastily they formed a group called the Executive with a floating line-up of friends, Jamie Gould, Tony Bywaters, Andrew Leaver and David Mortimer, roping in Andrew's younger brother Paul on drums. By this time George had put aside his own percussive ambitions in favour of a more upfront role. But this was little comfort to his mother, who was reluctant to let them practise at his home. Eventually a deal was struck, and rehearsals alternated between his house and Andrew's; Andrew's parents seemed relieved that at last their chaotic son was becoming committed to something.

Before long, Lesley Panayiotou's patience broke. She was so perturbed by her son's growing obsession with music that one day she told him he couldn't rehearse at home any more. An indignant response stopped her dead in her tracks: 'If you stop me doing this, I'll leave school.' From then on, there were no more parental problems.

The Executive made an ignominious début at the Bushey Meads School Scout hut on Bonfire Night 1979. Excited by the enthusiastic reception for their simple ska here, they proceeded to gig as much as they could locally, albeit never graduating very far beyond shambolic school and youth club shows, which put the emphasis firmly on having fun. But their ambitions did extend to sending out a crude demo tape which would have been unlikely to secure them a record deal, even if it had been listened to by the most open-minded of moguls. The sort of material they were producing at the time was exemplified by one track unimaginatively entitled 'Rude Boy'. Post-2 Tone luminaries the Beat had set up their own label, Go Feet Records, but they, too, gave the Executive's efforts short shrift, dismissing these latest pretenders as feeble Specials copyists.

Anonymous bands cold-calling with demo tapes rarely reap dividends to warrant the cost of postage, and the Executive soon boasted a dossier of thanks-but-no-thanks notes from those companies honourable enough to reply. As is often the way, George Panayiotou eventually sought favour through a friend – a friend who was later to make, and ultimately conspire to break, Wham!.

Mark David Dean's family lived at 25 Chiltern Avenue, only a few doors away from Ridgeley, but he had attended school further afield at Rickmansworth. At nineteen, Dean was three years older than Andrew and had little more than a nodding acquaintance with him, although occasionally the two would bump into each other at the local pub, the Three Crowns. It was an age gap that seemed like a chasm at the time. While Ridgeley was still getting a thrill out of under-age drinking in Bushey and embarking on a fraught relationship with local girl Shirlie Holliman, Dean was already busy making his way up the record industry's greasy pole. The only characteristic they shared was naked ambition; but while Ridgeley was still a defiantly unfocused dabbler, Dean had already found his *métier* in the music industry's back rooms and boardrooms. Having worked his way up from the bottom as a school-leaver, he now had a job with publishing company And Son. Dean's intimate acquaintanceship with the post-punk mêlée had helped him to make his name signing up leading mod band Secret Affair and a number of lesser outfits that emerged in their wake. As Secret Affair notched up a sequence of hits, including the stomping Motown terrace chant 'Time for Action', Dean began to scale the corporate ladder. He was also becoming involved in the nascent West End club scene that was later to blossom as the New Romantic movement. As a favour to his mother more than to Andrew, Dean listened to the Executive's demo tape, but it made little impression on him. Even Dean, ever on the look-out for new talent, wrote off the first compositional efforts of George Michael: 'He must have always had talent, but his early Executive stuff was shit. He had to start believing in himself before he could write.'

With their ambitions coming to nothing, the Executive suffered motivational problems, and interest within the ranks fizzled out. Two days before a local college gig in autumn 1980 the rest of the band jumped ship and the Executive became a duo of George and Andrew. Rather than cancel the show, the nucleus decided to go through with it and just enjoy themselves. During the ramshackle set, Andrew chose to indulge in a rare outburst of cross-dressing, changing into a kilt with a bow in his hair. While George was still an awkward live performer grunting away and supplying the effort, Andrew was the driving force in terms of fun, panache, bravado and all-important assurance. But after a few more gigs there was still no glimmer of the success the pair would later find, and shows began to peter out along with the following for ska.

Aware of the impending threat of nine-to-five drudgery,

they continued to persevere at song-writing. As 2 Tone euphoria died down and they returned to their first love of fluid, simple soul, one of the songs they came up with was 'Careless Whisper', christened rather uncharitably by George's sister Melanie as 'Tuneless Whisper'. In the run up to A levels in the summer of 1981, studying and music vied for attention. George dropped out of his A level music class, tired of so much theory, and Andrew's one-day-a-week college course turned even more part-time as he and George started to go clubbing on a more regular basis.

The scene was in a state of transition. *The Face*, launched in May 1980, had shifted from its original post-punk 2 Tone axis and was beginning to cover the emerging New Romantic and soul scene. In its attention to the vagaries of fashion and lifestyle, *The Face* effectively set the agenda for the eighties, dictating styles and trends way beyond its initial musical brief. It heralded an era of dichotomy, when street credibility was accommodated within a new kind of careerism. Bands like the British Electric Foundation and Public Image Ltd adopted knowingly ironic corporate identities; the former's *Penthouse and Pavement* album expressed the ideological ambivalence in its title. The appropriation of downmarket subculture became the latest in upmarket business tactics. *The Face* itself went from being a glossy music fanzine to a hip *Harpers & Queen*, chock-full of essential grass-roots gossip for both proletarians and aspiring professionals, replete with an acreage of tittle-tattle from the battle zones of each successive style war.

Disco was beginning to bite back by now, and succinct, funky tracks like the Gap Band's 'Burn Rubber on Me', which charted in early 1981, recaptured George's attention. Yet, as the music was becoming more traditional, the clothes were becoming more outrageous. Amid the public coming-out of the New Romantic movement, George continued in his quest to be a style setter. He took great pride in claiming to be the first person to wear dungarees in Bushey, and boasted a pair of Chelsea Girl jeans he had bought from Shirlie Holliman. The friends were becoming more adventurous in their socializing, and forays were made into London to sample the delights of the most fashionable clubs, the Wag and the Camden Palace. The latter was a regular haunt on Thursday nights when the prime mover of the New Romantics, Steve Strange, would hold court at his 'Club For Heroes'. But George's local club was Bogarts in Harrow, where erstwhile professional cockney Gary Crowley spun a diet of American soul and a sprinkling of the Jam, punk's first pop superstars and fellow upholders of suburban rituals – in their case, the grail of mod.

In lanky front man Paul Weller, the Jam had a voluble, articulate spokesman who built up a powerful reputation as a youth figurehead through a succession of hits that combined powerhouse rock thrashes with intense neo-soul vocals. During the late seventies and early eighties Weller became increasingly politicized, speaking out regularly against the Tory Government and social issues. The Jam's first number one, 'Going Underground', in 1980 was a thinly veiled condemnation of nuclear weapons while 1982's 'A Town Called Malice' was a damning critique of urban deprivation under Thatcherism set to a thumping Motown beat. In many respects Weller seemed to be a spiritual first cousin of George yet they were never to see eye to eye. In later years Weller and George Michael thrashed out some of the principles of Red Wedge, the left-of-centre pop coalition formed to engage youngsters in political ideas, but George refused to join the group, considering Weller's idealism too naïve.

The lives of Paul Weller and George Michael have followed uncannily similar directions, only occasionally overlapping, but always echoing each other. Weller was also from an upwardly mobile, hard-working family from a satellite of London – in his case Woking in Surrey. Both chose to split up their groups at their commercial peaks. Both were to attempt a more mature version of the music with which they had made their names, though with varying degrees of success. Both are staunch supporters of nuclear disarmament and other left-wing causes, though they manifest their attitudes in fundamentally different ways. They even shared the bill – with divergent results as we shall see later – at the Royal Festival Hall Miners' Benefit of 1984. As Weller's star has fallen of late, Michael has remarked that Weller doesn't have quite the intelligence to carry through his beliefs. And finally the two have tended to overlap musically, sharing the same parochial flirtation with the soul-boy credo. And although the slightly older Weller made his name first, take a look at the Style Council's video for their single 'The Lodgers', made in 1985. The choreography of the two-man, two-woman line-up is reminiscent of an early Wham! show. Moreover, one of George's first backing singers, D. C. Lee, later left Wham! to sing with the Style Council and more recently gave birth to Weller's child.

In the summer of 1981, George put aside his dreams of stardom to face up to his A Levels, gaining two passes in English and Art. The recalcitrant Ridgeley had by this time all but abandoned his education, convinced in typically cavalier fashion that certificates were not the stuff that legends were made of. Already, differences were emerging. Even though George was still set on a pop career, he had tried to garner the safety net of some academic qualifications, albeit through residual academic ability rather than any effort on his part.

Ridgeley signed on the dole immediately. His suburban, middle-class approach to his putative poverty differed dramatically from events around the inner cities that summer. In July the Liverpool district of Toxteth was the scene of some of the worst riots in living memory. Shops were looted and property destroyed by unemployed working-class teenagers facing a distinctly unpleasurable lifetime of signing on. The northern insurgence went down in history as the first time CS gas was used on the British mainland, but the uprising was soon repeated in Brixton in South London, Handsworth in Birmingham and other centres of social deprivation and discontent; but the disturbances were smothered long before they reached Bushey, whose youth was more concerned with dressing up than revolt. As one of the London club slogans of the day prescribed: 'Dance, don't riot.'

Constantly in conflict with *arriviste* parents who were keen to see their only son fully ensconced in professional studies, George responded to his new life differently from Andrew and his poorer contemporaries. With his parents' ingrained attachment to the work ethic, the dole was a stigma. Andrew's industrious friend, now using the more comfortable name of George Panos, looked for work of any kind. His decision not to go into further education had led to a series of parental battles before an agreement was struck whereby he could pursue his pop fantasies for a while before settling down to either a professional career or a permanent involvement in his father's thriving restaurant business.

A series of jobs followed that summer, some more suitable than others, but all on a temporary basis. Three days' hard labour on a building site was enough for George, and he was sacked from British Home Stores for being scruffy. But he already had a vision of the kind of music he wanted to make. Stacking shelves to the accompaniment of bland, anonymous muzak and hearing other workers talk about what they had watched on television the previous night made him see that people going about their ordinary lives needed a certain amount of escapist fantasy to get through the day. In the next decade he was to do as much as *Dallas* and *Dynasty* to provide the ultimate escapist soundtrack of the eighties.

One of his better jobs was that of cinema usher. The pay was bad, but it meant he could sit through endless free viewings of *Saturday Night Fever*, studying the steps and paying careful attention to the smallest details of disco deportment. At one stage George thought he had found his milieu when he tried his hand at deejaying. But he ended up working a long way from the bright lights of the West End in some of suburbia's more sleazy dives and restaurants, where the crowd was more interested in the supper than the soundtrack. 'It was terrible,' George recalled. 'Half the time you got really obnoxious little restaurant managers who didn't know what the hell they were talking about, telling you to play the wrong stuff. The worst bit was when you said something and everyone in the restaurant turned round and looked at you. I felt like a prat!'

Once he managed to persuade Andrew to rise from his bed and go with him to get a Saturday job at Texas Homecare, where David Mortimer, their friend from the Executive days, was working. At the time, the height of their New Romantic period, Andrew was going through a particularly camp-trendy phase and turned up wearing eyeliner. George, ever conscious of the necessity to provide a pleasing front where work was concerned, coerced him into washing it off, but neither was given a job.

The friends often competed to outdo each other's dandyish excesses. Even in 1981, Andrew's appearance in cherry-coloured satin trousers with Red Indian-type plaited hair inspired by Adam Ant must have caused something of a stir amid the refinement of Radlett, topped only by George's frequent outings dressed as a timewarped Robin Hood, sporting a Sherwood green waistcoat and matching hat. The elder burghers of Bushey might have raised eyebrows and questioned the duo's sexual preferences, but their eccentricities did little to deter the female population of Hertfordshire.

Between the freewheeling fancy-dress sessions, the friends would sit at home and talk of a grand future success, never quite knowing whether the other really thought it would happen. They even managed to come

23

up with a name for their imaginary superband, culling it proudly from one of their own anthemic compositions. Having played around with the phrase 'Wham Bam' for a while, the song became known as 'Wham! Rap' and the protagonists became Wham! – with the all-important exclamation mark.

Wham! was a name that resonated in ways that George was unaware of. Pop art painter Roy Lichtenstein had added an extra 'a' for his explosive cartoon-picture *Whaam!* in 1963. George may have spotted a reproduction of the picture on *Top of the Pops* when Paul Weller sported a guitar embossed with a reproduction of the brash pop art graphics. There had been a vivid comic called *Wham* in the sixties, but the word had other connections too. Rock and roll impresario Jack Good had tried to follow the TV success of *Oh Boy!* with a number of short-lived pop programmes. One of them, consigned to broadcasting incidentals in 1960, was called Wham!!. In America, by the seventies, the word had become associated with an altogether different kind of youthful activity: WHAM was an acronym for 'Winning hearts and minds', the slogan that advised people to send drugs to draftees fighting in Vietnam, both to keep their spirits up and to distract them from the insanity of the war. Certainly this last connotation was one that George remained unaware of as he settled back in satisfaction, having found a suitable name for his pet project.

3

Boys Will Be Boys

When 1982 rolled round, Andrew was developing a reputation as a lounge lizard, while George was trying to
avoid his friend's parlous predicament and his parents'
admonitions by taking whatever casual jobs came his way.
Both continued to hatch plots about how they would soon
make musical history, but their partnership had its rockier
moments. For a while it seemed that George would make
pop history not with Ridgeley, but with ex-Executive
guitarist David Mortimer, a friend since the age of two.

In many respects Mortimer was remarkably similar
to Ridgeley. His family was less upwardly mobile than
George's, he was extremely loud and cocky and, most
important, he was desperate to be a pop star – in the
end, too desperate. His language was punctuated by the
most vulgar of epithets, and he could hardly have met
with Mr and Mrs Panayiotou's approval any more than
Ridgeley. But Mortimer played a mean acoustic guitar, and
he and George would occasionally make busking forays into
Leicester Square tube station to pick up some extra money
by performing Elton John and Carly Simon songs. For
George this was big adventure – with a purpose – but as
far as Jack Panayiotou was concerned, his only son was
falling in with a bad crowd and a bad lifestyle, and the
sooner he snapped out of it and moved on the better.
Jack tried to keep George on the rails by encouraging
him to help out behind the bar in one of his restaurants.
Unfortunately George proved to be something of a liability,

doling out over-generous measures to the patrons' delight but his father's despair.

The alchemy of pop is a magical thing. As much as shrewd manipulators such as Mark Dean and later manager Simon Napier-Bell might concur that you can build up a star in the music industry, both would be forced to agree that you cannot make stars from anyone. However much better Mortimer might have been than Ridgeley as a guitarist, success simply wouldn't have come Wham!'s way if that combination had stuck. Even the fact that Mortimer was intensely ambitious seemed to count against him. It was as if he tried too hard and just made things tougher, whereas Ridgeley's aimless insouciance eased him effortlessly into his pin-up role. Prevailing logic would have been for the musicians, Mortimer and George, to form the nucleus of the band – their busking experiences ought to have paved the way for greater things – but somehow it seemed destined not to be for Mortimer.

Mark Dean also remembers that Wham! should really have been George and David Mortimer, but he is quick to emphasize the significance of Ridgeley on George's formative years: 'Andrew designed George. Without him George could never have made it. Andrew had the ambition to be a star; even at the beginning of Wham! George was too insecure. Remember, Andrew co-wrote "Careless Whisper" and "Wham! Rap". But he was not a musician, however great looking he may have been. On the other hand George was not great looking and had to work at himself, with Andy's help. Even so, it was a great combination. If it had been David and George, I don't think they would have made it.'

As the Wham! set-up developed and became more serious, an understanding was reached between George and Andrew. It had become apparent from early on that George was far better motivated than Andrew, as well as more gifted. Wham!, then, would basically be a vehicle to launch George's career. It was mutually agreed that Andrew was only there to bolster George's confidence, and that once he was no longer needed, the two would go their separate ways.

Meanwhile, Mark Dean had moved on. By the early months of 1982 his apprenticeship at Bryan Morrison's publishing company, And Son (which handled the Jam's catalogue), had established him as a youngster with an eye for success. His virtually wholesale signing up of the vibrant mod scene, led by Secret Affair, impressed his elders, and soon his enthusiastic, amiable, whiz-kid exterior had helped him to work his way into a job in the A&R department of Phonogram Records as one of their posse of talent-hunters ever on the look-out for the Next Big Thing. Mark Dean was the archetypal hyperactive-on-the-make, far more so than the younger George and Andrew; he was a hardbitten veteran of the burgeoning London club scene, and had been one of the first to offer New Romantic mavericks Spandau Ballet a publishing deal.

At Phonogram, Dean became something of a stylemaker. Back in 1977 punk had shaken the foundations of the music industry, and the ripple effect had engendered a sense of confusion in the corridors of power; even in the early eighties the doors were still ajar for trend-wise young men to earn a lot of money, where before they would have spent their early years making the tea and opening the post. Dean's first success was to license the *Some Bizzare* compilation album of quirky electronic bands to his new label, the record's ensuing chart success meeting with gleeful approval from above. Later, he signed the best of the Bizzare bunch, synthesizer duo Soft Cell, in their own right, but better things were to come. Having journeyed to Sheffield on a tip-off, he discovered a band who were in the process of changing from an electronic outfit to a funk band. Dean was so impressed he had to catch his breath. Vice Versa, led by a blonde-quiffed ex-fanzine editor, Martin Fry, were about to become ABC, destined to lay down a blueprint for eighties white pop soul with their début album *Lexicon Of Love*. They wanted Dean to manage them, but the young entrepreneur, excited by his new-found status and power as an A&R man, did not want to get bogged down in booking studios and gigs for the new band. Instead he acted as their agent, forcing Phonogram to bid for the band along with everybody else. Impressed by Dean's patronage and the band's impressive demos, Phonogram had little hesitation in taking on the unashamedly commercial northerners.

With the help of Trevor Horn, hi-tech genius of the mixing desk, ABC, along with the aforementioned B.E.F. and Public Image Ltd, were to typify the early eighties shift from the post-punk idealistic avant-garde to commercial accessibility. Various strands were about to collide with explosive results. The anti-establishment DIY ethic of punk was evolving into a more self-contained corporatist credo, where these bands sought to function as businesses as much as groups of musicians. It was this appropriation of the success ethic and the dicta of Thatcherite free enterprise that would play straight into the hands of critics who were waiting to cry 'sell-out'. This new opportunism also fed into the New Romantic movement, soon to give birth to 'new pop', as colourful, photogenic bands used the growing popularity of pop videos to help them skate into the charts without the need for enthusiasm-sapping tours. Spandau Ballet were the torch bearers of this cross-over, having gone through their own dubious synthesizer phase to drive a wedge through the charts with their crisp commercial form of funk. Dean still remembers fondly the idealistic, if eminently contradictory, excitement of that early scene as he chatted to Spandau Ballet guitarist Gary Kemp, who wanted on the one hand to recreate the thrill of punk while reaping financial rewards, but on the other to keep their left-wing credentials intact.

The clearest indication that a sea-change was taking place in pop attitudes in the early eighties could be gleaned from many an earnest interview in the music press. Until now, any band that wanted some kind of critical credibility mentioned seeing the Sex Pistols as a prime motivation for forming a band. If everyone who claimed to have seen the Pistols really had, they would have had a residency at Wembley Arena rather than Oxford Street's modest 100 Club. Even Duran Duran, alongside Wham! the apotheosis of punk, initially set out to be a cross between the Sex Pistols and Chic, and Spandau Ballet and ABC waxed lyrical about the energy of punk. Suddenly, reference points were changing. The punk influence was dropped, seemingly overnight; instead bands seemed to have grown up on a diet of seventies soul. The new meritocratic Mecca was not the 100 Club but Wigan Casino, the shrine of northern soul that every band on the British mainland appeared to have hitched to at some point. Bands were no longer selling out, they were buying in, going for disco popularity in a big way and cashing in their credibility for commerciality. *Saturday Night Fever* had finally become an epidemic. The balance was tipping and Wham! were to be the first major band never even to pay lip service to punk's lasting influence.

ABC's contribution was to usher in the age of post-modernist pop with a distinct brand of eighties music that nevertheless harked back to past styles; even their name self-consciously nodded towards one of the Jackson Five's hits. Of course, post-modernism to its supporters was plagiarism to its detractors – George Panos would have to get used to the pejorative.

Dean had developed a reputation as someone with his finger on the pulse. In a profession over-populated with superannuated rockers whose bands had broken up and who had cloth ears when it came to spotting something new, Dean was a valuable commodity. Here was a man who could function without succumbing to the bullshit-riddled pop jargon of his elders. He enthused about music in a way that could only come from someone who knew what he was talking about. As his bands clocked up the hits, his stock rose; in the incestuous record company world of long lunches and limitless gossip his fame spread fast. What started off as friendly meals with associates turned into job offers. Dean carefully weighed up each one, but the most attractive came from the powerful CBS Records. In a part-bluff spiel he proposed a deal whereby they would finance his own label. Rather than employing him, CBS would pick up the tab in exchange for a slice of the profits. In theory it seemed like the ultimate entrepreneurial dream: financial independence without the financial risk. He had seen precedents elsewhere: Spandau Ballet's hip quotient had given them the muscle to negotiate their own label, Reformation Records, through Chrysalis, but they had not signed any other bands. The same company had struck a similar deal for Jerry Dammers' 2 Tone Records once his band the Specials had taken off. They had autonomy and a budget and 2 Tone would be able to release records by Dammers' own band as well as sign others. Meanwhile, the strategy was followed by the Beat's Go Feet Records, with less success – although it might have been a different matter if they had been a little more sympathetic to the Executive's plight and offered to nurture the young band. Dean's ambition, however, was to set up a dance label that would be like a British version of the early Atlantic Records, 'starting off really, really hip'.

Dean was well aware that there was no such thing as a free lunch in the music industry. The deal was not a philanthropic aberration on the part of CBS; he knew there would be a price to pay, but at the age of twenty-one what better launch-pad could he want for his career? The fortune he could worry about later. All he needed now were some hit records, and that required the signing of some bands. Dean could feel the dynamic of punk beginning to die down. He had gone through mod, 2 Tone and New Romantic, but now felt the market was closing up. He needed to find a band that could compete with the likes of

Spandau Ballet and Duran Duran, already firmly ensconced as regular *habitués* of the Top Ten.

Wham! were still making little headway with their latest demo tape, apart from brief encouragement from EMI who approved of their looks but suggested they went away and wrote some hit songs. Morale was low when Andrew Ridgeley once again proffered a demo to his acquaintance. This time it was a rather more professional job, recorded at home on a four-track recorder.

Dean had listened to Ridgeley's tape the first time because his mother had said that Andrew was such a nice boy. In agreeing to listen to the second one he was, once again, indulging his mother. This time, however, he was impressed by the rough twenty-second snatches of 'Wham! Rap', 'Careless Whisper', 'Come On' and 'Club Tropicana'. The tape was relatively crude and brief; little did the aspiring mogul realize that his future stars had used a broom handle for the mike stand, and that the snatches were short not just to capture the attention of the impatient A&R man, but because George's mother kept putting her head round the door and interrupting them. Asking Dean today what went through his mind when he first heard the tape still elicits a response in hushed, reverent tones: 'Special. It was very, very special. That tape said they could go all the way. There was an energy. I couldn't believe it, but I had stumbled on stardom on my doorstep.'

Mark Dean had found the first signing for his fledgeling label, christened Innervision. Professional sessions were hastily arranged, and in February 1982 – only a month after the pair had adopted the name of Wham! – contractual negotiations were underway.

By the end of March a deal was struck, one that all parties would come to regret. For the first and last time George made a foolish business decision, rushing into a contract that was not just miserly, giving the duo a paltry £500 advance, but was also ultimately to prove unworkable.

Wham! later claimed that Dean had persuaded the duo into signing because they needed to be signed up before CBS could put them on their release schedule, an accusation that Dean, to this day, strenuously denies. George's solicitor, Robert Allan, a man with experience in the industry who had been recommended by a customer of George's father, was instructed only to negotiate on legal points. Dean himself took the contract to the Halligan Band Centre in Holloway, North London, where Wham! were rehearsing on 24 March. Retiring to a café, George saw written amendments on the contract. Thinking that negotiations with their solicitor were completed, they signed the contract immediately. But unbeknown to George, many of Allan's amendments had not been included in this draft, while Paul Henry Rodwell, Dean's solicitor, had made changes which Allan had yet to see. This, at least, was later to prove to be some kind of blessing: on past precedents it would be almost impossible to legally enforce a contract which had not been overseen by an independent legal adviser.

One did not have to be a Tin Pan Alley professional to realize that a hard bargain was being struck by Innervision. Eight per cent royalties on singles and albums was tough even for an unknown band with no track record. Robert Allan had clawed back some of the severest demands, such as Wham! having to foot the bill for the producer, but it remained a rigorously tight agreement. George should have realized that he was signing not just a one year contract; Innervision had first option on retaining Wham! for the following four years, and each year they were entitled to one album with an extra one if they so wished. Thus, on a very frugal agreement, George Michael could be compelled to make ten LPs in the next five years. In fact, should Wham! split within the duration of the contract, Innervision could demand another ten albums from each artist!

It was no consolation to George and Andrew that Mark

Dean's hands were tied in that he was only passing on the raw deal that his new company Innervision had received from CBS. In his own way, Dean had been as impetuous in signing to CBS as Wham! were in signing to Innervision. But it was not the first time a group of musicians fired by ambition rather than avarice was landed with a poor deal. The days of the Beatles and Rolling Stones getting a penny per sale were not long gone; Frankie Goes To Hollywood were to sign to ZTT for a pitiful £250 advance and a five per cent royalty – and ZTT were not squeezed as tight contractually by their parent company, Island, as Dean had been by CBS.

If the figures all became a blur, one clause at least should have stuck out to the DJ side of George. The duo was to get no royalties at all from twelve-inch singles sales. In the past, twelve-inch releases had been mainly a promotional gimmick dispatched to radio stations, but the disco boom of the late seventies had seen them become a commercially viable commodity in their own right. Even if the extended tracks did not get played on daytime radio, they got so much exposure in clubs that the public was buying them in quantities comparable to seven-inch singles. Even the most unlikely rock records were released simultaneously in the larger format. Occasionally they featured extra exclusive tracks, but the larger size meant that the sound quality was always superior, and the commensurately higher price made the profit margins greater.

Who could blame the pair for signing with the first company that showed interest in them? Particularly as it was someone they knew and felt they could trust rather than an anonymous corporation. Was George actually mistakenly led to believe all his lawyer's amendments had been included in the contract? Dean referred to the ramshackle state of the rehearsal rooms they currently inhabited, and promised that if they signed they could move into much more amenable surroundings befitting their new status. In the event, George and Andrew did not seem to need any coercion; the pair brimmed with excitement over the realization that their wildest daydreams appeared to be turning into reality, and the whole affair had seemed to be simplicity itself. Not for them the slog of the pub circuit and pleading with unsympathetic A&R men to come and see them play. As George and Andrew cheerfully signed away the remnants of their adolescence, it was becoming apparent that while both parties were developing a hedonistic cavalier streak, George was showing at least the makings of a sharp business mind, having been responsible for carrying out an independent company search on Dean before negotiations were underway. Nevertheless, George was so thrilled by the momentous events in the café that he went out and celebrated by having both ears pierced.

It may have been naïve of George to accept Dean's offer, but there were certain pressures being exerted on him by another party. Jack Panayiotou's tolerance was running out. He had indulged his son's nebulous notions of pop stardom long enough. The real world beckoned. Relations had become strained to the point where incessant arguments had given way to a war of attrition until eventually father and son simply stopped talking to each other. Jack saw little chance of George's ambitions being realized, and in the summer of 1981 had given him an ultimatum: he had six months to make it or he would have to leave home. So by March 1982, that ultimatum was looming fast for the eighteen-year-old.

In Dean's defence, he, too, had fallen foul of the same youthful impetuosity in his dealings with CBS. Eagerness to enter the pop fray had resulted in contracts being drawn up on both sides that no one would want to be held to.

The youthful threesome felt they were going places as they toasted their new alliance in Innervision's new offices on the third floor of 64 South Molton Street, an exceedingly swish address for the prospective Tycoon of

Tycoon of Teen. Looking out over the city, it really appeared that the world was their oyster, and as they looked down on all that disposable income, it seemed as if all they needed to do now was release some records.

4

Rap Attack

'Wham! Rap' was the obvious choice for Wham's début single. The title would instantly identify the unknown band; it was also catchy, obsessive and even contained a socially observant message that would give the duo a credible profile. And its rap subtext would show that this band knew the direction in which soul and pop were moving. As early as 1981 Blondie had shown that rap could chart with their own homage to the New York street argot, 'Rapture', and George shrewdly chipped in with his own tough pseudo-pavement chant in the middle of 'Wham! Rap'. But rap was really a misnomer in describing the song as a whole; Wham! were playing safe by associating themselves with the hippest style of the time, but the real structure of the song was as conventional as any sixties pop song.

A few subtle changes had to be made to give the record a realistic chance of being a hit. First the four-letter expletive of the rough draft in 'you don't take no shit from the benefit' had to be discreetly excised, while elsewhere the more moderate expletive 'crap' was deemed acceptable for daytime broadcast. As for the name George Panos, it may have been a marked improvement on Panayiotou, but it did not really fit the bill. George Michael was chosen as a simple, racially ambiguous *nom de guerre*. The new name represented a break not just with his anonymous past, but also with Greek culture, which had always tugged at him from one side while the other side was being tugged that bit more strenuously by his English friends and all that pop music. But Michael was also the name of one of Kyriacos' six brothers, so George managed to flatter his family and retain a clandestine link with his roots. He wanted to please his peers as well as his parents; it was a successful compromise in this battle for George's soul.

Ironically, holed up in another part of London at the same time, New Romantic face 'Boy' George O'Dowd and his new multi-racial band Culture Club were concocting an image that exploited their own ethnic roots, as well as some that they lacked, appropriating rastafarian dreadlocks and Hebrew symbolism to make themselves polynational as well as polysexual. George Michael was having nothing to do with any kind of ambiguity; Wham! were going to be the Anglo-Saxon heterosexual antidote to Boy George's heterogeneous hybrid.

A producer needed to be found that would add polish to the 'Wham! Rap' track but retain some grit. George's choice was Bob Sargeant, who had made his reputation working with the Beat and recent cleancut teen-idols Haircut 100. To George's chagrin he turned them down, and after some deliberation they turned next to Bob Carter. Carter had been the champion of the brief-lived Brit-funk scene. Groups such as Junior and Linx stamped out a blueprint for this indigenous hybrid of soul that took its inspiration from American R&B traditions but grafted on a distinctly British pop sensibility while maintaining the highest standards of lyricism.

Linx, led by affable vocalist David Grant and bebereted bassist Sketch, notched up a number of hits including the vivacious 'Intuition', and the wry, nearly too cynical, 'So This Is Romance'. Like Wham!, they were a studio-based group who had achieved chart success without proving their live mettle. The Brit-funk movement turned out to be more seminal than saleable. Among its other achievements, it persuaded Spandau Ballet to move away from their Euro-dance music into a brash, purer form of funk, which reaped best results on 'Chant No 1 (I Don't Need This Pressure On)', a collaboration with the brass section of Light Of The World which celebrated the hedonistic hothouse that was London club culture, and reached number 3 in the summer of 1981. The short-lived Brit-funk formula was remarkably similar to the format that Wham! had adopted for 'Wham! Rap'. The butch American accents were fooling no one; this was the unmistakable face of high gloss Brit-pop.

During the summer of 1982, 'Wham! Rap (Enjoy What You Do)' was unleashed on a nation still high on the jingoistic euphoria of the Falklands War. This bellicose tub-thumping respite from recession had helped win Margaret Thatcher a second term in office, even though unemployment, particularly among the young, seemed to be soaring uncontrollably, the total figure now being well over three million. Wham! were not the first group to tackle the unemployment issue, nor were they the first to glorify it; a year earlier, Malcolm McLaren's protégés Bow Wow Wow had also positively celebrated the advent of adult leisure lifestyles on their single 'W.O.R.K. (N.O. Nah No! No! My Daddy Don't)', which contained the rather more anarchic credo, 'Demolition of the work ethic takes us to the age of the primitive.' Wham!'s opening volley, though more pro-social security than antisocial, seemed somewhat out of step with the Rule Britannia *Zeitgeist*.

Choosing one's moment correctly is essential in having a hit: the Sex Pistols had been performing 'God Save The Queen' for over a year before its release, immaculately timed, put it at the top of the charts during the royalist frenzy of the Queen's Silver Jubilee in 1977. But if 'Wham! Rap' represented the resilient anguish of a nation's disenfranchised youth, why was no one listening? Even the sanitized version of the single failed to notch up much airplay or appear in the charts; it seemed that the bored shelf stacker had been right – the nation wanted escapism, not gritty realism, even a gritty realism played out against a frenetic funk backdrop, though astute club DJs started to show source interest in this new English duo. The real problem, though, was the lack of all-important radio play. It seemed that the credo of the song, that things were *not* so bad on the dole, that it was even hip not to have a job, did not find favour with cosy Radio 1's influential programmers. Without their whole-hearted embrace of the single it would never be a hit. Perhaps George was aware that a high political profile would marginalize the band and he tried to allay suspicions of Wham! as soul subversives by saying the record was being taken too seriously. It was just a bit of fun reflecting his own decidedly transient situation. But it seemed that unwittingly a message *was* getting across: seventy per cent of 'Wham! Rap''s domestic sales were reputedly in the economically depressed north of England.

For George, the summer months appeared somewhat less gloomy. Clubbing now gave him that extra *frisson* of being able to hear his own single played alongside those of his heroes. Life seemed like one long party, one where they were always playing his tune. Thursday nights would be spent at Steve Strange's Club For Heroes in the Camden Palace. There was no success to go to George's head yet; he was just excited that he had a record out. It was not so much arrogance as high-spirited optimism that he would make it. He spoke keenly about Innervision, suggesting to a number of contemporaries with an eye on stardom that they should contact the hippest mini-mogul in town. Friends remember that he would always buy plenty of drinks, but also that he would always have a few himself: 'He was just a real lad.' Although George presented a brash, clownish front in a crowd, he still became awkward and clumsy when attempting to ask women out: his drinking sprees were primarily for stocking up on Dutch courage. He and Andrew had a distinctive sense of humour which continued to amuse their peers. Yet while George was growing increasingly confident and communicative in a crowd, in private with women he was diffident and reluctant to declare his intentions.

Many times he would stagger home in the early hours of the morning to face his parents' disapprobation. One night the disco dipso did not dare go home and slept at Andrew's house. His friend's mother knew what to expect by now and left a basin at the foot of the bed for George to throw up into. As he proceeded to do this he fell face first into the bowl, an event which he seemed to relish rehashing for his friends for some time afterwards.

If George's alcoholic haze contributed to the confusion over the 'message' in 'Wham! Rap', the response of the critics at the time did not help to clarify things. 'Wham! Rap' may not have had the fermented bile of the Sex Pistols' début 'Anarchy In The UK', but the soul-boy sonata's pseudo-political cant won praise from a rock press that was normally as dismissive of dance music as the denizens of Bush House. The credibility-obsessed post-punk publications had found something they could identify with; the *New Musical Express* had taken on board the principles of Brit-funk and Spandau Ballet's working-class hero ethic, and was beginning to accommodate club culture into a world-view that had previously been restricted to the decaying rock circuit.

Off the record George himself was dismissive about the sincerity of the sentiments of their first single. As Mark Dean says, 'What did they know about being on the dole? George's dad was a millionaire, they lived in a really nice house in Radlett. When he left school he worked as a cinema usher for fun.'

Certainly, listening to the single today it seems more like the kind of parody of rap that you might get on a BBC variety show, taking the traditional 'get down' clarion call of funk and inviting people to 'get down to the DHSS'. At the time, it seemed pertinent and vital; in retrospect, 'Wham! Rap' is the tackiest début single ever released by a major act.

George had actually absorbed, almost by osmosis, some of the lessons of punk. He was unintimidated by the pop process; he thought that anyone could do it and felt it was Wham!'s inalienable right to be a part of the industry. They were reacting against pop being run by grey-haired, cigar-chomping executives, as were the young punks looking to replace geriatric rockers like Led Zeppelin and the Rolling Stones, except that Wham! wanted to usurp the *bêtes noires* of disco, the likes of Dollar and Bucks Fizz, who were well into their late twenties and owed more to outmoded showbiz traditions than the eighties notion of New Pop. It seemed perfectly natural to George that a nineteen-year-old would know what other nineteen-year-olds would want to listen to. As he commented at the time: 'We've got two things going for us. One, we are young; and two, we are not singing about ordinary disco stuff.' But while that ordinary disco stuff continued to clog up the charts, 'Wham! Rap' did make 'Single of the Week' in that usually hardy rock bible, *Sounds*. The pin-up press shots that were circulating editorial offices and increasingly finding their way into print didn't detract either, but more of that later.

The duo was assailed for its first interviews. At the time, few had seen the faces behind the dashing vocals that ranged from macho slang to ball-clenching falsetto. When the pair met the press it was Andrew Ridgeley who was the rent-a-mouth of the two and was assumed to be the front man; his swarthier half was more pensive and introverted. Copy-hungry journalists artlessly pigeon-holed George Michael as boring.

Hailed as profound social realists swimming against a tide of superficiality, Wham! seemed to fill a subcultural vacuum. The New Romantics had been absorbed into the establishment, and Boy George was destined to be enshrined as England's pet eccentric. By comparison, Wham! were the unlikely standard bearers of pop's latest counter-culture. They seemed tailor-made to accompany

The Face's manifesto for 'Hard Times', the pseudo-political August cover feature penned by Robert Elms that championed a kind of backs-to-the-wall stance against the downside of Thatcherism and long-term youth unemployment. In the face of such ferocious fashionability, George and Andrew seemed to fit the bill; who cared that 'Wham! Rap' was simply a mealy-mouthed, leafy-laned albino retort to Grandmaster Flash's edgy pop psychosis, 'The Message'. Who cared that the meek streets of Hertfordshire had nothing on the mean streets of Harlem.

Wham! suddenly found themselves called upon to offer some style counsel of their own on the etiquette of 'Hard Times' chic for the glossy teen magazines. George's years of attention to appearance above and beyond the call of duty began to pay off as he became something of a garb guru. By now Wham!'s stylistic excesses had made way for a back-to-basics look: 'Levi 501s with tears, faded not bleached' was his prescription of the day.

The charts had yet to be conquered, however. Promotion was still needed. For a band whose natural habitat was the disco, they opted sensibly for PAs (personal appearances) around the country. Since the last days of the Executive, George had keenly attended to the dynamics of dance and he decided to inject some sex appeal into Wham! by introducing a pair of female dancers.

Wham!'s first consorts were school friends Amanda Washbourn and Shirlie Holliman, lately Andrew's paramour. Amanda, then sixteen, recalls that George managed to shed the remains of his puppy fat by sweating the night away, either at the disco or, failing that, by pushing the furniture into the corner of the room and setting up an *ad hoc* dance-floor at home. But George's conviction that success was imminent was not shared by all. Amanda Washbourn decided to leave the band because she thought she would make more money as a hairdresser. Another version of her departure, however, sheds some light on the sense of professionalism creeping into George's approach.

He allegedly deemed her tender years and accompanying naïvety something of a liability, as the group would
be called upon to make promotional public appearances
around the country. She was usurped by the more worldly
ex-model Diane Sealey, professionally known as D. C.
Lee. George demanded a full-time commitment from all
participants in Wham!.

The club promotion racket was a hectic affair. Rather
than one evening show, the quartet would undertake a
whistle-stop tour of as many venues as possible, miming
to a tape of the single and doing their floorshow before
moving on. Inevitably, there were upsets. At one of
George's old haunts, Lasers in Harringay, they turned
up expecting to mime to their single when DJ Norman
Scott played the instrumental B-side, forcing George to
sing along while going through his breathless callisthenics.
At Stringfellows in the West End, one of George's high
kicks sent a shoe flying through the air. Every inch the
professional he continued regardless and returned later to
retrieve his footwear. Chart success still eluded 'Wham!
Rap' but the series of fleet-footed PAs saved George the
effort of putting a live band together for endless support
slots. By the time Wham! came to tour they would emerge,
seemingly overnight, as a fully formed headline act. It was
indeed the best of times and the worst of times as George
and Andrew found themselves occupying a half-way house
between success and failure.

'Wham! Rap''s follow-up, 'Young Guns (Go For It)',
released in September, was therefore all the more crucial
when it appeared in the charts at number 72. The following
week, it had risen to number 48, and the dream of an
appearance on the ailing but ever-prestigious *Top of the
Pops* looked like turning into a reality, until the following
week when it slipped down again. But daytime play,
frantic glad-handing PAs and judicious plugging combined
with some genuine word-of-mouth interest began to reap

dividends as the single did a sudden *volte face* and raced up to number 3. The defiant brashness of the Wham! shows seemed to declare their right to be stars, and George, whose CV could now boast choreographer besides everything from shelf-stacker to lyricist, was vindicated. Having appropriated Rocky's credo, 'Go For It', George was now making it work for himself. His musical skills were also being acknowledged by experts. Anne Dudley, who arranged the brass parts for 'Young Guns', and who was to go on to become an integral cog in ZTT Records' musical success, quickly noticed how George's musical sensibilities were sharpening when he confidently informed her during recording that she had changed round a chord. She had merely swapped the inside parts around, but George immediately spotted the difference. Whereas other aspirants might have been content to delegate tasks to experts in each field, George demonstrated his plans for a distinctive brand of hands-on self-determination.

Once again the subject matter of their single drew attention from the rock press. The *NME* made it 'Single of the Week', but the song's sentiments were not universally endorsed. Having already told the youth of Britain to avoid work, 'Young Guns' was telling boys to avoid girls, who only ever want to tie them down when they should be out enjoying themselves. It was an unbridled declaration of teenage male independence, the macho tribal gang mentality set to a disco beat. In subject matter Wham! were harking back to the 2 Tone days, when the Specials had penned a number 1 single, 'Too Much Too Young' which condemned teenage pregnancy, and an LP track 'Stupid Marriage' which advocated a wariness of matrimony and drew adverse notices, not for its social awareness, but for the anti-female line of its celebration of male bonding.

The criticism from feminists for its smug laddish stance failed to halt its progress up the charts. When George was invited to make the leap from living room to *Top of the Pops*, he expressed distaste for the badly put together show, which made even the brashest of pop seem pensionable, and insisted that the band should perform its own dance routine. Their appearance set pulses racing throughout England: George and Andrew's combination of athleticism and tight jeans played havoc with a nation's hormones. Putting personalities as well as pin-up faces to the music made 'Young Guns' the breakthrough, and, as if to confirm that Wham! had been doing the right thing all along, Innervision rereleased 'Wham! Rap'. This time it claimed its rightful place in the Top Ten, dispelling the suggestion that the band might be merely the latest in a long line of pretty-featured one-hit wonders.

George found it difficult to treat the business as seriously as his critics. Thrust suddenly onto the treadmill of promotion, this was a time when he was still happy to have fun, even at his own expense, rather than appear like a po-faced professional. One stunt involved the duo shooting a photo-story session for teenage weekly *My Guy* where they were to act out the narrative of 'Young Guns'. On the day of the shoot the magazine received a call telling them that Andrew was sick and could not make it. But then George rang to say that his best friend from Bushey, David, would come up and do it. So the story co-ordinator waited for George's arrival. The problem was that when the receptionist rang to say George was on his way up, the staff of the magazine suddenly realized that no one knew what he looked like. In a frantic panic they managed to find a writer who did, and she discreetly pointed to the young man in the foyer clad in jeans and leather jacket.

The shoot in and around the offices, employing such glamorous locations as Waterloo Station and the Stamford Arms pub, was a surreal scenario. When David Mortimer, rechristened David Austin, finally arrived they shot it as if he was the other member of Wham! acting out the role of the mate who had married a harridan. The punchline of the plot turned the song's lyrics on their head, however: George's character, having condemned his friend for his premature marriage, returns one day having also tied the knot.

These *My Guy* skits were always done tongue in cheek, but George really wanted to go over the top. 'He had this idea that he ought to wear three pairs of sunglasses and really camp it up. He was a complete lunatic,' remembers another member of the cast. But beneath the clowning lurked a burgeoning determination to succeed: 'It's strange how he was completely mad then, but today he hardly ever even smiles.'

Already George Michael's song writing had garnered attention. Apart from 'Careless Whisper', most of the demos already recorded were credited to him alone; Andrew seemed content to sit back in an advisory capacity. Among the publishing companies bidding for the rights to his catalogue, the firm of Morrison/Leahy Music secured a deal. Bryan Morrison, described by Dean as 'a tough cookie', was a music industry veteran with a reputation that went back to managing the Pretty Things in the sixties. In the late seventies he had gone into publishing with the company And Son and had made his name, not to mention a small fortune, by handling the Jam's lucrative catalogue of hits. The same Morrison recognized the need for young grass-roots talent spotters and hired Mark Dean, who returned the gesture by introducing Wham! to his cigar-consuming ex-employer. Dick Leahy was also a music business heavyweight whose greatest success had been as managing director of Bell Records, the outfit that dominated the teeny-bop market in the mid-seventies, recording acts like Gary Glitter, David Cassidy and the Bay City Rollers. With Dean's loyal endorsement and their track record, Morrison/Leahy Music Ltd. found themselves handling a catalogue, albeit a small one, of immensely bankable pop songs.

What Wham! really required now was management that would match the mettle of their publishers. George was keen on self-determination and wanted to handle himself, but things were patently destined to get out of hand. Dean had worked wonders for the duo, or so their chart success suggested, but as the man in charge of a record company – whose *raison d'être* is to 'exploit' its acts (albeit in the purest sense) – as well, there was a conflict of interest. Dean was already under pressure from parent company CBS to promote Wham! at the expense of the rest of his roster, which was a colourful mix of pop and pretentiousness including Jimmy the Hoover, Space Monkey, Animal Nightlife and Steve Walsh. Outside stewardship was needed and a team big enough to match the might of Morrison/Leahy was to be found in the form of one of the unlikeliest partnerships in the history of pop management.

Jazz Summers had started small and until he heard Wham!'s demo tape while passing through Island Records' offices in the first half of 1982, it looked like he would stay that way. Management had not been his earliest vocation; persuaded to sign his adolescence away and join the army at the age of fifteen by his military father, Summers spent nine gruelling years in uniform before leaving to train as a radiographer while drumming in various bands in the evening. By the early seventies he found himself managing the folksinger Richard Digance, but he only really got the bit between his teeth with the commercialization of the punk explosion in 1977, when he saw in it an energy similar to the sixties beat boom that had first attracted him to music. Various punk signings failed to hit paydirt, and although he had big hopes for the day-glo pop of Blue Zoo, who were to have a fleeting brush with stardom with the hit single 'Cry Boy Cry' in the same month as 'Young Guns', by 1982 he had his eye on two bands – Wham! and another unknown duo, the Eurythmics, both of whom had a fresh dynamic sound that he was convinced would be massive.

Simon Napier-Bell's genesis is possibly even less straight-forward. In twenty years he had had a hand in the careers of the Yardbirds, Marc Bolan and Japan, but his dilettantish nature and fate had always conspired to snatch his charges from him either at their peak or before they had made it. Napier-Bell's approach to management was the same as his approach to his own life: he was an unmitigated hyperbolist. With a florid wit and keen imagination he could always be assured of a career in tabloid journalism if pop management ever ceased to fire his enthusiasm.

Napier-Bell gives an account in his autobiography, *You Don't Have To Say You Love Me* (published in a typical burst of vanity, by his own company, Nomis Books), of the now legendary story of how he discovered Wham!. As he remembers it, he was watching the then increasingly monotonous *Top of the Pops* when on came these two leather-clad lovelies with sharp dance routines, which he knew must have been devised by the group and imposed on the director. He believed the sexually and racially ambiguous duo had a universal appeal. By the time the performance of 'Young Guns' was over, Napier-Bell had already hatched the mythical film plot of two young cow-boy adventurers who come through a welter of drama and romance, where 'one gets married, one goes to a brothel, but by the end of the film they ditch the girls and ride off together into the sunset'. It was crass and commercial, but so was Napier-Bell, and Wham! were not much different. Since the demise of his most recent protégés Japan, Napier-Bell was restless and looking for a new challenge. Enthroned in the opulence of his Bryanston Square apartment overlooking Marble Arch, money was the least of his interests. But the thought of a place in history and visions of overseeing the biggest band in the world fired the wistful trooper into action.

Jazz Summers had put himself forward as a manager for Wham! as soon as he had overheard the demo at Island Records' offices, but he had got no further than Bryan

Morrison. As publisher and something of a mentor to Dean, Morrison and Leahy were to exert considerable influence over the direction, both musical and managerial, of Wham! and indeed would find their position even stronger when Dean found himself ousted from Wham!'s inner sanctum. At this stage Morrison was hard but fair to Summers, dismissing his enquiries with the frank response that he was too small-time. Already there was talk of teaming up with Americans Freddy De Mann and Ron Weisner, at the time responsible for the careers of Michael Jackson and Madonna. Wham! were never a duo that took things lightly; how many new, untutored bands made their first appearances complete with dancing girls and choreographed routines? George may have had his moments of camp mischief during bibulous nights at the Camden Palace and while shooting that eventful photo-story, but his eyes were always firmly set on the top even at this early stage.

What Summers needed, then, was a powerful partner. Timing was of the essence, and by the time music business veteran Neil Warnock match-made a meeting between Summers and Napier-Bell, each man had Wham! in mind as his next major interest. Summers also enthused about the Eurythmics, but Napier-Bell's sights were set exclusively on the two boys. All they needed to do now was convince the Wham! camp that they were the team for the job, something which would take them another six months to achieve.

May 1983 should have seen Wham!'s world domination campaign begin in earnest. The release of the third single, 'Bad Boys', suggested, however, that George Michael was already thinking along the same lines as his aspiring manager Simon Napier-Bell. They may have come from different generations, but they seemed to share the same poetic/homoerotic vision of Wham! as real *Boy's Own* stuff. 'Bad Boys' was a caricature of two rebels taking no lip

George Michael

from anyone, going their own way and sticking together, with musical accompaniment from their prototypical soul rubric. If the song dripped with clichés, the video was even more damning, featuring George and Andrew in an over-the-top leather look that George later admitted was completely phoney.

The 'Bad Boys' image had a distinct homoerotic *frisson*. Their motorcycle chic owed more to film-maker Kenneth Anger's muscle-bound hunks and standard gay clone garb than the James Dean rebellion the duo once aspired to. George was entirely responsible for the style: he had always made his own decisions about presentation and was not about to relinquish artistic control now that Wham! were successful. And where their previous dance routines had been with women, here they seemed to be dancing with each other. On their publicity shots they looked less sullen and less brooding than vulnerable and feminine, a neo-'New Man' look that begged the question of their sexuality for the first time. Besides, they may have been bad, but they were still only boys. Social notions of male bonding dictated that young males grouped in groups larger than two, whether drinking in pubs or performing in bands. To compound matters, Wham!'s unashamed wowing of the gay disco audience was tangibly helping them to carve a hefty slice of the Pink Pound, regardless of their own sexuality.

Nonetheless, 'Bad Boys' rounded off George's first trilogy of releases as the third in a soul trinity that gave him a place in pop history: he was drawing on themes that were undoubtedly both contemporary and eternal: the escape from the humdrum, the pursuit of fun and the rejection of one's elders. In 'Wham! Rap', 'Young Guns (Go For It)' and 'Bad Boys' George Michael had dipped into the collective teen psyche of recent history that had only been encapsulated better by Eddie Cochran's 'Summertime Blues', 'C'mon Everybody' and 'Somethin' Else' in the late 1950s. 'Summertime Blues' had also celebrated in alienated

50

fashion the eternal leisure of youth. But for Cochran the leisure was the result of finite school holidays rather than unemployment created by an economic recession that stretched into the foreseeable future. 'Young Guns' resounded with the free-wheeling spirit of 'C'mon Everybody' while 'Bad Boys' was the formularized synthesis of facets of rebellion chic in 1959's 'Somethin' Else'.

While all competitors sang of love and universal harmony it would take the surreal wit of journalist-turned-Svengali Paul Morley to shunt Frankie Goes To Hollywood towards Cecil B. De Millean concepts of sex, war and God for their opening pop shots of 'Relax', 'Two Tribes' and 'The Power Of Love'. Frankie's arrival marked an unwitting start to the global-consciousness-as-sales-pitch that was to reach its apex, or nadir, depending upon one's level of cynicism, with Live Aid. Frankie's triple-pronged assault on the charts would do battle with Wham! for the domination of 1984's charts, but that was all ahead of George and Andrew. For now they could sit back and accept the passionate clinches of the pop press. In the process, the last vestiges of rebellion were being replaced by preening passive narcissism; a severe case of premature emasculation.

'Bad Boys' helped to make Wham! the first pin-up of the first edition of teen magazine, *Number One* on 7 May. Set up by *NME*'s publishers IPC, *Number One*'s aim was to outgun their rival EMAP's ever-flourishing *Smash Hits*. The publishing success story of the 1980s, *Smash Hits* had been launched in the autumn of 1978 and by the summer of 1983 boasted sales of over 400,000 per fortnightly edition. Having astutely latched onto the rebirth of scream pop, *Smash Hits* had taken Culture Club and Duran Duran and clutched them possessively to their hearts, in the process virtually becoming Duran Duran's house magazine.

Number One opted for Wham!. Tying in with the release of 'Bad Boys' they printed the lyrics and put the notorious picture of the pouting leather duo on the back page, hailing the single as an 'unashamed poppy flash of disco'. The following week George found himself fixed up on a blind date with Bananarama's Karen, and the week after that, in a bid for the Wham! vote, George revealed in a fashion feature that his mum bought his white soul-boy socks in bulk from Marks and Spencer's. Later that year they were to notch up an impressive three cover features for the magazine, a helpful and attractively irreverent aid to their cause. The final magazine of the year was to put the seal on the birth of the so-called New Pop, squeezing George, without Andrew, onto the cover with Spandau Ballet's Tony Hadley, Boy George and Simon Le Bon, as if to proclaim that a festive *entente cordiale* had been reached between the rivals. Why squabble? There were more than enough fans to go around as they took it in turns to mount the charts.

Wham! were now considered worthy of Fleet Street's burgeoning pop newshounds. The coverage at this stage was either superfluous or cheekily scandalous. One premature story on a Wham! split 'revealed' that their backing band was breaking away to form a group called Fantastic. This, by a happy coincidence, happened to be the title of Wham!'s début album, due for release a month later in July. Elsewhere, George and Andrew played upon their fictional image as bad boys, happily feeding the press stories of their insatiable love life in a way that was inevitably to backfire on them.

Suddenly it had become difficult for George to walk the streets or frequent the Wag Club and Le Beat Route. Until Fleet Street turned their gaze on Wham! George had not even had too much difficulty going home to Radlett by train after his *Top of the Pops* appearances. Now the duo found themselves in the public domain, vying for front page space and bold type headlines and photo opportunities with the Royal Family and sundry soap stars. Life was tough for George when he had to avoid his usual watering holes. For a while he tried the

plush but tacky surrounds of Stringfellows, the scene of
his early shoe-jettisoning triumph. Out of the price and
taste range of the ordinary clubber, this West End haunt
a stone's throw from Leicester Square did play classic
seventies disco, George's first love and inspiration. But
eventually he found himself pursued and cornered by
fans even there so he ended up back in the cooler more
street-credible outposts of clubland, where the inevitable
frank exchange of views would only take place at the end
of the evening when his sterner critics had been fuelled by
alcoholic bravado. George fiercely refused to succumb to
the star syndrome of going out with minders, preferring
instead to talk his way out of trouble.

George looked on 'Bad Boys' as the nadir of Wham!,
the albatross that would forever haunt him. It marked
the point where he realized that there was a formula to
making pop records. It had been a suffocating time for
him, as he became swamped by the process and demands
to complete the group's début album. Andrew had never
been that involved in writing the songs and by now he was
quite happy to graciously take a back seat, acknowledging
that even if he tried to write tracks, George would always
come up with better ones. Instead he could continue to lead
his lotus-eating life that was later to become so interesting
to the British press.

George meanwhile retired to rethink his strategies and
work his way out of the critical conundrum he had become
embroiled in. 'I'd been given this kind of young-social-
commentator halo, and I just wasn't comfortable with
it. The way I saw it, I was going to get found out one
day anyway, so why not be honest and start making pop
records.'

For all its flaws, 'Bad Boys' had enough impact to be
their highest chart placing to date, reaching number 2.
The way it shot up the charts immediately rather than
building up sales showed that there was an audience out

there clamouring for more Wham! product. But at the same time the shortcomings of the Innervision contract were manifesting themselves as George realized that there was no substantial increase in their earnings. A début album had to be completed both to satisfy demand and to earn the duo some money. George finally conceded the need for professional management to handle their increasingly hectic affairs. Their solicitor Robert Allan had handled them for three months but all parties agreed that there was potential for a clash of interests. Having been courted by them for six months, a cautious George Michael decided to take on Simon Napier-Bell and Jazz Summers' Nomis Management Company in June 1983. The wily Napier-Bell and the efficacious Summers could rejoice in the fact that they had an act made up of friends that would never be in conflict with each other rather than a large group, which invariably made golden geese become barren and rooms shake with the sound of colliding egos.

Crucial to George Michael's agreement to the deal was the fact that the contract had an unusually short notice period of just three months. Summers' and Napier-Bell's confidence in Wham! was so great that they knew the deal would be mutually beneficial. They also realized that Wham! knew the strength of their bargaining position and that if there were any difficulties they would look elsewhere for management before even such a short-term contract was signed. George also hoped that with the aid of Napier-Bell's forceful ego and not insubstantial experience he would be in a better position to renegotiate Wham!'s contract with Innervision, leading them into penury, not profit.

One more single was required to trail the long-awaited album. 'Club Tropicana' sealed Wham!'s fate and ended their honeymoon with the music press. Any credibility they had once had was well and truly dissipated by the seemingly unashamed decadence and loss of social concern in this dizzy disco strut. George had intended

'Club Tropicana' to be ironic, having written it before his success, but any last vestiges of irony were lost with a video that ought to have been sending up the recent cocktail-swigging club craze in general, and Spandau Ballet, who had namechecked Le Beat Route in their single, 'Chant No. 1', in particular. But the video shoot saw the group jetting off to Ibiza to combine film with fun in something that was not that far removed from the Duran Duran travel guide promos that Wham! really ought to have been sticking the knife into. What was claimed to be a critique was obviously so subtle it seemed to all intents and purposes to be a celebration of the lifestyle it should have been lampooning.

Wham! appeared to have made the same political *volte face* as Spandau Ballet, who had started as a proud working-class socialist group and eight months later were lapping up the pop star life and travelling round in Rolls-Royces. Mark Dean defends Wham!, saying that their comfortable backgrounds meant that, unlike other bands intent on retaining that post-punk strand of credibility, 'Wham! were being honest from day one: they were just fun-loving lads who had always wanted to live on the beach and have sun tans.' Their songs about the dole were simply about what they had been going through back then. As such, they were indeed the prime exponents of Thatcherism in pop music. In its ostentatious celebration of success for success's sake, the dumb hedonism of 'Club Tropicana' effectively set the agenda for the 1980s every bit as much as *The Face*.

The duo seemed further than ever from their DHSS-financed beginnings. Yet the real irony was that while they behaved like brash, well-heeled pop stars and were being slammed for their affluent arrogance, they were hardly better off financially still having to scrape together the bus and train fare to get to the *Top of the Pops* studio. But pop's love of illusion and the fact that they were behaving so affluently meant that the public was buying up their image wholesale with an alacrity that ought to have made the fantasy real. A recuperative holiday in Cyprus interrupted by George flying back to England just for a haircut made good copy, and only accentuated the illusion of wealth. Even though the coffers were empty, it was evident that George was in fact developing a taste for lotus-eating and for anyone that had once praised George as a cool spokesman for a generation, after the abrasiveness of his early work, 'Club Tropicana' seemed to be confirmation that he was now suffering from terminal sunstroke.

Worse still, the lame-brained 'Club Tropicana' was musically their weakest single to date, the ultimate lazy pop pastiche unencumbered by originality. Matters were made worse when the keenly anticipated début LP *Fantastic* was released. Record company pressure, combined with George's self-professed unprolific output, conspired to make *Fantastic* a profound disappointment, albeit one that topped the charts. With the four singles included on it, there were approximately only seventeen minutes of new material, and part of that was a pedestrian cover version of the Miracles' disco classic, 'Love Machine'. Andrew took up the cudgels to defend the group against criticisms of political apathy, demonstrating only how very apathetic he was: 'If you start thinking about politics you get wrapped up in it all and your life becomes a misery. So it's best not to think about it at all.'

For D. C. Lee it was the end of an era. Dissatisfied with being consigned to the background, she decamped and went to work with Paul Weller's more overtly socialist soul fraternity, the Style Council, in an attempt to kick-start a solo career. In her place the exotically styled Pepsi De Manque slipped into the line-up next to Shirlie Holliman.

In the meantime there was growing pressure for Wham! to stop their sun-worshipping and succumb to the traditional rigours of stardom: a promotional live tour. When the financial comings and goings were assessed, Wham!'s debilitating contract soon became apparent. Constrained by Mark Dean's increasingly unworkable agreement, Wham! appeared to be making a fortune but were only seeing a pittance. The Nomis team saw that for the sake of Wham!'s financial future the contract would have to be renegotiated before too long. Even with the chart-topping success of *Fantastic* Mark Dean would find it difficult to finance a tour of the magnitude warranted by such a popular band. But for immediate exigency, Napier-Bell hastily hustled a licensing deal worth £50,000 to underwrite the Club Fantastic Tour. The deal with the Fila sports company presented Wham! with their outfits for the proposed tour. It was an unwittingly shrewd move, tying in neatly with the recent fashion boom in designer sportswear which had replaced ripped jeans as true working-class chic. Kitted out in athletics shirts and thigh-hugging shorts like a couple of tennis seeds, the duo confronted their biggest challenge yet; looking sheepishly like they were about to step out at Wimbledon they faced living down a decidedly un-pop image. As if that wasn't enough, they were also about to find themselves in an altogether different kind of court.

5

Litigation and Shuttlecocks

Now that Nomis and Wham! were working together, the first objective was to sort out the Innervision contract. Neither party was happy with the existing deal. Even Mark Dean was aware of the absurdity of the situation where the band with the number one album in the country was having to travel home by public transport after increasingly frequent TV appearances. Dean went to CBS to ask for renegotiation following the band's meteoric rise but came away empty-handed. In principle, a settlement could have been reached that was agreeable to all parties. The real villains were CBS, who had driven such a hard bargain with Dean, and who had latterly refused to renegotiate in the light of Wham!'s success, which was feeding no one's coffers as much as theirs.

But Simon Napier-Bell had different ideas. Having spent the best part of twenty years striding into the head offices of the biggest corporations in the world, he was not about to start chatting amicably to the youthful Dean, whom he seemed to view with a cocktail of condescension and disdain. The relationship between George and Andrew and Jazz and Simon was close but strictly professional. For the latter's part, they were fortunate in having taken the reins of a band with a number one album behind them; the hard graft of initially breaking Wham! had already been done by Dean. Jazz Summers remembers Wham! as having very clear ideas about their future by the time he sat down with them: 'Both George and Andrew were really bright people. They really knew what they wanted. It was not just that they wanted to be rich and famous, they also had ideas about presentation and direction. George was already learning the intricacies of his trade and becoming as astute as any businessman: he knew he wanted to go onstage and go to America, but he also wanted to look at his photos and talk about his producer. George had been in bands since he was fourteen; he'd been playing drums since he was eleven . . . They wanted to be successful without being manipulated and they learnt the business incredibly quickly.'

George was more succinct about the strengths and weaknesses of his management team: 'Simon is a real asshole,' he said; but he was also aware that Napier-Bell was the kind of asshole you wanted batting for you rather than against you. Vanity prevented the fabled figure from letting Dean, barely half his age, have even half an opportunity to get the better of him, and he considered that the best form of attack was attack. His passion for corporate politics and boardroom games led him to negotiate directly with CBS behind Dean's back, much to the chagrin of his easier-going partner Summers. One of his early casualties in what was to prove a fierce war of attrition came in August, when Robert Allan was replaced by heavyweight music business solicitors Russells.

After a series of quasi-amicable exchanges, Mark Dean received a lengthy letter from Russells on 7 October 1983, marked 'Strictly private and confidential: for the attention of Mr Mark Dean and for his eyes only.' In nitpickingly thorough and uncompromising terms the lengthy document listed the alleged failings of Dean's handling of George and Andrew, drawing the conclusion that the contract with Wham! was not legally binding. In fact Russells was of the opinion that Wham!'s case against Dean was so watertight that they were entitled to seek a recording contract elsewhere, taking with them the rights to the master recordings they had already delivered. It was claimed, for instance, that the weekly £40 that Innervision had been paying Wham! was not concomitant with a band of such stature and that the contract had been obtained by fraudulent representation in the outset, in circumstances of unequal bargaining power. The Bad Boys were suddenly poor innocent victims of a combination of avaricious and incompetent dealings. In effect, Nomis had abandoned any ideas of renegotiation with CBS via Innervision; their intention was to escape from the contract and strike a more favourable deal elsewhere.

George, Andrew and the Nomis team were not the only people who assumed that such a successful act ought to be rivalling Croesus. In America a band also called Wham! took out a lawsuit against its English namesake demanding the sum of $19.6 million in damages. Sympathetic fans sent George and Andrew pound notes through the post in case they lost the case. The American band was no doubt under the impression that the chart-toppers would by now be in a position to pull the money from their petty cash. Napier-Bell was intent on assuring that the word Wham! became the sole property of his charges. Hearing of an independent label calling itself Whaam *pace* Lichtenstein, he offered it £500 to change its trading name. Eventually the matter was settled for a relatively paltry £2000. It was not the first time a band had tried to patent the strangest of facets for marketing purposes. Adam Ant had once tried to patent the white stripe of make-up across his nose in order to monopolize the merchandising of his image.

Dean's immediate response to the letter from Russells was to seek a temporary injunction restricting Wham! from signing a contract elsewhere. Court proceedings ensued during that November, and Wham! began to take a back seat to their learned legal representatives. Their major legal requirement was to sign autographs for the QC's children. With Wham! gagged, Mark Dean chose to release the 'Club Fantastic Megamix'. Originally, the next single slotted for release had been 'Careless Whisper', but Morrison/Leahy suggested holding fire. Before the court case George had wanted to put a megamix out himself, but he had wanted a distinctive New York production job on it to give Wham!'s fans something extra rather than a workmanlike in-house CBS number. If ever there was an opportunist episode to the affair it was this. As if the 'Fantastic' album was not a specious release anyway, the megamix strained both the music and credulity further by seguing 'A Ray of Sunshine', 'Come On' and 'Love Machine' into a crass disco special. Wham! issued a statement asking fans not to buy the record, but in their insatiable lust for Wham! the record reached a respectable number fifteen, bought, presumably, by fans who already had the album. Perhaps, in fairness, the profits were helping the put-upon Dean to underwrite the £80,000 the court case had so far cost him.

It was in this strange, muted atmosphere that Wham! set out on the Club Fantastic Tour. It was a tour that took its toll on them. At the same time as dates were being cancelled when even Andrew came down with laryngitis, an unprecedented demand for tickets meant that more and more London shows were being added. At least this was a manifestation to CBS that Wham! were worth fighting for should things get to the stage where the group was looking for a fresh contract.

On the eve of the tour that November, the fearless duo not only faced legal conundrums but also the most severe journalistic encounter of their career: being probed and prodded by Paul Morley for *Blitz*. Morley was the last surviving *agent provocateur* of post-punk New Journalism who had formerly plied his trade at the *NME* in its heyday before it was squeezed out by the teen mags and the glossy style bibles. He was also in the process of setting up a new record label and working on his own McLarenesque manifesto for an unknown Liverpool band called Frankie Goes To Hollywood.

Morley's main intention seemed to be to reduce Wham! to tears, to strip away their new-found assurance rather than ask them what songs they would be singing on tour. For the first time, George and Andrew, accustomed to tabloid asininity, were out of their depth as Morley harangued them. He was taking a metaphysical approach to the Wham! phenomenon, and here were two suburban teenagers, caught up in a strange world, who just wanted to get their hair right for their photo shoot and talk about their album and tour. In a more comfortable moment George started to explain and make sense of everything Wham! had done up to that point: 'What I think we're celebrating is simply what certain years of our lives mean to us and what they mean to most people. Valid things . . . energy and optimism, you know.'

Faced with Morley's barbed presumptions, Andrew's retorts became increasingly aggressive; in George there was an almost tangible sense of self-examination taking place; it was the nearest pop journalism could ever come to John Freeman's legendary 'Face to Face' TV interview with Tony Hancock. Like Hancock, George was confronted with his instinctive art and compelled to intellectualize about it. The difference, however, was that where Hancock began to analyse himself literally to death from this juncture, for George Michael it marked a shift forwards. But while George gained wisdom from the experience, Ridgeley remained a chump.

For George the tour became more of a challenge than ever. There was no way Wham! were going to present a traditional show. Instead they opted for recreating the suburban disco of their childhood around the concert halls of Great Britain. Bogarts' DJ Gary Crowley was co-opted onto the Wham! bench to spin the discs before the band came on and to introduce 'those bad boys from Bushey'. With no live band to speak of, Wham! called on an *ad hoc* session crew, Dream Merchant, put together and led by journeyman bassist Deon Estus who had played on *Fantastic*, and George Michael's old friend David Austin. With Shirlie Holliman and Pepsi De Manque in the background, the line-up was complete.

When the band came on in their Fila gear they decided to

add to the sporting theme by playing badminton onstage. In gestures of unbridled sexual teasing, George and Andrew stuffed their shuttlecocks inside their shorts before hitting them out into the audience; where else could they put them? For once, genuinely spontaneous gestures garnered them blanket coverage in the press. Simon Napier-Bell's well-oiled publicity machine appeared to be grinding into motion, but contrary to popular belief this was an off-the-cuff idea of George's rather than one hatched by his manager's fecund imagination; however, it did imply that they shared the same wavelength when it came to public relations exercises.

Regular meetings were convened to devise future strategies. Bryan Morrison and Dick Leahy, whose publishing position saw that they survived the Innervision purge, joined Summers, Napier-Bell and George and Andrew for brainstorming sessions. George paid extremely close attention to every aspect of his career, coming up with many of the ideas which Nomis would put into effect. Napier-Bell shared George's ambitions and used his organizational skills and long-standing network of press contacts to disseminate George's ideas.

The major innovation of the shows occurred when the band was offstage. During the interval they somewhat vainly aired their home movies gathered since childhood, giving the audience a chance to gasp at their antics as toddlers and fledgeling teenagers. The moments of sickly ordinariness congealed to relieve the mundane but slick efficiency of a show that basically ran through the much-aired *Fantastic* album plus a cover of Chic's 'Good Times' and the new, slower number 'Careless Whisper'. But whatever their critics might have remarked, Wham!'s fans came away smiling and more convinced of the godlike stature of their all-too-human idols.

1984 started with a kind of phoney war for Wham!. Stars without pop portfolio, they spent the first three months frustrated and bored. They were gossip column staples without a product to promote. Frequent mentions, from George's alleged romance with Hazel O'Connor (who perhaps not so coincidentally shared the same solicitors) to Andrew's rather lacklustre twenty-first birthday party at Foubert's nightclub, may have kept the band in the public consciousness, but the coverage was very much the calm before the storm. Indeed, it was serving a higher purpose: Nomis's PR putsch for Wham! everywhere but on vinyl helped to remind CBS (and other labels) that when Wham! were inevitably freed from the Innervision shackles they would still be a highly marketable commodity. Meanwhile, Andrew used the break to work on his skiing and tan while George concentrated on his songwriting in preparation for a resolution of the legal battle.

The litigation that had prevented the band from recording was finally settled out of court on 23 March 1984. Dean's capitulation lost him Wham! in exchange for a 'handsome' pay-off in settlement. But it had been a taxing time for him. He claims to have received anonymous phone calls telling him to leave town. There was a considerable amount of relief on his part that the ordeal was over. Dean's real gain was wisdom; having suffered the ignominy of being on the receiving end of proceedings with people he once considered friends and his own employer CBS, the disabused Dean was determined to go on to bigger things. George and Andrew, meanwhile, signed to Epic (ironically a CBS subsidiary) on a considerably higher royalty rate in line with their recognized potential. Simon Napier-Bell and Jazz Summers could rub their hands in satisfaction at the job they had done. They had more than earned their reputed fifteen per cent slice of Wham!'s profits.

For George in particular the whole affair was a chastening experience which left him both warier and harder. He was grateful to Dean but felt far from indebted to the young entrepreneur, remarking in *Time Out* in the spring that, 'In some ways he was very good to us. But somebody would have broken Wham! some day. You don't have to thank people for trying to make money out of you.' Although he had been confined to the legal sidelines George could now bring a seasoned businessman's acumen into play in his discussions with his management, publishers and record company. When he first entered Epic Records' offices in Soho Square, just off Oxford Street at the opposite end to Innervision's sanctum, he didn't just visit the visible publicity and A&R department, he also made a special point of showing his face behind the scenes in the copyright office, the legal office and the credit control office. He wasn't going to fall into another web of anonymous wheeler-dealing again so quickly. For George Michael, Dean was not in the same league as him any more; he just was not big enough for Wham!. Rather ungraciously, George felt that he did not need to thank Dean for breaking Wham!; he believed that in time they would have broken through anyway.

It is a shame that Dean has been written out of George's life. Acknowledgement of his role in their 'discovery' has been lessened by George's *post hoc* claims that he inevitably would have been 'discovered' anyway. Who can say that George would have persevered long enough? Would his father have tolerated his son's ambitions for much longer? Of course the success of Wham! had helped to cement his relationship with his father. Indeed, both sets of parents bristled with pride at their son's achievements. For George and Andrew it was an odd time: still living with their families, they would find fans camping out on the doorstep during the day. Andrew's address was still in the phone book and when girls turned up at his house his father Albert gave them socks as souvenirs. But if success hadn't come so quickly, would George and Andrew have been prepared to fly the cosy Radlett nest and patiently work for their success?

Dean's predicament was priceless in shaping his own future ambitions: 'Small labels don't work. At the end of the day the corporation rules.' In the intervening years he has been an independent mogul again but has developed a fondness for the corporate structure that today sees him working for A&R at MCA Records in America and thinking of a move into movie production. As George would also learn in his own time, Dean's experiences have taught him a thing or two about the British attitude to success: 'Britain hates anyone that does well. When you have success here they don't just run you over, they reverse the car to check that they've got you.'

In retrospect, the six-month moratorium on Wham! releases was probably an ideal sabbatical. Any longer and they might have been forgotten by the public, any shorter and they might have been in danger of over-exposing themselves as their closest rivals were doing. Late in 1983 Culture Club had peaked with the international success of 'Karma Chameleon'. The media had been utterly drenched in Boy George's dreadlocks and easily palatable pronouncements and was visibly beginning to tire of him. He may have always made good copy but the incessant appearances of the pansticked poseur were beginning to lose their immediate shock value. Not only that, but the band's waning commercial popularity had brought with it internal strife. George Michael had seen this backlash coming and, learning his lessons well, was already concocting ways to keep the demand for Wham! rising.

Napier-Bell's tactic was one which both exposed Wham! and maintained public interest in them. His approach was to get as much press as possible, but keep TV appearances to a minimum. Television, Napier-Bell believed, was a medium everyone had access to and was no longer special. He wanted to create a mystique for his stars and he believed that the best way for that was to feed the newspapers stories. Napier-Bell was more than capable of rising to the challenge of creating mystique; in the past his charisma had enabled him to clinch record deals for bands that had not even existed outside his hyper-active imagination, so myth making around a bona fide band came as second nature by now. And he was swift to realize that, even more than television, the tabloids were also involved in the business of peddling fantasy. With the aid of his loyal press officer Connie Filippello, whose efficacious 'dahlings' could entice the most cynical of hacks, Napier-Bell had a field day supplying the British tabloid press with 'silly stories'. George and Andrew were not averse to playing the game, exaggerating their sexual exploits until their braggadocio conspired to backfire on them.

Wham!'s enforced sabbatical created just the right bal-ance of expectation and salivation to make 'Wake Me Up Before You Go Go' climb swiftly to become their first UK number 1 in May 1984. Recorded in Pittsburgh, Pennsylvania, the new single marked the shape of things to come, hinting at the lush American pseudo-Motown sheen that was to become George's stock in trade.

Hunger for something new from the duo was so great, the single sold 700,000 copies as fast as the tills could ring up the prices, 64,000 in one day alone, knocking the spots off strong competition from the current, more authentic, black soul invasion of Rufus and Chaka Khan, Womack and Womack and the Pointer Sisters. The demand virtually outstripped the supply, indicating the efficacy of the perfectionist pop star's decision to shelve the comeback single they initially recorded, 'Whamshake', which to this date remains unreleased. George was aware enough that Wham!'s growing band of supporters would have snapped up 'Whamshake', but he wanted to return with a more sophisticated, less contrived style that would be indicative of his imminent direction. 'Go Go' saw Wham! pitching themselves back into the battle for teen pop supremacy against latest challengers Frankie Goes To Hollywood and reigning champions Culture Club and Duran Duran. In their absence, particularly insipid second-rate bands had made their challenge and found a certain naïve notoriety, almost by default. But the second division of New Pop, particularly the worst offenders, Howard Jones and Nik Kershaw, were soon to fall by the wayside. 'Go Go' deposed Duran Duran's 'Reflex' from the top spot, but was dethroned itself by Frankie Goes To Hollywood's apocalyptic dose of pomp, 'Two Tribes'.

The 'Wake Me Up Before You Go Go' composition typified George's techniques. The title had been inspired by a note that Andrew had left for his mother one night back in Bushey. For those that were totally dismissive of Andrew it was nice to know he still had some creative input in the band. It was the product of a cocktail of inspiration, impulse and apathy that still exists in George today. Part prima donna, part enigmatic muse, part sloth, even when making the *Faith* album he would book studios at £1000 a day and not turn up if the mood was wrong, regularly rising from his bed at one or two o'clock in the afternoon. George did a demo at home with just a bass line and vocal and by the time they got into the studio, still unable to write music having dropped out of his A level class, he sang all the parts to the musicians and they recorded it in one take, the rehearsal resulting in virtually the finished copy.

At the time the best way to come up with a new hit was to fall back on an old hit. The singles charts were being consumed by retro-pop, pastiche and re-releases. Bob Marley, dead for nearly half a decade, vied for a chart placing with comedian Nigel Planer's alter ego 'Neil the Hippy', who had recorded a joke cover version of Traffic's psychedelic hokum, 'Hole In My Shoe'. The charts were often a barometer of the nadirs in popular taste, but this was now compounded by the cynicism of marketing records by dead people and fictional TV characters. If one did not actually cover an old song, the next best thing, and one which meant you kept the publishing royalties, was to lift melodies and lines from classic songs. This was the downside of the postmodern condition, as pop folded in on itself by failing to come up with something new.

The abiding rumour of the time was that Boy George would turn up in the studio with three old Motown records. He would take the bass line from one, the hook line from another and the rhythm from a third. Certainly the introduction of his hit 'Church Of The Poison Mind' was reminiscent of two Martha Reeves numbers: 'Dancing In The Street' and 'Nowhere To Run'. It was an accusation that would be levelled more and more at George Michael too. His defence was that if his songs reminded listeners of old ones it was because his mind had been absorbing classic pop from the radio and his beloved tape recorder for over ten years: in other words, pop had infiltrated his psyche. Besides, his intention was to write good pop songs; he did not say anything about them being original pop songs.

Totally responsible by now for Wham!'s musical output, the muse could strike George anywhere. One night, while watching 'Match of the Day' at Andrew's family home, he decided that Wham! ought to have a Christmas hit in the bag; making pop-writing look ludicrously simple, minutes later he had composed their forthcoming hit, 'Last Christmas'.

Meanwhile the war on pop's home front was being fought between Wham! and Frankie Goes To Hollywood. Frankie were making the brazenly epicurean Wham! seem rather feeble. Where Frankie's 'Relax' had been banned because of the sexual nature of its lyrics, 'Go Go' could have come straight from the clean-cut stars of the fifties. In the same way that Pat Boone had bleached out all the blackness of early rock and roll records, so George was squeezing the sexuality out of eighties pop, relinquishing his social commentator mantle in the process. In interviews George and Andrew frequently declared their support for the Labour Party because of their nuclear disarmament policy (they had hoped to play a CND benefit at Wembley but it proved to be logistically impossible) but refused to be

drawn on political issues in their music, sticking to personal
politics with the somewhat spurious argument that opera
did not have any political content so why should pop.

To compound the contrast, where 'Go Go''s video saw a
frisky pastel-hued Wham! in their shorts in a pop playpen,
jumping from monochrome to dayglo shots, the 'Two
Tribes' video followed the lurid lyrical content of the song
by moving away from the band members and presenting
a head-on USA v. USSR fight in a circus ring between
Reagan and Chernenko look-alikes. The difference was
made explicit: one was ultraviolet, the other ultra-violent.
The public was buying up both, but if Frankie were selling
more discs, Wham!'s pandering to the cult of personality
was helping them to win the pin-up battle. A measure
of the new-found arrogance of Wham! was the way they
purloined Frankie's big bold lettered T-Shirts, customizing
their own with the words, 'Choose Wham!' and, most
cuttingly, 'Number One'. Plunder appeared to have been
appropriated into the rules of pop – Frankie could hardly
complain; they had themselves borrowed the designs from
terminally hip *haute couture* designer, Katharine Hamnett.

Success was now a reality for George. And at last he had
complete control while his nearest rivals were ostensibly
ZTT's puppets on a shoestring salary. He boasted to *Time
Out*'s Simon Garfield: 'There is not any aspect of our
presentation or recording arrangement which is engineered
by anyone else.' With the elegantly constructed 'Wake Me
Up Before You Go Go' however, the honeymoon with
the media was well and truly over. Wham! were about
to find themselves partially willing participants in Fleet
Street's open season on pop. Preoccupied momentarily
by the charts, they saw Frankie holding on to the top
spot for a staggering nine weeks with 'Two Tribes'. But
if the Liverpool group had any illusions about owning the
freehold to the top spot they were about to be shattered.
George Michael had other ideas.

6

Soul Mining

In the midst of his success George Michael found himself
becoming more and more isolated from Andrew Ridgeley.
As events catapulted them to greater heights they handled
their predicament differently. The sensationalist tabloid
press, not known for its deftness of touch, reported
Wham!'s success and swiftly accrued wealth with a
condemnatory relish that was at times barely containable.
George and Andrew diligently played right into Fleet
Street's hands by claiming to live up to their Don Juanish
images. They clearly did not realize that by feeding the
beast of Fleet Street to make a name for themselves, they
were also setting themselves up for a backlash as it became
difficult to get the hype without the hypocrisy.

At first the popular press loved Wham!. They had other
whipping boys to arraign with their self-righteousness.
Frankie's outrageousness made them the corruptors of a
nation's morals, Boy George's bisexuality made him prey
to the homophobic hacks. Wham! by contrast appeared
to be the archetypal boys-next-door whose sheer normality could be used by the press as a stick to beat their
polymorphously perverse contemporaries. And in the case
of Frankie, the suburban soul stylists George and Andrew
made explicit the economic north/south divide. Frankie
were defiantly scouse, George and Andrew were elegantly
south suburban. Wham! were still living like your average
well-heeled teenagers, returning from glamorous West End
openings such as the première of *Saturday Night Fever*'s

sequel, *Staying Alive*, to their comfy out-of-town family abodes. And the image that George had choreographed on *Top of the Pops* two years before for 'Young Guns' was genuine: they really were close friends who would do anything for each other; they really did share a distinctive off-the-wall sense of humour which, through a series of shared, private experiences, had by now become almost a secret language, impenetrable to the outside world. The problem was that the pact they had made to split once George's career was established was getting harder to fulfil all the time. Things had got so quickly out of hand, and what they had not allowed for was Andrew getting hooked on the pop star lifestyle to the point where it seemed impossible to back down. At the same time, his self-respect made it difficult for Andrew to constantly live in the shadow of his partner. Andrew's difficulty was finding a viable way of living with these contradictions.

They could not avoid the schism that was developing, and the subtext of their respective press coverage hardly needed to be deconstructed to reveal their different aspirations and preoccupations. Andy had sold his archetypal soul-boy wheels, a Capri, and was looking at ostentatious Jaguars and Ferraris. George had yet to pass his driving test.

While George and Andrew continued to frequent the same clubs and restaurants together, the press homed in on Andrew as the more newsworthy. Even when the duo was cornered together, it was always 'Randy Andy' who qualified for the sleaziest of reportage. It was almost as if George had struck his own pact with the press with the sole purpose of bringing down his friend.

With Parliament in recess, summer is always a thin time for hard news, thus justifying its 'Silly Season' title. But the summer of 1984 was the silliest season of all, particularly for the tabloid press, which did not give much coverage to hard news at the best of times. Royal gossip would quite easily capture the front page at the expense of a declaration of war and Wham!'s copy-worthiness was almost as high as Princess Diana's. So when a report rang out that Andrew Ridgeley had been involved in a fracas in a London nightclub which ended with him in hospital, imaginations began working almost as feverishly as Wham!'s press office had done earlier in the chain of events.

According to one report, George's sparring partner David Austin had been swinging an ice bucket and lobbing drinks at Ridgeley because he was talking to his girlfriend. Another talked of him being slashed with a bottle. A third homed in on the tragedy that Ridgeley's face had been scarred for life. All in all it seemed to be an eventful night for Andrew. The story was widely reported with different emphases on events. Some innocuously called it a prank while others haughtily condemned it as a brawl. The only consistent 'fact' appeared to be that the happy-go-lucky pop star was blind drunk. The front page coverage was carefully engineered to run for a staggering four days. As different stories were leaked from the bowels of Wham!'s headquarters in W1, no one dared not print for fear of missing the truth. It was an object lesson in the way Fleet Street rivalry caused the tabloids to chase each other's tales.

In reality the story was being used to conceal something more furtive. Andrew Ridgeley had had another operation on his nose. Not for the first or the last time, Napier-Bell and the press had created maximum publicity. The pop entrepreneur took an almost unseemly pleasure in calculating the column inches gleaned for his young charge. The throwing of the champagne bucket was a particularly nice touch, raising the tone of the supposed escapade from a lager loutish pub rumpus into a rather glamorous jet set altercation.

The egomaniacal half of the management team was revelling in his position as unofficial king-maker, revelling in his old style manipulative tactics. Not only did he help to infiltrate the tabloids, he also raised his own profile in the quality press when he talked to the *Observer* and unusually coyly explained his shrewd managerial talents: 'There are ways of making sure that people buy them from the chart shops.' This way number ones could be achieved by selling a quarter of the real number needed. He revealed that the demand for Wham! on their return had not been as effusive as it first had seemed. There was at least some genuine demand but it was the perfect timing of the release of 'Wake Me Up Before You Go Go' that gained it fourteen days of constant airplay before it reached the shops. This created a bottleneck effect, in turn assuring such an impressively high initial chart placing. From then on the hype could be replaced by genuine interest created by yet more airplay earned by its high position.

Meanwhile the misdemeanours of Mr Ridgeley were vying with the peccadilloes of Princess Di and Margaret Thatcher for the front pages. Where the first was lovable and the latter formidable, Andrew's gimmick was his metamorphosis into the archetypal rock monster. But under closer scrutiny he was hardly in the same league as the debauched larger-than-life legends of the sixties and seventies. There were no Cadillacs driven into swimming pools, no bacchanalian orgies of sexual excess. His sins of heavy drinking and minor lechery were just the going rate for the average twenty-one-year-old. In the fifties it was Presley's below the waist movements corrupting our children, in the sixties it was drugs and devilry. The seventies heaped still more gross self-indulgence into the headlines. What had the eighties to offer so far? Cosmetic surgery combined with nothing more than someone getting rather rowdy and randy.

What was more interesting was the way that George was ignored, as if he was at home each night penning the next best seller. It was a situation strangely reminiscent of the exploits of the Beatles and the Rolling Stones two decades earlier. While the press played them off against each other as evil corruptors and white knights, the two bands actually got on quite well and happily mixed socially. But when the Stones were busted for drug use, the Beatles had also been present, the constabulary conveniently waiting for their departure before making their entry. The Beatles were so much a part of the establishment by then that they were almost beyond reproach. The question asked was whether George was being set up as the 'Mr Clean of pop', as the *Star* dubbed him, just to bring him crashing down. Fleet Street was a fine example of the great English disease of despising success. Would hubris have its way with George?

By Wham!'s own admission the rock and roll clichés of groupies and drugs didn't interest them. Their background was not in rock, they had paid their dues neither as musicians nor as avid fans of live music, they were simply letting their suburban lifestyle escalate as their careers advanced. And while the press hounded Ridgeley for every nuance of naughtiness, George's own exploits went unnoticed, even though high bounty was offered for stories relating to his sexual predilections and prowess, or lack of it.

George recovered some respectful press coverage for the band that August when, significantly solo, he was the pin-up star of the *Sunday Times* colour supplement spread celebrating the return of the Hawaiian shirt. In a bright-lit layout George found himself in the illustrious if unlikely company of a similarly apparelled Noël Coward, the Duke of Edinburgh, and perhaps rather more appropriately Elvis Presley. If the publication gave Wham! a certain amount of kudos, the angle was somewhat retrogressive. A year on, Wham!'s tongue-in-cheek 'Club Tropicana' look was still being taken at face value; unfortunately the prestigious photo opportunity was too attractive to turn down, particularly as it coincided with George's promotion of his début solo single, 'Careless Whisper'. Andrew, meanwhile, had his own fashion spread, modelling shirts in David Litchfield's *Ritz*, the chic broadsheet of Chelsea's moneyed airheads. Appropriately he was modelling the 'rich and happy look', something more in tune with Wham!'s current state of affairs than George's palm tree nirvana.

Having prepared for the photo sessions, a retreat from continued exposure was found in the isolated château Minerval of jazz composer Jacques Loussier in the south of France. In the recording studio there George was able to polish up his compositions for the crucial second album. France held various attractions for the duo. Not only did it help them escape from the glare and hysteria that they had encouraged the media to whip up, but it also had tax advantages. The duo were becoming ever more money conscious. At the same time it was not too far away for George to whiz home for promotional appearances, a crucial factor when the sojourn coincided with the success of his first solo single, 'Careless Whisper'.

Inevitably the release of 'Careless Whisper' in July 1984 prompted further speculation about a split, but it was strenuously claimed by both the temporarily solo star and his PR mouthpieces that at that point nothing was further from George's mind. What its hidden agenda did reveal was that George was not only growing away from his easily satisfied friend, but he was also moving away from his hormone-charged teenage audience and their limited attention span that demanded non-stop frivolity. Ironically it was one of the few songs to be co-credited to his partner, a remnant from the original demo tape, though legend has it that George did the bulk of the work while sitting on the top deck of a London bus, and lyrically it was certainly claimed that it was grounded in his own experience.

The version of 'Careless Whisper' that arrived in the shops that summer was produced by George Michael himself. He had originally gone out to record the song in Muscle Shoals, Alabama, the summer before with legendary soul producer Jerry Wexler, whose track record included such showbiz tyros as Aretha Franklin and Ray

Charles. The veteran producer had honoured George by
asserting that he had the nearest thing to a black voice he
had ever heard from a white European. At the time the
single was intended as an impending Innervision release,
but things did not work out well. An increasingly self-
confident George was dissatisfied with Wexler's work and
he shelved the results (although they eventually surfaced
briefly on a limited edition twelve-inch release of the
single for Epic Records). After a second recording session
with an outside producer, George decided that he was the
best judge of his own material and produced the track
himself, demonstrating an impressive ability behind the
mixing desk as well as in front of it. From the beginning
of his career George had insisted on producing his
own material and he had now proved that he could
arrange, orchestrate and record his own songs better
than the best. The ensuing sales that took the record
to number one within the month, knocking Frankie's
second successive nine-week chart-topper 'Two Tribes'
off its pedestal seemed to indicate that the arrogant streak
of self-determination was vindicated. Indeed, 'Careless
Whisper' eventually topped the charts in an impressive
fifteen countries.

'Careless Whisper' demonstrated that George's aspirations stretched further than finger-clicking-good dance
exercises. This was an intensely personal, deeply languid
ballad that seemed to project George in a more adult,
sincere, worldly light. It was hard to believe that it had been
penned by an insouciant, slightly awkward seventeen-year-
old. One lyrical couplet in particular, 'I'm never gonna
dance again/guilty feet have got no rhythm', was bursting
with the kind of emotionally packed imagery that even
acknowledged wordsmiths like Elvis Costello and Randy
Newman would have been proud of. Amid the rumours
of a split George was quick to explain that the two careers
had to be separate but could easily co-exist: 'As Wham!
the only constant identity we have is that we're up-tempo,

lightweight pop. I love writing Wham! songs but I've enjoyed doing my own solo record, too.' You did not have to peer deeply between the lines of the verbose press puffs to realize that the Wham! formula, successful as it was proving, was still very much a finite, musically limited affair that in many respects Andrew was as keen to be freed from as George. In America 'Careless Whisper' was released under the name of Wham! featuring George Michael, which only helped to compound the question on the lips of many a pop pundit: was Wham! a group any more?

With plans afoot for the solo single even before the imbroglio with Mark Dean, one of the first things George did when the Innervision settlement was reached in May 1984 was go off to Miami to film the video. 'Careless Whisper' was like a vinyl version of *Dynasty*: a soul symphony and soap opera combined and condensed into three minutes, a steamy tale of love and betrayal that almost sat up and begged for the film rights to be snapped up. The storyboard religiously traced the single's narrative as George embraced his role as full-blown sex symbol and pandered to the worst facets of his vanity. Cravenly refusing to send up the decadent excesses of pop, this gauchely competed with Duran Duran's 'Rio' clip, the benchmark of New Pop's hedonistic self-indulgence. Without a hint of irony George opted for a similar scenario of sun, sea and scantily clad women. Here George romped playfully with an actress in champagne-bathed bedrooms, silhouetted against a golden Florida sunset. Rumour had it that while filming the steamy bedroom scene with one of the two women featured, George's partner passed out. His apologists put it down to the authenticity of the passion that had left his co-star breathless while his critics suggested that her still slightly chubby consort's girth had been the cause of her gasping for air.

When casting, George had reputedly taken a leaf out of actor Richard Gere's book – during the filming of *Breathless* he wore trunks when auditioning girls to see their response. With the first day of shooting completed George decided that he did not like the way his hair looked. The Florida heat had turned it frizzy and made him 'look like Shirley Bassey'. Shooting had to be repeated at an extra cost of £17,000, after a quick snip from his sister Melanie, echoing the rather unlikely tale of his flight back from Cyprus just to have his locks chopped. Only the most generous of commentators could praise this as an example of an acute awareness of the subtleties of image in contemporary music. To many this was simply the most expensive haircut in pop.

Where Andrew's press-worthy misdemeanours seemed to revolve around his alcoholic excesses, George's concerns centred upon his crowning glory and his battle to contain the curls that waged war around his scalp. This was a story that would run and run. When Andrew was asked what George's most irritating habit was he had no hesitation in replying that it was that he spent so long on his hair.

During the filming of 'Careless Whisper' Andrew and David Austin kept George company in the exotic Mutiny Hotel, a watering hole renowned for its theme rooms. George's was called 'Luna Dreams', a disco dream come to life replete with a panoply of neon tubes and lights around the bed, and mirrors on the ceiling, even in the kitchen. George had to mix his pleasure with business. Still unable to write musical notation, he carried a portable cassette recorder around with him, so that if a bacillus of inspiration struck he could preserve it. Even if he did not have his cassette with him he worked on a simple principle that he felt would maintain the quality of his output, one that did go some way to explaining the paucity of originality; if a tune came up which was good enough to be a hit it would lodge naturally in his head and he would not need to write it down.

The release of 'Careless Whisper' was undoubtedly a case of George testing the waters to see if he was a commercially viable entity without Andrew. The single's swift ascent in the charts proved his theories beyond doubt. Had 'Careless Whisper' been met with a lukewarm response, Wham!'s future plans might have been extended indefinitely; but the confirmation that Andrew was superfluous to George's success instilled the singer with a hitherto unacknowledged confidence. He had finally overhauled his friend in the one role in which he felt he had always lagged in the shadows: George too had the charisma to carry off stardom. While boys wanted to be George Michael, girls wanted to bed George Michael; and sometimes the sexual dividing line was not so clearly drawn.

Not only had George now become the first person to have a number one record in the same year both as a solo artist and member of a group, but he had also knocked arch rivals Frankie Goes To Hollywood from the top. After nine weeks at number one this was the beginning of the end for Frankie; their inexorable rise was rapidly to become their inexorable fall. The momentum of two of the biggest selling singles in history could never be maintained or lived up to. It was a challenge that George, himself, was only too aware of.

It was while staying at Minerval that George first met Elton John. In typical fashion, a helicopter landed on the lawn outside the château and out stepped the diminutive foppish rock star that George had idolized as a child. Elton had to go to France to record a voice-over for a French TV commercial and took the opportunity to meet the new pop wunderkind. Elton's reciprocated admiration of George soon turned the day into an unceasing bout of back-slapping as they found that they had many things in common. Elton John was also a product of North London's suburban sprawl, albeit from an earlier generation, having been born in Pinner in Middlesex. He retained a passion for the area long after he had settled in America, and had become chairman of Watford Football Club, not a million miles from Radlett, pumping over £3 million into their coffers and seeing the lowly Fourth Division side reach the First Division and the FA Cup Final. Like George's, Elton's success reflected a triumph over early difficulties: here was a small, bald, myopic figure slipping into middle age not particularly gracefully – the unlikeliest international sex symbol of them all. Like George, he had changed his name, from the uniquely mundane Reg Dwight. Both of them realized that the real secret of success was not just talent, but solid hard graft.

Their public friendship and increasingly fulsome mutual endorsements revealed more sinister behind-the-scenes powerbroking. Wham! were clients of promotions high-flyer Gary Farrow. From Bromley in Kent, Farrow had carved himself a niche working for Elton John's Rocket Records as a record plugger and now in his late twenties was branching out into public relations. From his humble beginnings, his streetwise yuppie-cum-barrow-boy patois had helped him to establish an influential network of contacts in the media industry that had lubricated his quasi-ascendance from hyperbole-clogged record plugger to hyperbole-clogged 'PR, marketing and promotions'. His clients included Paul Young, Bob Geldof, Elton, David Bowie and George. While Nomis's loyal press officer Connie Filippello threw titbits to the press, Farrow busied himself stage-managing events of a more respectable nature. In recent years an uncanny quantity of tabloid stories have numbered various permutations of the afore-mentioned dramatis personae in their cast. In suitably oily fashion, Farrow was instrumental in easing George's transition from teen-idol to mature artist by associating him with other mature artists from the outset of their professional relationship. It was certainly a fruitful, close team, George going on to become a close family friend and godfather of Farrow's baby daughter.

Elton's flying visit was one of the few breaks for George during the recording of the new album. There were very

few occasions when the duo could let their hair down.
For George, weighed down with orchestrating the proceedings, there was little chance to unwind. There was
only one occasion, a cruel parody of their youthful high
jinks, that broke the tedium for George and Andrew.
The duo drove down to the south of France where a
night of drunken revelry culminated in Andrew haranguing
Joan Collins's quayside yacht and asking her to show
them her curlers. It was an incident in which George was
drunkenly complicit, but the following day, as he nursed
a retributional hangover and was thoroughly ashamed
of himself, Andrew considered the event just another
caper. But this break in the routine, combined with the
inspirational fillip of Elton's visit, spurred George on to
greater industry and by the end of the summer, following
a brief remix in Paris, George was back in England with the
second album ready for release in time for Christmas.

Much to George's chagrin, Wham! were still at the epicen-
tre of the notoriously shallow pop scene, simultaneously
symbols and symptoms of Thatcherite *laissez-faire*. Even
the more mature, reflective outpourings of 'Careless Whisper' and the indulgent excesses of the video had done
little to restore his political credibility. Staunch defenders
of the Left did a double-take when it was announced
that Wham! were to be performing at the Royal Festival
Hall on Friday 7 September 1984. The event was the
final night of a series of concerts entitled 'Five Nights
for the Miners'. The performances had been set up in
conjunction with the National Union of Mineworkers
to raise money for miners and their families. They had
been striking to save their jobs since March and many
communities had been forced beyond the poverty line by
the action. A family of four in Yorkshire, for instance,
had to eke out their existence on a weekly payment of
£45.50. The prospect of their homes being repossessed
by building societies as mortgage payments were not met

was becoming a reality. As Chairman of the National Coal Board, Ian McGregor had indulged in the most discompassionate kind of asset-stripping, closing twenty pits and consigning 20,000 miners to the dole queues. Two years later, after an acrimonious and increasingly violent strike had petered out, McGregor would be awarded a knighthood for services to British industry. Fund-raising events and benefits had been taking place throughout the dispute, but this was pop's biggest contribution to the fight. Most of the acts confirmed were known supporters of the Left, bands such as the Style Council and Working Week, who were to go on to form the hardcore of the political consciousness-waking front, Red Wedge. They were complemented by the burgeoning radical talents of the alternative comedy ranks, in particular Rik Mayall and Alexei Sayle.

Among such champions of the oppressed, Wham!'s inclusion seemed perverse, but Jazz Summers had accepted the invitation and put it to Wham! who had agreed to perform. Even though George had declared that he had voted Labour in the previous year's General Election, this was still a spectacular coup for dogmatic militant Miners' Leader Arthur Scargill. George's intentions were fundamentally honourable, but there must have been a thought lurking somewhere in his mind that he could regain some of the credibility of Wham!'s dole days by striking this blow for socialism.

But what could have helped to redeem Wham! and gain George capital with his much-desired adult audience cruelly backfired. Unable to use their usual backing band, the duo chose to mime to tapes. Eighteen months earlier this would have been second nature to them. But the once ceaseless round of club promotions had been replaced by the skilfully co-ordinated live shows, miming was confined to *Top of the Pops*, and the increasing use of the videos in the place of studio appearances had made even that more and more rare.

Wham!'s lack of musical match fitness, combined with an audience that was not, for once, wholeheartedly partisan, conspired to set things off on the wrong foot. Matters were exacerbated when the tape started and George found himself introducing the wrong song. Instead of praise, Wham! only gleaned worse press. One paper cruelly suggested the concert should have been called the Mimers' Benefit.

Backstage George met Arthur Scargill. After the shambolic events of the evening, a bitter George came away with a negative impression of the Miners' Leader: he felt that he was enjoying the strike too much and in the process damaging his own industry.

Reviews of the event failed to give George any credit for his contribution. Criticism ranged from his miming to his hairstyle and declined to praise his agreement to appear. The music press in particular revealed themselves to be completely out of step with the real world, suffering from the delusion that being rich meant one had to be right wing. The street-credible, left-inclined, post-punk stance was no longer a viable ethos for the eighties. Things had changed beyond recognition since the days of spiky revolt. The fragmentation of popular culture had dissipated any bedrock of a mass alternative lifestyle such as had been witnessed in the hippy counterculture and punk recalcitrance. The aspirations of the average youthful pop fan had perceptibly altered; the perceptions of the press remained firmly rooted in the past. Even George's political idealism was rapidly wilting; he would exercise more caution in aligning himself with specific political issues in the future. He was in a more realistic, individualistic frame of mind later on when he refused an invitation to join Red Wedge: 'That kind of idealism doesn't take account of human nature.' From the point of view of George's career, the miners' débâcle was another nail in the coffin of Wham!. Another reminder of how suffocating the expectations and format of pop could be.

Ten days later, on 17 September, it was business as usual

again when the duo released their bona fide follow-up to 'Go Go', 'Freedom'. Number one by the middle of October was an almost foregone conclusion for what was evolving into George's generic brand of pop – a dash of Motown, a stomping rhythm and a deliriously infectious, if corny, hook line; their fame even warranted a front page story in the *Daily Mirror* which stated nothing more than its position. Pop was taking a grip on Fleet Street in a way it had not done since the sixties; a simple grainy press shot of the duo was enough to raise a smile on the face of the Street of Shame's circulation managers.

Wham! were back in buoyant mood. They were consistently outstripping sales of their nearest challengers, Duran Duran and Culture Club, making them seem decidedly over the hill in the process. With 'Last Christmas' already earmarked as their next hit, it seemed that their only real threat for the Christmas number one spot came from the rather less sexually appetizing Father Abraham and the Smurfs.

Wham! were also intent on securing the top of the album charts with the release of their second album, *Make It Big*. Starving miners were a long way away by November when Wham! launched the record at London's Xenon club amid a champagne celebration that set them back £10,000. This was showbiz in excelsis as London's rentacelebrities crowded around the paparazzi to notch up some gossip column inches of their own. It was an unlikely cast that paid tribute to the sterling work of the capital's best agents as a troop of celebrities, half-stars and passing fads paid their compliments to the band. Ageing comics Frankie Howerd, Bobby Ball and Kenny Lynch, sixties star Lulu, wife of footballer George, Angie Best, grizzled actor John Hurt and more predictable pop personalities of varying status, Duran Duran's Simon Le Bon, archetypal flash-in-the-pan singing haircut Limahl, David Cassidy and Bob Geldof were among the throng. Former paramour of Prince Andrew, Koo Stark, put her head around the door but one look at the self-congratulatory spectacle was enough and she disappeared into the crisp autumn night.

Make It Big confirmed Wham! as big league pop, going straight to the top of the LP charts in Great Britain. In record time Wham! had become simultaneously the most reviled and the most popular band in Britain. The music press may have scathingly tainted them with the teeny pop tag or worse still the Thatcherite pop tag, but no one could deny the commercial success of George Michael. *Make It Big* had triumphed over the challenges from Frankie Goes To Hollywood's gargantuan, overproduced *Welcome To The Pleasuredome*, Culture Club's hurried, haphazard *Waking Up With The House On Fire* and Duran Duran's water-treading live outing, *Arena*. Even more significantly, the album release coincided with 'Wake Me Up Before You Go Go' topping America's Billboard Top 100, holding off all comers including Prince and Madonna.

In Britain the charts were as lacklustre as ever; as 'Freedom' drifted out of the singles race it was replaced by a new wave of pop minnows such as former lead singer of one-hit wonders Kajagoogoo, Limahl, whose exotic nomenclature belied a previously unparalleled blandness, and Jim Diamond, a squeaky solo artist of no fixed ability. In fact England seemed to be in the grip of seedy second-raters. *EastEnders* was still a twinkle in some producer's eye as doomed soap *Crossroads* and the antediluvian cloth-capped *Coronation Street* vied for the top of the UK TV ratings. In the publishing world the adolescent angst of *The Growing Pains of Adrian Mole* allowed author Sue Townsend to laugh all the way to the bank, challenged only by clairvoyant Doris Stokes, who with a blinding lack of insight which was hardly the best advert for her skills, failed to predict her own untimely death in 1987. It was little surprise that Wham! were so newsworthy; pop seemed to be the only thing England still excelled at.

Andrew's younger brother Paul, occasional drummer with the Executive, chose the release of *Make It Big* to slam his sibling in the *News of the World*, surprising no one by claiming that he was more talented than his brother. He went on to recall how he used to have to save Andrew from the school bully back at Bushey Meads, although he loyally added that the band could not survive without him. Not so coincidentally, perhaps, he also happened to be plugging his own new group, Physique.

The release of *Make It Big* was ample excuse for George's critics to lay siege to his musical abilities again and write Wham! off as tuneless pin-ups. George manfully defended himself: 'If a bunch of ugly bastards went up on stage and played "Wake Me Up Before You Go Go" it would still be a hit.'

No amount of bile could halt his progress. With the UK and crucial US charts conquered, the next objective was a tour to shore up their world-wide successes. On 5 December the UK leg of the global jaunt kicked off relatively quaintly at the Whitley Bay Ice Rink in north-east England. A modest venue whose name suggested pantos and synchronized dance rather than international pop sensations, the arena still held a substantial sell-out crowd of 4,500 screaming youngsters. And regardless of the increasingly economically depressed circumstances of the region, they each found £6.50 for the tickets.

All George needed now was a Christmas number one to make his year complete and to become the first artist ever to have four number ones in the same calendar year. Apart from his fears of Father Abraham and the Smurfs it looked like a formality. Indeed it would have been but for a little thing called Band Aid.

7

Now is the Time for All Good Men to Come to the Aid of the Party

It did not go unnoticed that on Sunday 25 November 1984, as the full complement of pop's current icons from Boy George to Bono turned up at Sarm West Studios in London, one of the absentees was Andrew Ridgeley. Some reports suggested that he had not been asked by Bob Geldof to contribute to Band Aid's 'Do They Know It's Christmas?'. Others enquired after his absence to be informed rather churlishly that he had not been able to get out of bed in time. Whatever the reason, his diminishing relevance both as pop star and part of Wham! – not to mention an untimely lack of humanity – was to drive an ever-widening wedge between the duo. The smug pseudo-Rabelaisian's continuing behavioural lapses could no longer be put down to the initial shock of his sudden success. He was simply unable to adjust to stardom as comfortably as George Michael.

As it turned out, George still sang on four number one records that year. His bravura front-line vocal contribution to the Band Aid single played its part in helping it to become the biggest-selling single in history, so he could hardly complain. *Primus inter pares*, even his fiercest rivals felt compelled to heap praise upon his style and professionalism. Amid the roll-call of the best of British pop, George's star shone brightest. Boy George's blue-eyed soul suddenly seemed desperate, Simon Le Bon simply seemed spent. Paul Young was old, Sting was subdued, Paul Weller past it.

It became yet more of a purple patch for George when 'Last Christmas' nestled at number two alongside the Band Aid opus, which went on to sell a historic three million copies in the UK (over seven million worldwide), raising 96.03 pence for every £1.35 single bought. George could afford to be generous, and donated the royalties for 'Last Christmas' to the Ethiopia appeal as well. In a somewhat indulgent show of his generosity which came across as a rather more ostentatious gesture than he had intended, he remarked: 'I want to feed a few more mouths myself.'

Pop seemed at last to have come of age and accepted some of its wider social responsibilities. In the past, adult rock bands had played benefits in aid of world causes such as the Bangladesh famine and the Kampuchea upheavals, but in an era of rampant cynicism, performers aimed predominantly at the apolitical juvenile pop market had turned away from their transient teenage constituency and tried to do something socially substantial. Band Aid was to trigger off a new age of global compassion which musicians would suddenly realize did no harm to their own careers either.

For the money men, it was business as usual. At all stages of the production and distribution of the Band Aid single fees were waived: only the Government soured the cause by insisting on levying the 15% value added tax on singles.

George's own magnanimous gesture with the royalties to 'Last Christmas' became embroiled in an acrimonious dispute when publishers Dick James Music had the royalties frozen, accusing George of 'stealing' the melody from their client Barry Manilow's hit, 'Can't Smile Without You'. It was a petty case, even though substantial sums were involved ('Last Christmas' and its impressive, undulating piece of Anglo-funk on the B-side, 'Everything She Wants', was a million seller), since the money was intended for charity. DJM could hardly claim that the alleged lift was from the housewives' favourite, Manilow. George's lawyers could cite eleven similar melodies dating back to the beginning of the century, and if any, the one that George's memory banks had probably filed away was his ex-idol David Cassidy's hit 'Day Dreamer'. When the case was finally dropped in November 1985 and the royalties freed, George made a little capital out of the rhetorical retort: 'If they had won, would they have asked the starving to give back the food?'

Band Aid was George's first serious political commitment since the miners' strike benefit. It was a chance for George to show the world that he was not just the pretty pop star that Nomis thought they were managing. It gave extra cause for celebration when the duo's tour reached Wembley Arena at Christmas. The North London venue was almost like a local concert for George. With two shows either side of Christmas Day, he was able to spend the festive season with his family, just a brief drive up the motorway to their Hertfordshire home.

The London dates marked the culmination of the war between the giants of New Pop. Wham!, Spandau Ballet, Paul Young and Culture Club all announced a string of dates at the Arena and had been trying to outdo each other. Wham!'s four shows may have been beaten by Culture Club and Spandau Ballet who played six nights each, but George and Andrew knew that their rivals had been around longer and had been able to accumulate a backlog of fans. In a comparatively short space of time – just over two and a half years, which included a substantial period on pop's benches during the Innervision travails – Wham! were well on their way to overhauling the others.

It was an occasion for unbridled hysteria. One banner which declared its loyalty for the lesser half made no bones about its upholders' interests being decidedly non-musical, reading 'Drop 'Em Andrew'. Less vociferous mutterings, perhaps of 'Drop him George', could be heard among the cynics, but the electorate was still divided, albeit in George's favour.

The tour took a heavy physical toll on George's voice, which could not have been helped by the ludicrously tight black matador pants he was shoehorned into each night. Topped off with a white shirt, cummerbund and ill-advised bum-freezer jacket, George looked like some obscene parody of Tom Jones. This was not his most stylish phase. Andrew's main musical contribution appeared to be to jangle the sleigh bells during 'Last Christmas' while Pepsi and Shirlie's ever-shrinking role consisted of self-mocking parodies of women through the ages, from cheer-leaders to Christmas fairies.

The dynamic of Wham! live had shifted dramatically since their last tour. Andy's antics seemed shunted into the background by this new George who appeared to be positively bursting out of his cummerbund with confi-dence. By the end of the set it was George far more than the illustrious imbiber on guitar who was dancing amid a sea of Marks and Spencer's underwear.

1985 saw the tour head out around the world. Wham! had conquered Great Britain, but that was only the beginning. From Japan to Australia to their American début in Febru-ary, this was the blanketing of the globe that George had dreamed of. In each territory the same process of adulation was repeated with minor regional and cultural variations. In America underwear was tossed on stage, in Japan it was sweets, in Australia a shower of miniature kangaroos and koalas; but each gesture conveyed the feeling that the fans could not get enough of George. And each full house had the same beneficial effect on George's bank account.

One of the problems with attending to foreign affairs was that home affairs could be concocted *in absentia*. If Andrew's nose operation episode marked the zenith of collusion between the press and the press office, the self-proclaimed 'soaraway' *Sun* now excelled their smutty selves by giving birth to a story which could hardly have been generated by anyone else. Entitled 'Hands Off My Andy', reporter Ruth Brotherhood interviewed two topless models who each considered themselves to be poor, put-upon Andrew Ridgeley's closest bosom buddy. In a tumescent litany of Andy's fascinating love-life, Elisha Scott revealed how she found out she was not Andy's only bedmate when she rang her best friend Jackie St Clair and Andy answered the phone. As she was quick to realize it was 8.00 a.m. and 'No one calls around for coffee at that time . . . I bet she offered it to him on a plate.' Not coffee it transpired. 'She's a wicked temptress . . . I'll scratch her eyes out. She's not going to steal my man.' Elisha went on to recall events when they had driven back to her flat one night: 'We were so turned on we didn't make it to the bedroom. We made love right there on the floor.' The story continued in a similar vein of gutter journalese about kinky clothes and turning men on, and was accompanied by two pictures, one of Jackie St Clair and the other of a topless Elisha Scott with one arm round a smirking inane pre-rhinoplasty Ridgeley. One had to read the small caption to discover that she was standing with a 'cardboard cut-out of Andrew Ridgeley'.

Wham! discovered the incident when Jazz pointed out the headline in the *Melbourne Truth* which read 'Wham! star in nude rumpus'. Andrew had never met the two protagonists. And as for one of them having cryptically nicknamed him 'Walnut Whip', even his mind boggled. It was a 'story' that was soon picked up by the *Sun*'s rivals, further news being that the singer's rivals would be flying to confront him in New York for 'The Saint Valentine's Day Love Massacre'. Having set the Fleet Street ball rolling there seemed little the duo could do to stop the stories running, regardless of the reality.

On 9 February Wham! broke into their tour to attend the British Phonographic Industry Awards in London's plush Grosvenor House. Apart from Culture Club, who were conspicuous by their absence, this was just another assembly of the New Pop alumni. Duran Duran collected the award for the best video for 'Wild Boys', Paul Young was the Best Male Artist, Frankie's 'Relax' won the Best Single of 1984 (the establishment typically slow on the uptake – it had been released in autumn '83) and Geldof got a special award for 'Do They Know It's Christmas?'. But for many it also marked their swan-song; all of the aforementioned had already fallen, or were about to fall, from grace. Boy George had finally emptied his heart on TV one time too many, Duran Duran were growing up painfully and Frankie had simply run out of subjects to shock. Paul Young's crooner days were numbered, while the first post-punk progenitor of pop, Bob Geldof, was about to attempt to relaunch his career on the back of his honorary sainthood but was doomed to fail miserably. Only Wham!, who collected the award for Best Group, were to go on to bigger and better things.

An unlikely guest at the occasion was leader of the Labour Party, Neil Kinnock. Shrewd negotiations enabled the aspiring ambassador to unconsciously stamp socialism's approval on the orgy of free enterprise that pop had recently become. Following his video appearance with comedienne and pop star Tracey Ullman and his support of Red Wedge, the balding Parliamentarian indicated the the influence of pop on impressionable young voters was not lost on the Labour Party.

Further acknowledgement of his prodigious talents came that March when a tearful George picked up an Ivor Novello Award for Best Songwriter for 'Careless Whisper'. Presented with the gong by Elton John, his friend conferred something of a mixed blessing in acclaiming him as 'the Paul McCartney of his generation'. It was a lot to live up to, but also a lot to live down. In many people's eyes the eternally teenaged McCartney represented the saccharine side of the Beatles; his most militant work of the early seventies, 'Give Ireland Back To The Irish', may have been banned but it was dismissed as something of an

aberration. Its successor, 'Mary Had A Little Lamb', was
more in keeping with McCartney's style.

1985's media buzzed with rumours of George's supposed affair with Hazel O'Connor again. In reality he
had simply been helping her out with some production,
but the overworked minds of Grub Street printed their
fictions just in case. Had it been true it would have made
a fruity feature indeed; the classic saga of *A Star Is Born*
all over again. O'Connor was the female star fading fast
and finding herself attached to the young man on the rise
as she watched her own career crumble. Hazel O'Connor
had been jumped to prominence in the 1980 rock movie
Breaking Glass, but a number of dubious record deals and
business machinations resulted in a failure to capitalize on
her instant fame. By 1985 she too had found the solicitors'
firm Russells defending her in a contractual litigation case
not dissimilar to Wham!'s. Unfortunately for O'Connor,
her case became so drawn out that the public had lost
interest in her by the time she was free to record again,
not just because of the length of the lay-off, but also
because *Breaking Glass*'s bleached punk image was too
firmly fixed in the industry's mind and seemed totally
outmoded. However much she tried to soften her look
she could not shake her history off. Worse still was the fact
that record companies lost confidence in her because of her
wayward, impulsive nature; charming in an acquaintance,
a nuisance in a business associate.

Essentially Hazel O'Connor wanted to be a star every
bit as much as George did but had gone about it in a completely different way. She was a hang-over of the seventies,
when contractual ignorance and commercial indulgences
left major stars signing on at the dole office after their
hits had petered out. George, a crucial number of years
her junior, may have had artistic pretensions of a sort, but
he had taken a leaf out of Thatcherism's rule-book and
approached pop like any other business. More importantly,
George was peddling an image and a style of music that

was timeless. Where O'Connor could have emerged only in the early eighties, George could have broken through with the same melody-based music, the same clean cut look, twenty, even thirty years earlier.

Meanwhile Ridgeley lurched further and further into his role as Fleet Street's favourite reprobate. In late March they got to hear about his antics at a rugby club party in Bristol's luxurious if rather stiflingly upright Dragonara Hotel. With not inconsiderable pride, Ms Lynn Brown confessed to her 'stolen night of love' and 'my saucy antics with Andy' when she drew out the rock and roll reptile's animal desires simply by flashing her green knickers. The sequence of events as recalled had all the makings of a French farce with a touch of seaside postcard humour thrown in for good measure, a strange emphasis on the colour of underwear making the story particularly outstanding. Briefly, Andy was caught *in flagrante delicto* in only his canary-coloured underpants by her boyfriend who arrived with a fire extinguisher but was first soaked with water by Andrew. When interviewed he chided his partner by saying 'she's a naughty girl'. Reportage seemed rather awry. In the *News of the World*, who reputedly paid £500 for the story, Ms Brown gave her aspiring consort 'nine out of ten for effort and seven out of ten for style', while the less generous *Sunday People* reported her as bemoaning the fact that he was too drunk to do anything at all. Strangely, George had also been present at the evening but was presumably tucked up safely in bed by the time shenanigans ensued.

The *Sun* followed up with a salacious catalogue of Andrew's ice-breaking skills at another party, taking care not to morally censure his healthy heterosexual recreations. He had organized a big boobs competition, taken down a girl's trousers, offered autographs in exchange for gropes, tweaked girls' suspenders and fondled a man in drag, mistaking him for a woman. He was a busy man.

Rupert Murdoch's *Sun* at least approached the Lothario for an exclusive interview. They offered him £50,000, but Andrew, not wanting to do it at any price, asked for a Rolls-Royce Corniche convertible instead. To his surprise they agreed, but finding there was a waiting list they asked him to suggest a different car. Coming up with a Ferrari Daytona convertible seemed to meet with mutual approval until Andrew realized he would not have control over the copy. For once prudence got the better of him and he pulled out of the deal, resigning himself to the fact that they would continue to write whatever they liked.

George seemed to be the press's sweetheart. By contrast the main story involving him revealed that he was planning to buy the country house that formerly belonged to Britain's answer to Monroe, Diana Dors, and her husband Alan Lake, for £250,000, which was kitted out with an indoor swimming pool, gold-plated doors, a mirrored bedroom and ceiling, and carpets deep enough to get lost in. 'I think it's just right for me,' George reportedly remarked. After Diana Dors' recent death her grieving husband committed suicide and a series of macabre events had led the housekeeper to conclude that the house was haunted. Not that this was too much of a hazard for George; the exorcism would have to continue in his absence, he was still spending most of his time in London.

George was not averse to speaking freely to the style magazines that graced him with a certain amount of respect as one of pop's more articulate personages, even though sailing too close to the wind could result in his quotes being taken out of context and relocated in the tabloids. George could fulminate until the cows came home, but he knew that trial by tabloid appeared to be becoming an occupational hazard. In *The Face* that July he discussed his own sexual mores in a world where AIDS was still a speck on the heterosexual horizon. The chances of a settled George seemed slim: 'I don't believe fidelity is all it is cracked up to be.'

But the press hounds did eventually manage to associate him with an overblown scandal over the goings-on at the London club, Taboo. George's profile was smudged rather than shattered when he found himself as a peripheral addendum to a hysterical story that detailed drug-taking at the West End nighterie. George had been a frequent *habitué* of the club, run by embodiment of eccentricity Leigh Bowery. Taboo was a hang-out for the weirdest peacocks of the capital's after dark population, and it was reported in the press that George had been sighted taking poppers there. The fumes of poppers, or amyl nitrate, were inhaled immediately after the small glass phial was broken. The pop alluded to the crack of the bottle, but also to the feeling inside as one's heart started to race towards a brief euphoria.

Although used as a recreational drug rather than for pre-scribed medicinal purposes, amyl nitrate was perfectly legal and freely available, particularly in gay-orientated shops. The popularity of poppers among the gay community had linked it for a while as a possible cause of AIDS, since most of the Western victims to date had been homosexual. Inferences drawn from this about George's sexual prefer-ences were strenuously denied. The sexual link had added a lascivious moralistic *frisson* to the whole coverage, which contributed to the closure of the club, although the regulars simply regrouped in more underground haunts to rethink strategies and were later to become prime movers of the Acid House scene in the summer of 1988.

In *The Face* George revealed an understanding of British youth which helped him to steal a march on his rivals, who placed their faith in pop's traditional tribal mentality. After punk, post-punk, 2 Tone and New Romantic, the cyclical nature of youth culture revolving around a distinctive form of music appeared to have run its course. He had spotted the yuppie trend coming and the fragmentation of any distinctive counter-culture when he remarked to Tony Parsons: 'The music press is living in punk ideology which

97

is not the way the kids on the street live.' Like George they wanted a comfortable life; even the most politically aware still demonstrated a keen self-interest, looking for good jobs and dressing smartly as well as listening to music. Pop would in future be an adjunct to a lifestyle rather than a lifestyle in itself. Innocently George was heralding the dawn of devout Thatcherism, the decade when suits replaced jeans and leather as the uniform of the British youth; a style which was to make George's *Faith* rocker image seem all the more contrived and 'showbiz': George was wearing his jeans and leather for 'work' in a schmaltzy theatrical way, in the same way Springsteen wears his blue-collar garb. Both are outfits needed for their work. Hammering the last nail firmly into the soul on the dole ethic, pop was proving to be just a job after all.

For a few fleeting moments, there seemed to be a conspiracy to paint George as some kind of womanizer who would make Don Juan seem like the Bishop of Durham. Stories in the British tabloids painted a picture of George the superstud that many must have found it hard to recognize. David Baptiste, saxophonist, recalled in the *Sun* how he was in a bar in Osaka with George one night when some local women engaged the pair in conversation. After a while George whispered to Baptiste that he was going off and could he get someone to pick him up at noon tomorrow. 'The next day one of the security guards and I went down to pick up George. When he came out his eyes were glazed and he looked totally smashed. He'd been with the three girls all night and there were scratches and love bites all over him. What a mess.' His band members' tabloid testimonies may have put paid to any possibility of the gay slurs sticking, but they were a crude and uncharacteristically sordid light in which to paint their employer.

'Baps' went on to single out Andrew as the prime purveyor of groupiedom on the Japanese tour, recounting a particularly imaginative incident in the lewdly named town of Fukuoka. These were tense times for the friendship between George and Andrew: the duo seemed to be growing apart both publicly and privately. While George was Mr Reliable, Andrew was rendering it impossible to take Wham! seriously. Simon Napier-Bell's summing up of his wayward charge emphasized both the harmless nature of his activities and his trenchant immaturity: 'He sits on a bar stool in a stupor and dribbles, and then he has to be taken off to bed.'

George's ever-growing self-confidence was further bolstered when Elton John invited him to provide complementary backing vocals to his forthcoming single 'Wrap Her Up'. Events like these only added to George's increasingly acute awareness that Wham! was an awkward, even unwieldy vehicle for an artist of his stature. The intended split was becoming more urgent. But George remained publicly loyal in his defence of his band and his partner when he assessed the secret of his success. In *Record Mirror* he revealed a somewhat pompous side that almost reflected Conservative minister Norman Tebbit's 'on your bike' attitude that anyone could make it if they were prepared to work hard enough: 'I don't believe there's one band in this country who have worked as hard as we have this year. If people think that we don't deserve success and that they should be getting the same success as us, they should try working a bit harder.' He also made some telling remarks about the isolation he was beginning to feel, which had been brought into relief by his work with his older former idol: 'We don't have very much in common with our age group.' George was being forced to grow up too soon. Still only twenty-one, there was a distance between himself and his contemporaries that was now impossible to break down. Relaxation was becoming increasingly difficult; whenever he wanted the rollercoaster of success to slow down it actually seemed to go faster.

8

Chinese Whispers

By the spring of 1985 George Michael's career had proved itself to be one of success pursued by success. But everything had been done by the book. Apart from the contractual hiccup which took him out of circulation for half a year everything had gone according to plan, but nothing Wham! had done had been new, Wham! had always been mainstream. The rock press had chided them for not paying their dues, but their relatively instant success was typical in a decade where TV exposure and video had enabled many groups to bypass the staid pub rock circuit and hit the top with their initial intentions – whether banal or brilliant – intact. Besides, if scream bands had had to go through the draining traditional rock apprenticeships they would have had all those cheesy smiles wiped off their press shots long before they ever had a sniff of stardom.

Cast an eye over the lined faces and receding hairlines of the pop champions that paid their dues. Gary Glitter abandoned moisturizer for Polyfilla years ago; the Pet Shop Boys docked five years off their ages and were still well into their twenties when they first made it; even the former heroin addict Eric Clapton seemed to have taken out shares in Grecian 2000 to become the most perverse candidate for pop iconography, allowing, of course, for the oldest teenager in town, Tina Turner, who regardless of her vocal talents had to be squeezed into something that was not so much a micro-skirt as a pelmet before she could make her comeback. What Wham! had on their side was youth, and compared to the opposition they had it in spades.

George's New Pop rivals thought that their punk credentials made them as well-versed in handling the media. Boy George had even briefly been employed by Malcolm McLaren to sing backing vocals for Bow Wow Wow and the potency of media myth-making had not been lost on him. Paul Morley had multiplied McLaren's situationist ethos by ten and added his own romantic flourish to the notion for Frankie. Spandau Ballet's manager Steve Dagger had also lived through punk and had created a myth around the élitist nature of Spandau Ballet that got the record companies flocking to their obscure gigs in warehouses, on boats and in late-night cinemas. Dagger was also reputed to sleep with a copy of Machiavelli's *The Prince* under his pillow. Then there was Duran Duran's increasingly spurious schizophrenic concoction of Chic and the Sex Pistols as one of the early motivations. And nearly all the above celebrants of New Pop were by now closer to thirty than twenty. Except Wham!. By comparision Wham! may have been mere children, but they were positively geriatric in their approach to success. They may have written their own material but in every other respect they reeked of Tin Pan Alley. They had rejected Mark Dean, the one man who had identified their potential position in the postmodern market-place, in favour of seasoned players of the media game who looked as if they had just fallen from the pages of Wolf Mankowitz's seminal showbiz satire, *Expresso Bongo*, written a quarter of a century earlier. Dean had gone off Wham! after the first few singles when they had 'gone soft'. By now he must have looked on George and Andrew as singing marshmallows. Jazz Summers and Simon Napier-Bell were old school. Napier-Bell's reputation was built more on his own bluster than any star-spotting talent, while Summers had systematically failed to hit the big time until he chanced upon Wham!. With *Fantastic* at the top when he and Napier-Bell took over, success simply fell into his lap. The sixties' gad-about-town Napier-Bell had boasted about how he had to find time for management between a heavy schedule of eating out. By the seventies he was permanently out to lunch. His handling of punk symptomized a latent inability to cope with anything new, and Summers, too, failed to spot any true stars.

Both managers had separately attempted to carve themselves a piece of punk history only to find themselves lumbered. Napier-Bell had returned to the fray first by signing anachronistic glamrockers Japan before being gobsmacked by a working-class band called London, whose frantic fans showered their heroes with adulatory spittle. Napier-Bell impetuously signed them and promised big things for this uniquely anarchic band before discovering that every church hall and pub back room was boasting a similarly primitive collection of 'musicians' inspiring the same form of devotion. Japan were eventually to hit paydirt when the New Romantic scene brought things full circle and back to glam, but Napier-Bell's dreams were prophetically scuppered when enigmatic pin-up David Sylvian announced that the band was splitting up just as his pansticked persona turned a profit. Napier-Bell's penchant for pretty boys (Marc Bolan, Sylvian, George and Andrew) appeared to be his most efficient method of talent-scouting.

Summers for his part had been genuinely excited by the sheer effusiveness of punk but when it came to spotting stars he found himself as much at sea as his current co-manager. His first ventures capitalized on the cleaned-up residue of punk, pigeon-holed and packaged briefly as 'powerpop', taking under his wings forgettable acts such as the Stukas, the Crooks, the Autographs, Mark Andrews and the Late Show. The last notched up a little success and when the Stukas metamorphosed into the pop-orientated Blue Zoo he found himself with his first, albeit brief, encounter with real teen success. Summers could boast a wide range of acts but none that had stamped any identity on pop history.

To his credit it has been Summers that has rallied since Wham!. Taking on the Soup Dragons because they shared that original punk energy was a financial *faux pas*, but they eventually came good and with DJ Coldcut under his wing he has recently latched onto the sharp end of the UK Hip Hop scene, while Yazz, who he latterly married, has also learnt a lesson or two from her time hanging around Wham! and looks set to be vying with George Michael for press coverage for the next couple of years at least. Napier-Bell has notched up yet more column inches with the likes of Blue Mercedes and thespian fop star turned pop star Rupert Everett but has failed to come up with any lasting protégés, proving, if nothing else, that looks and publicity alone account for little.

The Nomis team had their differences over the methodology of management, as Jazz Summers recalls: 'I was the first person to say to George, "We have to stop people taking pictures of you," which has become a fetish now. Simon would say, "No No No. Get London Features [a Fleet Street photo agency] down, get more publicity." I said, "No, hold them back." Less is more. There was a time I really had to take quite hard control about how much and what went out of our office. Those papers are always there. So are the managers. It is the artists who come and go.'

To shunt Wham! into the superleague Nomis had to trailblaze, do something new. Simon had few groundbreaking ideas, but when he had them they tended to be big ones. One that had been germinating for some time was about to take shape. Back in 1984 he had hatched the seemingly hare-brained scheme of touring China, and with a powerful streak of liberalism hailing a cultural 'open door' policy he believed he might just be able to pull it off.

Napier-Bell's timing was perfect: by the time the tour was confirmed and underway the door was being eased shut and the wholesale embrace of the West was being questioned. Wham! were not the first Westerners to play behind the Bamboo Curtain – Jean Michel-Jarre had been there with his electronic extravaganza in 1981 – but they would be the first bona fide pop stars. The globetrotting Police, Mick Jagger and Rod Stewart had all tried to breach the rock-resistant wall of China to no avail. A stiff-necked succession of bureaucrats had been singularly unimpressed by their supposed artistic and cultural worth.

Rock was far too decadent a symbol of cultural decay for the East, but disco? That was something they could relate to. In recent years there had been a massive development of Chinese youth culture. Dancing, once frowned upon, was accepted as an essential part of a healthy lifestyle. As the *China Youth Daily* expressed it: 'Play is also a form of production. Only with an adequate amount of wining and dining and fun and games will the productive power of the workers be restored.' Napier-Bell was quick to notice that Peking's mayor had opened a dance competition saying that 'Social dancing tempers the body and strengthens the spirit.'

Chinese popular culture was opening up for the first time. There was even a record industry of sorts in Canton releasing well-intentioned if clumsy interpretations of Western hits. The cultural missionary aspect of the proposed tour was nice for the manager's soul, but with 200 million people between the ages of eighteen and thirty-two, the real thrill to the unashamed monetarist Napier-Bell was derived from the thought of breaking into the Chinese market.

Having approached the cultural attaché, Napier-Bell had succeeded in getting a team of delegates to view Wham!'s concert in Hong Kong in 1984 to see exactly what they might be letting themselves in for. An especially sterile show was met with approval. His next hurdle was to be endorsed by the All China Youth Federation, who had to issue an official invitation for the band to get permission to play. They presented Napier-Bell with the thorny problems of wanting a translation of George's lyrics and a chance to view their videos. To the West Wham! might have been reviled in certain quarters for their anodyne content but their shrewd manager was only too aware that 'Wham! Rap' could only be viewed in China as subversive. And as for their videos, each seemed to catalogue the symptoms of Western life that China sought to condemn: decadence, infidelity, promiscuity, rebelling against one's elders. Carefully a particularly antiseptic *Top of the Pops* performance of 'Freedom' in the mortuary atmosphere of a BBC studio was promptly dispatched, Napier-Bell going to great pains to explain that it was a love song and not a political demand. A positive reply came back, though like some tetchy neighbour the Committee asked the group to keep the noise down.

The news of the tour was a mixed blessing for George. It was too unique an opportunity to turn down, but he hated the treadmill of touring at the best of times and having only just completed the American leg of their world tour in February he was hoping for a more substantial break. Napier-Bell had to ooze more charm than ever before to impress upon his charges the sense and significance of the occasion.

Back in England George was much in demand as a friend to the stars. In March he found himself providing backing vocals for one of his childhood idols, David Cassidy. As a youthful heart-throb in the early seventies, Cassidy had experienced both the upside and downside of mass popularity. Inspiring an almost savage loyalty amongst prepubescent girls, the pressure had taken its toll while the press had refused to take him seriously as an artist. Eventually he had retired from music, but now in his thirties was making a comeback. His single, 'The Last Kiss', was a marginally breathy advance on his juvenile *oeuvre* of old which reached the Top Ten, thanks in no small way to George's svelte backing vocal arrangement.

In the run-up to the China trip George had a brief

opportunity to unwind between tours. Making the most of it he put paid to the media myth of a vicious rivalry among the gods of pop when he joined Frankie Goes To Hollywood onstage in Birmingham. After the gig he joined the Liverpudlians in a heavy drinking session and was honoured with considerable respect for his alcoholic capacity which resulted in him throwing up out of the car window on the way home.

By the time the Chinese tour was confirmed all possibilities of the two concerts in Canton and Peking being money-spinning ventures were forgotten. A contract as severe as any offered by a hard-bitten capitalist put paid to any hope of a profit. Wham! had to give up all the ticket money (at £1.50 per ticket compared to £22 for their nearby Hong Kong dates) as well as pay for the hire of all equipment, the rent of the hall and even for the printing of a free programme. Napier-Bell could only console himself by viewing the tour as a loss leader, hoping for a knock-on long-term effect when their records became commercially available in the Far East. And of course there were the column inches Wham! would be guaranteed back home throughout the jaunt, particularly once he had assured that gentlemen representing the *Daily Express*, the *Daily Star*, the *Daily Mirror* and the *Sun* had joined the beanfeast. If they did not make money, Napier-Bell was damn sure that Wham! would make headlines.

Leader of the hack pack ready to journey east was John Blake. A Fleet Street veteran, Blake had revitalized Rupert Murdoch's ailing tabloid, the *Sun*, with his scurrilous Bizarre column. His rise had coincided with a new generation of overtly successful pop stars. A number of factors contributed to his success and the change in the way that pop was publicized. No longer were chart figures isolated, élitist musos who spent their time locked away in their mansions when they returned from tax exile. The Conservative Government's reduction of tax in the high income bracket had helped to halt the exodus of pop stars, while conspicious consumption put an end to the street credibility of punk, when stars had shied away from publicity for fear of their proletarian image being tarnished. Suddenly pop's contenders and pretenders were scurrying *en masse* away from the specialist music press and into the mass circulation tabloids whose retarded editorial standards appealed to children and adults still addicted to the trivia of pop. Their relationship with Blake was an ambivalent one. While at one moment they would be condemning him for writing about them, at another the biggest stars invariably shared a virtual addiction to publicity. As Blake, so accustomed to writing hyperbole, overstated: 'They all want to do interviews because they are all bleeding egomaniacs. They all want to see their mush staring out of the paper. They all think they're wonderful and they want to be very very famous.'

Blake was so successful that in the mid-eighties he had become an unlikely 'victim' of a circulation war between the right-wing Rupert Murdoch and the *Sun* and the left-wing Robert Maxwell and the *Daily Mirror*. In a series of outbidding manoeuvres, which involved flights to New York for Mr and Mrs Blake and the promise of various ostentatious sports cars, Blake was eventually headhunted by Maxwell and fronted the *Mirror*'s White Hot Club with a brief to win over every *Sun* reader under the age of twenty-four with a daily diet of star names and exclusive stories. Perhaps one of the most ironic indictments of the decline of the press came from Blake who, on his defection, explained the lack of job satisfaction under media mogul Murdoch: 'There was a lot of pressure to exaggerate and distort because you've got this tremendous pressure on you five days a week to come up with something sensational.'

As the tabloids turned into comics they sought to win over the children with a new breed of probing journalists whose salaries were hardly pocket money. And the fact that record companies were willing and able to supply enough stories to fill daily columns reflected the fact that there was an undeniable mutual desire for coverage. It was in this atmosphere, and with Fleet Street's combination of a lust for Wham! copy and a fear of missing out to a competitor, that the *Sun*, the *Daily Mirror* and the *Star* all joined the trip. It was their job to find things to write about and effectively publicize Wham!.

Nomis's other coup was to film the epochal tour for future cinematic release. In February 1985 Jazz Summers had approached producer Martin Lewis, who had previously filmed the two Amnesty International benefits, The Secret Policeman's Ball and The Secret Policeman's Other Ball. Lewis helped to secure the skills of film director Lindsay Anderson to make a movie of the trip. The choice of director was made between the producer and the management. The esteemed British auteur was best known for his anarchic snapshots of modern Britain in *If* and *O Lucky Man*, but also had an impressive track record in making documentaries that stretched back to working with the BBC in the fifties. According to Anderson, it transpired that neither George nor Andrew had heard of the enduringly popular film-maker. None the less they acceded to this intrusive project which would confer a sense of posterity on the tour and also give an accurate insight into the offstage personalities of Wham! to counter Fleet Street's more fictitious moments.

The stern veteran was an ambitious choice for the task, but even the most reputable film directors were not averse to working with pop groups. Ken Russell, Martin Scorsese and John Landis had all made promotional clips for bands; even Anderson had supplemented his film income not inconsiderably by directing a video for Mancunian jazz popsters Carmel. But this was an altogether bigger proposition. From the very start the film-maker had doubts about trying to work with people from the music industry: 'I told myself it was rash to be mixed up with pop people. They are all liars and they behaved much more arrogantly than the film world.' Steeling himself for the ordeal, Anderson assembled a 35-unit Anglo-American film crew and shipped them to China on 31 March.

Wham!'s achievement in securing the tour sums up their appeal in many respects. Admittedly Napier-Bell had concealed some of the tackier effluvia of George Michael's career to date, but he had been able to get the band past the authorities because essentially they were peddling nothing more sinister than fun. As their co-manager perspicaciously pronounced: 'The boys have no controversial political or social message to put over. They have no problems with drugs or unusual varieties of dress . . . Pure and clean entertainment,' he added with a flash of his own pearly white teeth. In a nutshell, Napier-Bell had pin-pointed George Michael's major break with rock's traditions of rebellion. Here was a rebel without a care, happy to slide into the lounge suit and tuxedo of middle-of-the-roaddom. Any rebellion had always been merely cosmetic on George's part; his rise had taken that traditional route of revolt into style without the revolt.

As the tour party touched down in Hong Kong, where they were playing another gig to help underwrite the tour, and checked into the Regal Meridien Hotel, across the border in China they were preparing for the onslaught. In Peking fans queued for this unknown disco band overnight outside the Workers Gymnasium to be assured of tickets. Each purchaser had to have written permission from his work unit before he could spend what was the equivalent of two days' pay for the much-prized artefact. Corruption proved to be no respecter of national boundaries or ideologies. Free tapes that should have come with the tickets went mysteriously astray and ended up on the black market.

In Hong Kong, meanwhile, the duo undertook a lightning tour of the bustling city, ordering a few made-to-measure suits in the process. In an effort to stave off the glare of Fleet Street, the agreement was that they would join the trip in China. In the event each paper, fearful of a march being stolen upon them, headed straight for Hong Kong to file the first story of the tour. John Blake predictably led the way with a nice steamy head of paranoia concerning George having a tantrum and refusing to perform until all photographers and film crew had left his dressing room; a perfectly reasonable request immediately prior to such a significant concert. Blake revealed a tawdry tale of the change in George's personality that would make a schizophrenic seem positively single-minded. According to his story, poor old George was cracking up. First he had been happy-go-lucky, now he would not sign his autograph for a waitress and had made a complaint about her which would 'probably get her the sack'. In the light of Blake's probing, the lively set at the Colosseum Theatre was largely ignored and passed without incident, the only upset being the collapse, through exhaustion, of keyboard player Mark Fisher. This became a footnote to the hysteria alongside an unconsciously punning remark of how the loss-making tour was going into the red.

Arriving at Peking on Thursday 4 April was something of a comedown for George. No screaming fans awaited his arrival at the airport and the duo sped anonymously – as anonymously as two heavily tanned Westerners could – to their hotel.

They soon discovered that the city was not the bleak, hermetically sealed Communist conurbation they feared. In an attempt to reflate an ailing economy, Western styles of consumption had been appropriated. European and American cars motored gaily along, people drank Coke and even wore Levi's and there was a strong Western presence amid the throng of the vibrant capital city.

Wham! dutifully played up to the mixture of cultural emissaries and fascinated Western tourists. Cameras clicked like crickets on heat as the duo propped up the Great Wall of China, muttering inanities about its length, Andrew chipping in with a surly 'Who'd want to invade here?' This was

not the usual pop tour. There were trips and photo opportunities around Peking's Forbidden City and a somewhat
awkward lunch of crown of lamb combined with a flesh-
pressing meeting with the British Ambassador, Sir Richard
Evans. A man of inestimable diplomacy, Sir Richard Evans
had smoothed over the settlement of Hong Kong's expiring
lease for the benefit of East–West relations, so he had
little difficulty indulging in cocktail party small talk with
these two young men in strange suits. For once it was
George who was uneasy, finding himself socially out of his
depth among the reserved colonial enclave which boasted
impeccable manners but little knowledge or interest in pop.
At a banquet held by the Chinese Youth Federation in their
honour George announced his pleasure at the occasion in a
characteristically platitudinous speech: 'We just hope our
performance will represent a cultural introduction between
the young people here and in the West and help them to see
what goes on in the rest of the world. And I think I speak
for everyone when I say that this may be a small step for
Wham! but a great step for the youth of the world.'

The first bona fide Chinese pop concert on 7 April 1985
started unusually for Wham!. A silent auditorium watched
the entrance of Trevor, the breakdancing, bodypopping
support act who weaved through the audience, geeing them
up into the right mood like some warm-up man on a BBC
quiz show. What Wham!'s militarily precise plan had not
taken into account was the ban on dancing. That would
have been too much of a concession to Western decadence.
An announcement swiftly instructed the audience to remain
in their seats contrary to Trevor's ministrations. Many of
the audience may have wondered if this dark-skinned,
loose-limbed man was this Wham! phenomenon himself,
so it came as some surprise when an entire band entered,
followed by George and Andrew, doing their showbiz
athletes routine and darting around the stage. Fortunately
about a third of the 12,000 strong audience were of Western
persuasion – mainly overseas students, embassy employees

and journalists – and their cheers egged on the local contingent to join in. For many, their behaviour was in part dictated by a Minister of Culture saying two days before the concert: 'Enjoy it but don't learn', a direct contradiction of the usual cultural instruction which encouraged learning.

The show seemed to progress with a degree of insouciant sexual teasing, a shirtless George displaying his chest underneath his white jacket, while Pepsi and Shirlie topped up the sensual overload in short black leather skirts, the first of their frequent costume changes. The mandarins fearful of spiritual pollution must have been feeling vindicated by the sight of these two strapping young men at the front of the stage, their band name transmuted into Wei Meing, meaning mighty and vigorous.

If the audience was suffering from a heavy dose of culture shock, it was an equally strange sight for George as he gazed out at a sea of standard blue garb. Even more unsettling was their politeness. It may have been their way of enjoying a concert, but George would have preferred hysteria. And worst of all were the stern looks of the party officials in the privileged front rows usually reserved for the most hysterical teenage girls, who rather intimidated the younger fans behind them. For the only time in his life George found himself working through his repertoire of exotic gyrations in front of row upon row of octogenarians.

The concert ran efficiently but high spots were rare until 'Careless Whisper'. Thanks to Napier-Bell's cunning this was already one of China's most popular Western songs. Six months earlier he had encouraged numerous Hong Kong artists to record Cantonese cover versions of the ballad. Broadcast constantly on Hong Kong Radio the song was picked up and taped in nearby Canton and its languorous melody had been bootlegged right across the country.

'Freedom''s partly political broadcast had been relegated as a hands–across–the–water gesture, which Andrew introduced in a manner more suited to canvassing for votes: 'This is a number one hit in our country and I hope that one day it will be number one in China with your help.' George meanwhile looked hopefully at the most influential guest, Central Committee Member Hua Xiong, the seventy-year-old confidant of China's leader Deng Xiaoping, seated alongside a beaming Simon Napier-Bell.

During the second half of the show, the audience started to respond more energetically despite the guards' striving to keep them seated. Smoking was forbidden and at least one Chinese youth was arrested for refusing to put a cigarette out, rough treatment for an international act of adolescent rebellion. As the proceedings drew to a silent close without the customary encore, a jubilant throng emerged into the streets undeniably sweetened by their first taste of the most saccharine of Western pop.

In inverse proportion to the hyperbole of the British tabloids, Chinese reports of the concert were typically restrained. Many did not mention the concert at all. The China News Service gave the concert the thumbs up saying that they 'sang joyfully' and cutely failed to translate the colloquialism of 'Wake Me Up Before You Go Go', turning it into 'Wake Me Up Before You Leave'.

Throughout the trip the film crew, and Lindsay Anderson in particular, had encountered difficulties with the diffident stars: 'George Michael was totally uninterested in what we were doing. He never showed any interest at all in the whole idea of what film-making was. He was extremely bright in his own field, but he didn't want to learn. Of the two, Andrew seemed the more intelligent but they were both conceited.' While George occupied himself with an endless diary of photo opportunities, Anderson had dealt directly with Napier-Bell and Summers only to encounter further problems. Already there appeared to be talk of the inevitable Wham! split, and it appeared that George was developing a keen distaste for Napier-Bell. In an effort to restore their position, Nomis did everything to placate their employer in the hope of his continued patronage: 'The management were frightened of George. They would have put their heads down the lavatory to please him.'

One of the ironies of the trip was the revelation that the Chinese could be as opportunistic as their Western counterparts. Local bureaucrats and officials were as quick as any East End market trader to spot an angle and exploit it. Fees were demanded before the band's gear could be moved, a surcharge was imposed because the camera crew were using 35mm rather than 16mm film. The tour was never expected to turn a profit, but these expenses were hardly expected. Meanwhile there was a big problem with the band, discontented with being booked into different hotels to George and Andrew that were barely up to the standard of a third-rate British boarding house. By the time the weary expedition set off for Canton, a combination of extortion and exhaustion had conspired to dent the *esprit de corps*.

On the plane to Canton George talked candidly about politics, giving a rare glimpse of how superstar status was isolating him from his roots. He had always been cushioned by affluence, but his early staunch support of the Labour Party seemed to have buckled under in favour of admiration for the Prime Minister; besides, his support of socialism had always been on anti-nuclear, humanitarian grounds rather than any fundamental economic policies: 'I don't take a stand politically. I think that Thatcher has done a lot of damage. But she has given kids new drive. There was a lot of apathy a few years ago – but she's changed all that.' Fleet Street glossed over this revealing gem, however, when the flight carrying the rest of the band threw up an incident altogether more to their tastes. It is always hard to dissect the real truth from a news story, as one saw with Andrew's ridiculous nose operation saga, but the one factor that Fleet Street seemed to concur on was that the incident on Wham!'s specially chartered Boeing 747 should be blown out of all proportion.

At the back of the plane, trumpeter Raul D'Olivera apparently started screaming, pulling out a knife and placing it to his stomach. Minders were quick on the scene and relieved the Portuguese musician of his weapon, attempting to subdue the hysterical horn-man. Unable to calm him, the pilot had no option but to take the plane straight back to Peking airport, where a medical team was on hand to sedate D'Olivera before he was moved to the Peking Medical University Hospital (rather than the mental hospital as some later reported).

The sensation-starved hacks had a story at last. The *Sun*'s sub-editors had a field day describing the incident in the typically verbless headline of 'Wham Man In Hara-Kiri Terror'. The *Star* meanwhile carried minder Dave Moulder's description of how Raul went 'off his rocker . . . hallucinating and in a trance'. Descriptions of the self-inflicted wound ranged from a stab to a graze. One report went so far as to say that the trumpeter had broken into the cockpit and hi-jacked the plane, forcing it down. The real hysteria seemed to be among the journalists rather than the subject, as even the *Telegraph*, with no man on the spot, chipped in with a headline of 'Wham! man goes berserk'. The *Guardian*'s rather more liberal mores deemed the story worthy of the marginally more sober but no less nonsensical headline of 'Trumpeter Whams Himself', in the process adding a new verb to the lexicon of print journalism: 'to wham – to conjure up a front-page story out of almost nothing.' Indeed, the tabloids themselves had created news, forcing the broadsheets to cover it in their wake which lent a spurious credibility to the wholly negligible affair. It was the hyperkinetic self-fulfilling series of events that PR persons dream about; Wham! could rest assured that their China tour had been a historic one, thanks to Fleet Street's supple way with words. In the Epic Records press office the cumulative cuttings of Wham!'s annual exploits are contained in a single file; the China trip has a bulging file to itself.

Mr D'Olivera's behaviour was eventually explained as stress caused by the lengthy tour rather than possession by the devil as had been feared initially.

At Canton's Zhongshan Stadium the audience was less restrained and the guards seemed more interested in Wham! than disciplining the crowd. With its close proximity to Hong Kong there was a more liberal atmosphere all round. George was instantly able to lift his performance when he realized he was at last able to draw some response from the audience, accompanied by the feeling that perhaps Wham! had done their bit towards a cultural revolution after all. In reality, though, things only got worse. After the Tiananmen Square bloodbath, the very theatres Wham! had played in were used for show trials. The Bamboo Curtain had come down again.

Back in the comfort of Heathrow Airport after his seventeen-hour flight, George knew he was home when he heard the reassuring screams of his fans gathered to greet him. Some missed their O Levels and camped out to await his arrival. Their vigil was rewarded with a pensive George voicing serious misgivings about the experience. There did not seem to be any kind of gratitude or appreciation of the fact that Wham! had been the first Western pop group to play there; George simply felt that he had been used as a propaganda tool to persuade the West that China had welcomed Western music. His bitter remarks echoed his post-mortem after his gracious appearance at the Miners' Benefit. Perhaps it had momentarily slipped his mind that productive spin-offs would more than compensate for the hardship and exploitation.

The Chinese experience had not been solely an exercise in altruism. Towards the end Simon Napier-Bell announced what was financially far more of a coup than the tour itself. For some time now he had been negotiating for the release of Wham! songs in China and at last his protracted dealings had borne fruit. Straight after Wham!'s return to

England a selection of songs from *Fantastic* and *Make It Big* – effectively a greatest hits compilation – was to be released, followed by another release of five recordings and five Wham! songs covered by top Chinese pop singer Cheng Fang Yuen. After protestations from George Michael, she was to get a small royalty, estimated to earn her £50,000, which would substantially supplement her £15 per month statutory income. The initial run of 600,000 would be sure to sell out instantly. And incredibly the group had secured a full royalty for themselves; no doubt a considerably tougher bargain had been driven on their behalf than the one worked out with Mark Dean.

Tape recorders were more of an expensive luxury good than they ever were for Georgios Panayiotou, but the Chinese were so enthusiastic for Western music that they would make the necessary sacrifices to buy them. In time it was quite likely that China would become the biggest market for music behind America and Japan. With the expiry of the British lease on Hong Kong in 1997, Napier-Bell believed China would become more like Hong Kong rather than vice versa. He had reason to hope so: his companies were based there for lucrative tax avoidance purposes. Wham!'s tour of China might yet prove to be the biggest loss leader in the history of pop music.

As for the proposed cinematic release of the historic tour, that seemed destined to turn into something of a grand folly. It was later modestly mooted as a TV show but was destined to slip out as a video release only. Nomis and Anderson clashed over the production, while George decided that scenes had to be re-shot back in England when he was upset by footage of his perennially problematic hair.

The trip had borne fruit a long way from the Far East. The coverage had installed the band in the minds of rock fans everywhere and in America in particular. Napier-Bell's remarks two years on to writer Johnny Rogan hint at motivations similar to those that had lurked in the mind of Police manager Miles Copeland when he took his bleached boys to the Far East five years earlier: 'I told them . . . it was a challenge, it was great to help the music industry into new territories. But actually, to tell you the truth, it was a publicity stunt . . . a rather classier one than getting on page three of the *Sun* with a nude standing beside you . . . It was designed as a major image-building stunt to shove Wham! into the American consciousness.'

If China had been all Napier-Bell's doing, Jazz Summers was to be the brains behind the American operation in autumn 1985 but Napier-Bell had helped to lay the foundations. George wanted to conquer America the easy way. He did not want to undertake the traditional anonymous sixty-date tour across America, smiling for the camera in places he had never heard of, being interviewed about how he came up with the name Wham! by a string of faceless DJs. TV coverage of the Chinese tour had given them the blanket coverage in the US media that a year of concerts could never have achieved. Wham! had been planted in American consciousness far more by their tour of the Far East than their brief US visit earlier in the year. China may have appeared like hard work to George but he seemed to have been convinced of the tour's worth by the assurance that it would cut down considerably on the impending trek across America.

The Chinese adventure marked the end of another episode in George's career. Having first courted the tabloids and then lived uneasily alongside them, George now broke off contact with them. Indeed he returned to England to face another trial by tabloid over the bad management of the Wham! Fan Club. Immediately George set about putting the situation to rights by installing a new firm to oversee affairs. The press and the pop star had reaped a mutual benefit from the relationship but now George felt unassailable enough to continue without them; they had done their job in making his name, from hereon he could coast on his fame. He was all too aware of the risk of overkill; he was astute enough to realize that those who

Above: February 1986: The BPI Awards, London. The political interface: Elton John ~~~ives the belated award for his Russian junket, shadowed by Norman Tebbit. ~~king on L to R: George, Jazz Summers, Andrew Ridgeley, Simon Napier-Bell. *~~dication International.)*

~~w: The Agony and the Ecstasy. The emotion of Wham!'s Farewell Concert begins ~~ll on George and Andrew. *(Pictorial Press.)*

Above left: China 1985. George auditions prospective replacement for Andrew Ridgeley. *(RETNA Pictures Ltd.)*

Above right: Shuttlecocks Ahoy! George expands his repertoire during the Club Fantastic Tour. *(Rex Features.)*

Below: A Farewell To Alms: Live Aid. Bob Geldof leads the final chorus. L to R: Paul McCartney, Geldof, George, Andrew. Note Bono preparing a sermon in the corner. *(RETNA Pictures Ltd.)*

ve: Black on Black: 11 June 1988. George at the Nelson Mandela 70th Birthday
ert. *(Adrian Boot/RETNA Pictures Ltd.)*

: The birth of Pop. *(Pictorial Press.)*

Left: Taking no risks. George checks his belt and braces during the 'Faith' Tour. *(London Features International.)*

Below: Young Yog. I want your soc[k] *(Syndication International.)*

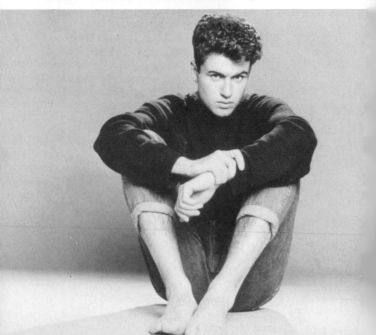

ɒe left: Happy Families: George and parents Lesley and Kyriacos.
(...dication International.)

ɒe right: The Oddest Couple. George sizes up a lascivious Elton John at Wham!'s
...well Concert. *(Syndication International.)*

...: Jeung Love. George endures an intimate 24th birthday meal with Kathy Jeung
... number of photographers. *(Rex Features.)*

Above: A rather subdued public appearance with Pat Fernandes *(Rex Features.)*

Below: Winner takes all. Man George offers commiserations to his vanquished pop rival Boy George *(Rex Features.)*

Above: Who needs BUPA? George explains the latest health cuts to a cosmetically re-aligned Andrew Ridgeley. *(Scope Features.)*

Left: A sickly George at home with cat. *(Syndication International.)*

Left: Pensive pop hopefuls. George and Andrew dream of stardom. *(RETNA Pictures Ltd.)*

Below: George at London Airport with excess baggage. *(Pictorial Press.)*

live by the word, die by the word (as was soon to happen with Boy George). George Michael's remarks to the *Sunday Times* a year later suggested a new-found haughtiness in his decision to stop giving them access: 'Quite simply I thought they had had their return for making us stars.'

The hiatus in hyperbole following Fleet Street's excommunication was soon filled by various cod-psychological analyses of George and Andrew, observing that where Andy got the screams at first and George was in the shadows the situation was now reversed. It was a crass representation but for once it was the truth. George had effectively inherited all of Andrew's plus points, his confidence, his style, his wit and his charisma, leaving his partner superfluous where he had once been essential to Wham!. The public rift the press hoped to conjure up was exacerbated when George was invited by Stevie Wonder to sing at the 'Motown Returns to the Apollo' celebrations in New York's Harlem that May. At last George stood alongside the kind of performers he had dreamt of joining. That was the kind of credible company that Ridgeley could not provide. It was also an event that made George a part of history giving him an edge over his New Pop rivals (though his closest competitor Boy George was also present). As well as singing with Stevie Wonder and Smokey Robinson, a special honour was conferred on George Michael when Robinson sang 'Careless Whisper'. George had always wanted his pop to be compared favourably to Motown's golden era of the sixties; this was the ultimate accolade.

George's appearance coincided with the 'Second British Invasion' reaching fever pitch in the Billboard charts. Thanks largely to the hyperventilating video jocks of MTV and accompanying wall-to-wall promo clips, eight of America's Top Ten singles that week were by UK artists, some of whose successes would be more shortlived than others. Howard Jones, the Power Station, Billy Ocean, Murray Head, Sade, Tears For Fears and Simple Minds all jostled their way to the upper echelons of the US charts. And there right at the pinnacle of the pile was Wham!'s 'Everything She Wants'. Having deposed Simple Minds' earnest 'Don't You Forget About Me', George himself was usurped two weeks later by Tears For Fears' celebratory 'Everybody Wants To Rule The World'.

That June George was reported to have bumped into the Queen at a polo match. Judicious ear-wigging revealed that they exchanged words about China, George passing on some tips to Her Majesty, who was due to follow in his footsteps when the Royal Tour headed East in 1986. Their visit was destined to be every bit as controversial as Wham!'s, with Prince Philip describing the Chinese people as 'slitty-eyed'. Royalist or not, George's meeting presented a timely coup for the excommunicated press; real royalty and pop royalty in the same story, and a vivid indication to George that his own refusal to speak to the papers did not mean that they would cease to write about him.

1985 was rapidly panning out as George Michael's year. The contemporaries that he once considered his closest rivals seemed to be falling by the wayside. Internal strife within the ranks of Frankie Goes To Hollywood and Culture Club manifested itself in their lacklustre or non-existent output; Duran Duran were visibly suffering from growing pains as the group temporarily fractured into the adult Power Station and the downright pretentious Arcadia; Spandau Ballet were wrapped up in their very own contractual dispute that had put their career on ice. They had served their record company Chrysalis with a writ in Februrary 1985 alleging mismanagement of their affairs and requiring their contract to be terminated forthwith.

Fame and famine make strange bedfellows. A scruffy declining pop star with a rapidly dwindling fan club seemed like an unlikely saviour, but when Bob Geldof saw the BBC's report on the debilitating famine in Ethiopia in

October 1984 he unwittingly set a process in motion that would change both the world's perception of pop and pop's perception of the world. Suddenly it seemed as if superstars were no longer disinterested decadent inhabitants of the *demi-monde* living out a kind of perpetual adolescence in the swankiest watering holes of the Western world. Live Aid made them accept a global responsibility way beyond the occasional crumb of comfort they had dropped in the past. George's contribution to the miners' strike fund had fed mouths but had hardly saved lives on a massive scale. And he was a relatively generous performer. Pop, as opposed to rock music, was seen as frivolous and uncaring. With Live Aid pop seemed to grow up. Stars accepted that they were so big they could influence the market-place and stir some consciences. Live Aid's naïve positivism effectively sounded the death knell for the negativism of punk; it was a cause over which pop's aristocracy could gather and close ranks; either you were there and you were someone, or you weren't and you weren't. It was no coincidence that the biggest band that failed to play, Culture Club, saw their stock plummet almost overnight. Live Aid managed to elevate a few new bands to a higher stratum too: U2 had been a rising middle-league outfit until that day, while George Michael was also to find himself elevated to the upper echelons of pop by the occasion, stealing a march on his New Pop peers.

The real repercussions of Live Aid occurred not in a drought-ridden country in the middle of Africa but in the pop charts that sandwiched the Atlantic. Those that were invited to take part acquired a hitherto unprecedented credibility. Until 13 July 1985 stardom had always been a precarious business, but this public act of uncharacteristic compassion gave participants an unfathomable degree of exposure and cachet that could never have been manufactured by a record company. In a decade of devout self-interest Live Aid looked briefly as if it would turn the music world on its head. By the end of the eighties charity events are still with us, but fully integrated into the commercial world. Even human tragedy was compelled to find a place for unconscious product endorsement when the 1988 Amnesty International Human Rights Tour was sponsored by the Reebok Foundation, a name more commonly associated with sportswear.

Live Aid took place at a time of domestic turmoil when a series of grotesque freakish events almost made one forget about Ethiopia for a moment. In Belgium at the Heysel Stadium, rampaging football 'fans' caused at least thirty-eight deaths in the crowd when a wall collapsed. This came little more than two weeks after over fifty fans had been killed when a football stand at Bradford City's ground had caught fire. Domestic tragedy vied with global incident for media attention. Only three days before Live Aid the Greenpeace flagship Rainbow Warrior was sunk by saboteurs in Auckland harbour where it was protesting against French nuclear tests in the Pacific. As the epochal concert loomed ever nearer it seemed as if the priorities of the world were more muddled than Geldof ever imagined. The born-again conscience of the Boomtown Rats demanded to know how Western leaders could destroy food supplies while the Third World was starving. No one could explain the sick iniquity, but Geldof could understand the skewed logic. He had been getting used to the British Government's callous cynicism in the face of dire poverty since the Government's insistence on imposing their 15% VAT on the Band Aid single when every other profit-making organization had waived its potential profits.

As the packed Wembley Stadium sweated it out in scorching heat, the stars fell out of the sky backstage, airlifted by DJ Noel Edmonds' helicopter firm. Fixer-to-the-stars Gary Farrow co-ordinated the operation and saw that they were swiftly whisked out of the 90 degree humidity and into their air-cooled dressing rooms.

That day, what began as a grand global call to alms became a roll-call of celebrity. Those of the past mingled with those of the fleeting present. Sade, Spandau Ballet, Elvis Costello and Howard Jones were among those that jostled with icons Sting, Phil Collins, Bryan Ferry, Dire Straits and the Who, reuniting just one more time. Queen's Freddie Mercury captivated the crowd with some dynamic if hackneyed posturing, while U2's Bono became a superstar overnight by spontaneously jumping into the crowd and picking out a lone female to dance with; for once, big gestures, however clichéd, were the only way to handle the event.

Wham!'s set pointed the only way possible for George. Rather than perform the statutory twenty-minute greatest-hits set, things were done differently. Elton John introduced his friend and then played the piano while George sang his 'Don't Let The Sun Go Down On Me'. Behind stood John's one-time foil Kiki Dee and Andrew Ridgeley, inaudible on backing vocals. But no one could fail to hear the young man at the front, belting out the classic ballad and winning over even the least committed of the audience with heart-stopping clarity and polish. Barely twenty-two, the bearded boy wonder suddenly looked every inch a man. As the show climaxed, the rumoured Beatles reunion was not to be but 'Let It Be' drew proceedings to a close before everyone hauled themselves wearily back onstage for 'Do They Know It's Christmas?'.

In Philadelphia old stagers ruled the day, as the time difference now shifted coverage to the other side of the Atlantic. Crosby, Stills and Nash reformed, as did Led Zeppelin. Tina Turner boogied with Mick Jagger while Duran Duran tried to convince everyone that they were the Rolling Stones of the nineties; they certainly looked exhausted enough. Hall and Oates, the American duo who thought they had cornered the market in boy/boy blue-eyed soul until Wham! came along, introduced their svelte mentors Eddie Kendricks and David Ruffin of the

Temptations, and Bob Dylan, Keith Richards and Ron Wood shambolically showed that not every rock and roller ages gracefully.

The aftermath of Live Aid added the obligatory titbit of scandal concerning Andrew. The *Daily Star* claimed that he was thrown out of the post-gig party at Legends for being drunk. Amid the acclaim that George was not only a star but a sex symbol he claimed to be unable to see what the fuss was all about. He explained in *Record Mirror* that he was not in the business for unseemly adulation: 'I see success in terms of selling records and writing better songs. Money is not what we are in it for now. You have to keep going for creative reasons . . . there is always a better record to make or more records to sell.' But he was also acutely aware of his position and its drawbacks: 'Sometimes I feel I am in a goldfish bowl with the whole world looking in.' It was a predicament which he was battling both against and for. He wanted to be a bigger, better star, but he was only too aware that if that happened there would be a lot more people queuing up for a piece of George Michael and there would be little that he could keep for himself.

9

Making It Bigger

Live Aid confirmed that George Michael was brimming over with big match temperament. If he could handle the hammiest, biggest soup kitchen in history he was ready for a stadium tour of America. Following in the footsteps of Duran Duran, Culture Club and the rest of the second British invasion, the foundations for the assault had already been laid by MTV. The twenty-four hours a day Music Television, launched in 1981, had clutched the carefree, sun-kissed videos of two photogenic boys to their collective hearts and had given them heavy rotation. With their help, Wham! had already notched up three number one singles in the USA, but their brief tour of large theatres earlier in 1985 had done little to test the live potential in America. Having initially called themselves Wham! UK to avoid confusion with their American namesakes, their success was topped off with a nice patriotic *frisson* and when their US counterparts sank from view the rather bellicose metaphor of 'invasion' seemed wholly apposite.

Setting up the American tour was not the formality one might have expected for a band that had seen so much chart action. Where Napier-Bell had been the driving force behind China and the Far East tour which took in Japan and Australia in January 1985, Jazz Summers had been concentrating on America. Summers might seem to have had the more placid temperament of the two but he was no less gifted when it came to business. Rather than promoters it was George who presented Jazz with the thorny problem of what kind of tour to undertake.

George's ill-disposition to another energy-sapping tour was testing Summers' entrepreneurial powers to the limit; the usual way to go about these things was to work up from grass roots support tours and small halls before the big stages. Even the likes of Bowie and Springsteen had been compelled to build up their following in this manner. But MTV had changed the groundrules of stardom; nervous promoters just needed to be convinced that record sales could translate into ticket sales. They got their confirmation in spades when a Miami Radio Station announced a Wham! concert on 31 May that had yet to be confirmed. Suddenly the venue was swamped with ticket requests vindicating Jazz Summers' audacity as the Nomis hotline started to burn from all the calls of eager American promoters. US and Canadian shows were hastily organized, the duo set to appear in front of a total audience of over 310,000 fans. Wham! took the opportunity to launch their own brand of designer sportswear. Drawing both stylistic and financial inspiration from the Fila livery they had once been sponsored to wear, they could now cut out the merchandising middle man and rake in the profits themselves.

George had another reason for wanting to appear in the flesh in America. When Wham!'s records were first sent out to radio stations they went out in anonymous white sleeves and ended up getting airplay at R&B records on primarily black radio stations. It was flattering for George's muso ego but he resented it, feeling that he had got in through the back door under false pretences. It was nice that his musical merits were noted, but an element of inverted racism had been involved in the selling of Wham! as an anonymous funk act. By the time the tour was underway things had changed. MTV had made sure that the faces behind the music were as well known as the voices.

Sure enough, Wham! were repeating their commercial success on the other side of the Atlantic with alarming speed. 'Wake Me Up Before You Go Go' had been number one on the Billboard charts for two weeks in November and December 1984, 'Careless Whisper' had dwelt at the top of the pile for three weeks in February and March 1985 while 'Everything She Wants' had followed suit for two weeks during May and June. With *Make It Big* enjoying an unbeaten run in the Top Twenty album lists since January including three weeks at number one in March displacing Madonna's *Like A Virgin* in the process, it now looked as if all of America was finally ready for Wham! in the flesh.

The itinerary for the tour was finally fixed to cover eight shows in America and one in Canada as follows: 23–25th August Poplar Creek, Illinois, 28th Toronto, 30th Hollywood Park, Los Angeles, 1st September Alamada County Stadium, Oakland, 4th Southern Star Amphitheatre, Houston, 6th Miami Baseball Stadium, Vets Stadium, Philadelphia, 10th Pontiac Silverdome, Detroit. In all, the band would play to an average audience of 40,000. Summers made sure, however, that there would be adequate days off between dates to allow for recreation, travelling, and most importantly, meetings with the American media.

The tour ushered in the adult George. His beard, which had only made fleeting stubbly appearances until now, cast a mature, sophisticated shadow over his youthful vigour. He wanted to be all things, boy and man at the same time. His new look certainly appeared to be making an impression on American womanhood; when comedienne turned chat show host Joan Rivers asked actress Brooke Shields which man she would most like to meet in the world her instant reply was George Michael.

George and the former child star met for lunch at the downtown Regent Hotel in Chicago and indulged in the noble art of the photo opportunity for the conveniently assembled press cameramen. Brooke Shields' high profile was no coincidence; her presence had less to do with the press froth about her infatuation with George and more to do with the fact that she was hard at work promoting her new book. Indeed, whatever rapport they established as the bulbs flashed away, she was absent from Wham!'s concert that night. In America Wham! had fewer credibility problems than in the UK and the audience consisted of as many serious soul fans as screaming teenagers. None the less, George was not averse to employing his latent sex appeal to garner endorsements. Had Ms Shields been there, she would have witnessed George scaling the heights of pop-schlock in torso-hugging black vest following Madonna's example and flashing his navel in front of the 25,000 packed house.

Having been savaged by the British press, George and Andrew were unsurprisingly loath to speak to the American media. Besides, everyone knew who they were, the tour was a sell-out and the records hardly needed promoting. In the end they spoke to television's *Entertainment Tonight* and the invariably hagiographic *People* magazine. The rest of the naturally disgruntled editors with showbiz columns to fill took a leaf out of their British counterparts' book and conjured up stories out of the ether attacking the duo for their arrogance. George and Andrew found themselves in a no-win situation again, but perhaps they had brought it upon themselves this time. The brevity of the tour, playing only a few big venues, was a lazy option and the lack of co-operation with the media smacked of conceit.

But in the face of critical flak the tour was a success. At the end of August Wham!, supported by the heavyweight soul of Chaka Khan and the somewhat incongruous no-nonsense guitar rock of Katrina and the Waves, were the first rock band to play Los Angeles' Hollywood Park since their intrepid forebears the Police. While the 50,000 strong crowd swamped the converted racetrack to see the new icons, Hollywood's élite paid extra to enter the VIP area, known as the Turf Club. There they could treat themselves to 'The Wham! High Sandwich'. For a mere $12.50 they could gorge themselves on 14 ounces of beef, turkey, ham and cheese or corned beef in a roll with salad and drink. On stage, Andy looked like a Bay City Roller gone mad in his ubiquitous tartan suit, while George's suede and studs, fingerless gloves and short hair lent an aggressively camp macho edge to his new Lothario-in-leather image which was accentuated still further when he tore off his jacket mid-set to reveal a black T-shirt and a belt that appeared to be constructed from an old motorcycle chain. A combination of sickly candy floss pop and mock rock managed to seduce any remaining sceptics in the crowd. Elton John joined them briefly onstage before they retired backstage to celebrate their latest triumph. But George's private revelries were to lead to more accusations of arrogance when he breached pop protocol by turning up late for his own party just as the glitterati were leaving. The high pressure demands of US stardom were of a magnitude unequalled in England, and seemed to be getting the better of George's good nature.

The tour was not without incident. In Toronto George was mobbed when he went to a funfair after seeing Bruce Springsteen disguised in a bandanna and cowboy hat, and his hat fell off on the big dipper. A more serious intrusion occurred after the gig at the Baseball Stadium in Miami when the band retired to a club to unwind. Bass player Deon Estus was casually chatting to a female fan when she suddenly pulled a gun from her purse. Fortunately one of Wham!'s now ever-present security men intercepted her and defused the situation, but it was the kind of moment when visions of John Lennon inevitably flashed through George's mind. He soon started to have premonitions of an unnatural early death that were to return to besiege him at regular intervals.

Inevitably the critics were the only dissenters. They were quick to identify smugness in the gauche swagger of the duo. Their aloofness manifested itself in their reluctance to acknowledge the audience; they neither threw much-demanded items of apparel into the crowd, nor picked up the flowers and gifts that rained down upon the stage. The most lasting, but justified, criticism was over their decision to play just a few isolated big shows, which revealed an unsavoury take-the-money-and-run attitude. To their fans Wham! could do nothing wrong, to the press they could do nothing right.

Returning to England in September, the antagonistic relationship with the UK media continued. Andrew seemed to be revelling in the star lifestyle and was rapidly acquiring all the accoutrements of the jet set brigade. His two and a half year relationship with Shirlie Holliman had been a tempestuous affair and had finally been terminated when the blonde singer announced her engagement to Spandau Ballet bass player Martin Kemp. Andrew didn't expect to attend the wedding for fear that when the vicar asked if there was any reason why the two should not be married he might put his hand up. Feeling jilted, he had recently found solace in the arms of Donia Fiorentino, the former teenage fiancée of Miami Vice TV star Don Johnson. As Andrew's new romance was spread across the papers, it was rivalled for importance by the news that he had taken up motor-racing. If this was an effort to prove that he had some gifts outside pop music it did not seem to be working. After being involved in a few minor scrapes in his Formula Three car he became uncharitably pigeon-holed as as hopeless a racer as he was a musician. While the autumn months should have been a period of low profile recuperation for the duo, it now turned out that having fed the tabloids with stories they could not shake them off.

In November 1985 the court case over George's hi-jacking of the melody of Barry Manilow's 'Can't Smile Without You' for 'Last Christmas' was finally withdrawn. For a while it looked as if George might become involved in the kind of litigious saga that had blighted George Harrison's solo career when the million seller 'My Sweet Lord' became the centre of a similar court case, where it was decided that the melody had been lifted from sixties group the Chiffons hit, 'He's So Fine'. George Michael's case seemed equally vulnerable until his lawyers and team of musicologists proved that there were countless other records before Manilow's that shared the same basic melody. Perhaps the fact that the royalties were destined for charity and not George's bank account helped to speed along the resolution. £250,000 in royalties accrued by the million-seller that had been frozen could now bolster the Band Aid fund. Such generous gestures reflected George's increasingly secure finances. Suddenly the £11,000 in royalties from Innervision's much vilified 'Club Fantastic Megamix' that he had donated to the miners' strike fund seemed like a mere bauble.

George's fate seemed once more to be intertwined with Elton John's. The same company, Dick James Music, that took George to court had signed up Elton's publishing rights for life back in 1967. Elton, too, had been involved in interminable legal battles to regain his own rights with DJM and after many years he won £5 million in unpaid royalties on 29 November, less than a week after George's victory.

George still had problems with his public image. His reluctance to speak to tabloids had cut off his most direct channel of communication with the public apart from increasingly vacuous press releases emanating from Connie Filipello's office and his records and performances. On 16 November he did a dramatic *volte-face* when an interview was offered to the Deputy Editor of the oft-reviled music paper, the *New Musical Express*. Danny Kelly was a particularly odd choice. The *NME* had sympathizers among its readers, but to Kelly, who favoured independent punk-inspired rock and the gritty new country acts currently emerging in America, the paper's pop constituency must have seemed like poor misled quislings. Damning George with faint praise, Kelly conceded that he could write a 'three-quarters way decent song'.

The most intriguing fact that the interview threw up was George's negotiations over the cover. In the past George had driven the hardest of bargains to guarantee that he would get maximum exposure when he deigned to speak to the press; rigorous contracts were drawn up to assure the star that he would appear on the cover of the respective publication; any digression from the contract and he would sue without hesitation. This time things were different; the contract stipulated that Britain's leading music paper would *not* put him on the cover. George's reasons remain unclear. Did he feel that his appearance on the cover of this publication would be so out of character that it could harm his career? Was he simply flexing his muscle and proving that he could pick and choose where his image appeared? Interestingly, his contract demanded picture approval (in fact, he would supply the pictures), while copy approval was not required. While he clearly enjoyed wielding so much power he was fully cognizant that in the 1980s image was far more powerful than the word. The *NME* could write whatever they liked about him; it could never damage him as much as an ill-advised photo-session.

George had one fundamental reason for opening up to the press again, a secondary one being to plug Wham!'s latest potion of pseudo-macho funk, 'I'm Your Man'. Since he had stopped speaking directly to Fleet Street the tabloids had either invented stories, exaggerated stories or stolen stories from back copies of *The Face*. George was tired of being categorized alongside Joan Collins and the Royal Family. He even seemed to be getting confused with the Royal Family – *Private Eye* was quick to spot his striking similarity to the Princess of Wales when his hair was longer, blow-waved and streaked blonde. *NME* would significantly place him in the company of other musicians and he could comfort himself in the knowledge that even if they did not like his music they would at least give him a fair and honest hearing and allow him more than a one-line quote. He also needed to speak out to prove to his detractors that while Andy was throwing up George was growing up. Since his return from China, George's major interviews had been conducted with Andrew *in absentia*. It was also a way of testing the waters to see how far he could be accepted both as a serious songwriter and without Andrew.

The *NME* head-to-head marked a significant change in George's approach to interviews. Invariably recent journalistic encounters had taken place in the plush, discreet confines of Blakes Hotel in Kensington, a short walk from George's rented apartment in Adam and Eve Mews, off Kensington High Street. Whether it was conscious or unconscious, the rendezvous in the Sarm West Recording Studio off West London's gentrified Portobello Road lent a musical credibility to the occasion.

George's ostensible lack of interest in the possibility of an influential front cover feature marked him out as haughty from the off. Perhaps George hoped to be pleasantly surprised by the paper's attitude, but he also knew that if it chose to slag him off it would be done intelligently and in a way that might help him to learn something about himself. At least he would stand more chance of recognizing himself within the *NME*'s florid prose than Fleet Street's monosyllabic clichés. At least George could enjoy a good verbal spar with a journalist rather than the usual diet of sycophancy and back stabbing.

Curiously, thirteen years earlier his recent vocal partner David Cassidy, then also twenty-two, expressed precisely the same motives when he consented to an interview with America's rock bible, *Rolling Stone* magazine: 'I had some hostility towards you, and I still do probably. The magazine is very anti-me and anything I have going for me – like commercialism and all that stuff. So I'm very defensive about *Rolling Stone*. I guess that's kind of a fucked way to be. But I would really dig reading something about me that wasn't, you know, the same old bullshit.' This was at the time when Cassidy's teen appeal had also reached unimaginable peaks; he had just broken attendance records at the Houston Astrodome by selling 56,723 tickets to two matinées on the same day, but he too faced the long haul towards adult respectability and the longevity that comes with it. George had grown up wanting to be David Cassidy ever since the early seventies when, avidly glued to the television, he saw his hero playing football on the roof of the TV studio. The camera panned to the edge of the building and there below were thousands of screaming girls. It was an image that had been forever etched in George's memory.

Danny Kelly set out to pick his way through the rubble of rumour in the hope of overturning a few facts. He was still living in an unfurnished rented flat with the stereo he had left home with. Money had not changed him that much; his only real indulgence was to replace his contact lenses with a new pair whenever they got dirty.

One of Kelly's unceasing fascinations, one shared with Simon Garfield of *Time Out* in his close encounters with George in the run-up to Wham!'s split, was the way George stood loyally by Andrew. Where Simon Garfield later heaped an unnecessary amount of scorn on Andrew, describing him as a 'revving boil', Danny Kelly contented himself with the slightly more generous epithet of 'idiot'. For once there was a chink in George's defence as continual squeals of laughter punctuated the conversation, revealing George's awkwardness and impatience about being in some way associated with his partner's consistently obnoxious behaviour.

Kelly's four-hour chat with George was an amiable affair that saw George playing mother and insisting on making endless cups of tea. Questions covered the familiar ground of his music and the power of pop and closed with some verbal jousting amid Kelly's continued attempts to winkle out a 'gay exclusive' angle. By now George was prepared for the onslaught. He was not about to commit himself in print, preferring instead to capitalize on the ambiguity. Bowie and Jagger before him had thrived on the vagueness of their sexual identities and had lasted a lot longer than the unashamedly camp Boy George. A defeated Danny Kelly came away still not won over by the music but impressed by the wit and clear-thinking of pop's boy king.

One significant subtext of the feature was the small amount of space it had been granted. A couple of thousand words would have been substantial anywhere else, but it reflected an underlying awkwardness in *NME*'s feelings about the Wham! phenomenon. Its high-flown philosophical tone of the day suggested it would be more likely to spend five thousand words debating the relative merits of various types of footwear. But George was more than satisfied with the piece when he read that he was good-looking and had nice hair.

Unbeknown to his persistent inquisitors of the time, George had that same month tackled the hardy perennial subject of Wham!'s split. The pact to break up was long overdue. The exhilarating whirl of Wham!'s momentum had simply prevented an opportunity to step back and work out the minutiae of the separation.

That November a meeting was finally convened between George and Andrew, Simon and Jazz, and Bryan Morrison and Dick Leahy to confront the situation. It was decided that there would be one final single, hopefully an album, and a grand farewell concert in July 1986. The timing had been chosen, the characters had been cast, all that was needed now was for the plot to be written. In the meantime the press would be kept guessing about Wham!'s future activities.

'I'm Your Man' was another in the line of unremittingly joyous chants that were becoming George's compositional trademark. He could come out with classic ballads occasionally, but he seemed to be able to dash off this superior confectionery with hideous ease. 'I'm Your Man' had been run off the assembly line during the American tour, on the flight between Los Angeles and Oakland. Increasingly aware of the importance of dance mixes, George had played an anonymous white label copy at London's terminally hip Raw Club in the bowels of Tottenham Court Road's YMCA to test the public response. Unannounced, the sound was unmistakably Wham!. The typically bouncy chorus and bubbling R&B bass lines were Wham!'s trademark by now. As for the macho bluster of the lyric, a totally over the top declaration of love, the kitsch quotient there could only point to George Michael. The infectious groove soon filled the dance floor. Even hard-bitten cynics have to admit that even Wham!'s corniest output was – and remains – eminently danceable to. His market research was vindicated when 'I'm Your Man' knocked ex-Undertone Feargal Sharkey's 'A Good Heart' from number one in late November.

As Christmas approached all looked cosy in the Wham! camp. George could take pride in his position of seemingly unassailable status and, as Elton John had once done for him, so he was able to offer his patronage to Paul Young, guesting with him at his Wembley concert that December. As 1985 turned into 1986 George could boast of his presence on four singles in the Top Twenty. 'Last Christmas' had been re-released and was back in the Top Ten (due in no small part to George's excellent exercise in undulating funk, 'Everything She Wants', on the B-side – his most American and truly soulful composition to date), as was Band Aid's 'Do They Know It's Christmas'. And when 'I'm Your Man' was starting to slip down the charts, George was simultaneously reappearing with Elton John, helping the stocky, ageing superstar's comeback by providing backing vocals on the high-spirited 'Wrap Her Up'.

Christmas was celebrated in jubilant style back in the

bosom of his family. Publisher Bryan Morrison presented him with a bulging Fortnum's hamper to mark the season and their continuing successful partnership, and the immaculately well-adjusted George demonstrated that he still retained a wholesome sense of value by sharing the food out with his friends and giving the empty pots to his family. George always showed immense loyalty to his family. When his sister Melanie was not helping him with his hair on tour, he had managed to secure her a post as hostess at his favourite London salon, Allan Soh's in Knightsbridge, where customers would be presented with a glass of champagne while they waited for their roots to be done.

The yuletide scenes in the Panayiotou household presented a picture of domestic calm and contentment; one which contrasted sharply with the storm-clouds that were gathering around George Michael's professional future. Behind the toothy smiles George and Andrew had reached a crisis point in their career. Having mapped out their activities right up to the split, Simon Napier-Bell and Jazz Summers were in the process of negotiating a deal to sell Nomis Management to another company. George was aware of the plans, but Nomis was theirs to do as they wished with. George intended to go solo after Wham!'s split anyway. But the split was still being finalized when a sequence of events was to force George's hand in a way that he had not expected and that was to test his powers of self-determination to the limit. In the meantime George continued to collect plaudits from his critics; on 27 January he was awarded two Grammy awards by the American Music Industry in Los Angeles.

The press's obsession with a possible estrangement between George and Andrew was given a fillip with the latter's decision to abandon England and take up residence in Monaco in early 1986. Facing a £600,000 tax bill if he stayed, part of the reason was tax exile, but the appeal

of press exile also hastened his departure. If he continued
his bread roll-throwing behaviour away from England he
would not have to read about himself the next morning
to find out what he had been up to. Monaco fitted in
with new-found motor-racing ambitions. He could mingle
freely with the glitterati at the Monte Carlo racetrack and
work on his Formula Three highway code. In England he
had pranged his cars once too often and given the tabloids
more sticks to beat him with; here he would work on
his technique in relative seclusion with the obligatory
model girlfriend, Donia Fiorentino, by his side. While
Ridgeley positively revelled in living out a Jackie Collins
pot-boiler, George was rather more torn between reality
and fantasy.

George was still prey to criticism from the unlikeliest
quarters. Rupert Murdoch's up-market broadsheet *The
Times* on 9 January was the unlikely quarter that accused
George of reneging on his original radical rock ethos:
'Wham! Rap''s rebellion had been a pose; George
was charged with mock rebellion. By this façade he
had brought rock's traditions of disenfranchisement into
disrepute. George deflected the idea that it was ever within
Wham!'s potential to achieve anything like that. They had
never set out to be the soul-boy Sex Pistols, but he could not
understand why nobody else had come in to fill that role.
The shifting sands of his brand of socialism appeared to be
on the march: 'That rebelliousness could never come from
us because we come from middle-class backgrounds. But
I can't understand why there isn't more rebellion around.
After all, things have never been worse.'

Perhaps the renewed inner city eruptions in Brixton,
Handsworth and Broadwater Farm were resharpening his
responses. George's views expressed to Mick Brown in
the *Sunday Times* the previous June before the latest disturbances also revealed how his background and current
position left him with little sense of the harsh realities
of growing up in the 1980s: 'I believe that when you

are seventeen or eighteen you have an awful lot going for you. You're young, you have your health, and a lot of people have optimism.' At the time, a medical report on the East End of London reported the return of rickets among the young and unemployed, a disease, caused by vitamin deficiency, thought to have been eradicated before the war.

George tried to convince his interrogators of his own socio-political awareness while simultaneously passing the buck, as if being middle class excused him from active service in the fight against urban strife. He was hardly starving but he did something for the Ethiopians; he had never been down a pit but he helped the miners. Why was he not prepared to preach the radical rock gospel now? A record 3.4 million people were on the dole now. George's socialism was of a distinctly selective kind.

In the sixties the middle classes had been only too keen to slum it and show solidarity with the proletariat. Mick Jagger, every inch the college boy, seemed to develop more of a guttersnipe drawl as the decade wore on. By the seventies there was a marked change, Jagger adopting a peculiarly eccentric home counties argot, while Bryan Ferry moved into an elegant flat in fashionable West London; by the eighties rock superstars were fully assimilated into the establishment. The likes of David Bowie were being sighted in the company of royalty until eventually the Prince's Trust concerts fused figures from pop and the monarchy firmly together. Equally other-worldly and adored, the public treated Charles and Diana like pop stars while they treated pop stars with the reverence usually accorded to the monarchy. It was all a long way from the Sex Pistols' three-minute burst of back-street bile, 'Anarchy In The UK'. Weybridge's stockbroker belt found itself adding ageing rockers to its electoral register, Jethro Tull's leader Ian Anderson positively luxuriated in his real-life role as country squire, and even passing rock revivalists Showaddywaddy took great pride in going fox-hunting.

Apart from the stuttered relapse of the punks, rock and pop has been upwardly mobile for the best part of a quarter of a century and George Michael was just joining the club. Napier-Bell explained the success of Wham!'s jet setting image and in the process summed up the social evolution and aspirations of Thatcher's decade in *The Times* in January 1986: 'Kids say look at Wham! and say I'd like to be like that. Parents say look at them and say I'd like my children to be like that.' Rock's traditional generation gap had finally been eroded.

But the gap between George and Andrew was becoming insurmountable. They had always been different, but as a team they had worked well together, complementing each other, bolstering each other's confidence and acting as a foil for each other. It had worked in their schooldays and had been one of the keys to Wham!'s early chemistry. But it was clear to George now that he really no longer needed Andrew; a quick glance at the Top Twenty would be enough to boost his confidence these days. On the American tour the difference had been drawn in sharp relief when Andrew chose to travel with old friends in tow as his drinking companions while George looked elsewhere for company. Andrew's latest erratic motor-racing escapades were a manifest attempt at self-assertion, a vain attempt to prove to the world and himself that he could steer his own destiny now that it was clear he could never be on equal terms with George within the world of pop music.

Ironically, it was Andrew who from the beginning had most easily embraced the pop star lifestyle, whether in the form of globe trotting, groupies or fame. George had let Andrew live out the worst clichés of stardom, he wanted recognition without some of the more hideous trappings. He was not averse to spending sprees, occasionally clocking up £1000 a month on clothes himself; but while Wham!'s pop star image was lived out more by Andrew, George knew that he could move on by leaving Andrew behind. Andrew's newsworthy indiscretions had kept George free to retain his sanity and carry on turning out the hits. One man alone could never have sustained both roles. George was not aware to what extent a solo career would test him to the limit.

In the meantime a heavily bearded George in voluminous stetson and a supremely sunkissed Andrew made their annual pilgrimage to the BPI Awards on 10 February where they found themselves on stage yet again with Elton John. Both Wham! and Elton were presented with special awards for outstanding merit, for taking British pop to China and Russia respectively. Elton John's award was a long time coming; he had blazed his own trail for pop *perestroika* back in 1979.

Their presentations were made by the Chancellor of the Duchy of Lancaster, the radically unhip Norman Tebbit. In the aftermath of Live Aid and Red Wedge's inroads into the youth market on behalf of the Left, the Government had finally latched onto pop as political propaganda and graced the affairs with one of their least docile ambassadors. Tebbit admitted that he did not understand pop music and preferred Gilbert and Sullivan; he compared it to the car industry, cracking a mildly amusing joke about the need for a Minister of Music, when in reality all he really wanted was someone to count up all the money pop was bringing into the country. In keeping with a Government that had stifled not only the growth of the Arts but their very survival, the ingratiating parliamentarian could only see pop music in relation to commerce. Elton John, not a man noted for political gestures, displayed his disgust for the squalid affair back in his hotel room by promptly smashing his tardy award.

Politics and pop, unlikely bedfellows as they might have been, were destined to precipitate the demise of Wham!. By February 1986 the minutiae of the split had yet to be worked out when George discovered to his horror that his worst suspicions were confirmed: Nomis were selling out to Kunick Leisure, a company that effectively owned most of Sun City, the giant leisure centre in the middle of South Africa. Unlike South Africa the location, Bophuthatswana, boasted equality for all creeds. In the eyes of the law blacks had the same rights as whites. But it was a decidedly cosmetic form of anti-apartheid. Blacks simply did not have the income to benefit from Sun City. While whites were cosseted in the opulence of the complex, blacks lived in the townships overlooking the site. In the hypocritical nature of its reform, Bophuthatswana was every bit as damnable as South Africa.

The labyrinthine network that led to South Africa ought to have been spotted by Nomis, and more importantly, should have caused them to pull out of negotiations. A year earlier promoter Harvey Goldsmith's company had merged with another to form Allied Entertainments. They in turn had gone public and were taken over by Kunick. A major shareholder of Kunick was Sol Kerzner, who owned thirty-four per cent of Sun Hotels, the chain that all but owned Sun City. The lattice-work of companies involved had blurred the trail, and the Nomis partnership were ignorant of the full involvements of Sol Kerzner, one of Kunick's biggest shareholders. Admittedly their diverse interests stretched from South Africa to an ice rink in Scunthorpe and the London Dungeon, but surely Nomis were aware of everything? George had asked Simon Napier-Bell about the South African connection back in November and met with pleas of ignorance. Summers was a vociferous opponent of apartheid, while even Napier-Bell should have been astute enough about the ongoing conscientious climate of contemporary pop to separate politics and profit.

In November 1985, Springsteen sidekick Little Steven had recorded the song 'Sun City', a Band Aid-type collective effort to which some of the biggest names in rock, from the Boss himself to Bob Dylan and Peter Gabriel, had lent their vocal support. The song was a musical condemnation of the South African system and particularly the leisure complex Sun City, where many rock stars had played, primarily for large fees but unconsciously endorsing South Africa's system of inequality. An unusually outspoken George had complained that he was not invited to sing on the record, saying that his stature would have added greater clout to the campaign; already vaguely aware of a South African wind blowing through the Nomis boardroom George was perhaps concerned about his position.

When George realized that the deal was going ahead, he gave Nomis the option of pulling out but said that if they didn't he personally would break away from Nomis as well as Wham!. The management had balanced the deal on something they ought to have realized George would object to and were about to suffer the consequences. When it became apparent that they were continuing (according to a tale spun by Napier-Bell, when in America George saw the headline 'Wham! sold to Sun City' in an American entertainment journal, variously the *Hollywood Reporter* and/or *Variety*), George was compelled to pre-empt events to salvage his own credibility. Although he was initially dissociating himself from Nomis, with Andrew's name absent from the press statement issued on 21 February it was couched in a way that left few people wondering if there was any future for Wham! as a group.

Napier-Bell, for his part, suspected that George was intending to split from Nomis anyway and chose this as an opportune moment to make his intentions explicit. As he succinctly put it: 'It's like if you plan to divorce your wife and you come home to find her in bed with somebody. It helps you make the decision that's probably a bit awkward to tell somebody.' But conflicting stories fell like confetti.

George's split from Nomis washed his political image whiter than ever. From supporting striking miners to starving Africans, George had always managed to balance successfully the pop/politics equation. Even his good friend

Elton John had succumbed to the lure of the lucre and had once appeared in South Africa, but in a more sensible frame of mind he later signed a pledge that he would never do it again. (A number of artists, George included, had yet to prevent their records being sold there.)

George's embarrassment over the affair was mixed in equal amounts with fury. But circumstances conspired to humiliate George's ex-partner-to-be even more. Andrew Ridgeley was in France motor-racing and hard as George tried, he could not reach him. Nomis had forced George's hand, which actually meant that George unwittingly turned the situation to his advantage by grabbing the higher moral ground and effectively breaking the news of Wham!'s split.

In the aftermath there were too many conflicting versions of the circumstances surrounding the deal ever to extract the reality. One is left to speculate on various permutations of the truth. Had Nomis underestimated George's integrity? Did Napier-Bell suspect George would want to farm out the lucrative American end of affairs to an American management team? Was Nomis suddenly not so confident about the stability of their three-month management deal? Was it not dumb of Kunick to offer such a large sum of money to a company whose only valuable asset was patently so precarious? Indeed, how innocent were Napier-Bell and Summers of the Sun City connection? Jazz Summers maintains that he was unaware of the Sun City link; he had a strong personal opposition to apartheid not to mention a half-black girlfriend in Yazz. At the same time a rumour circulated that Summers and Napier-Bell had in fact fallen out over their tenure of Wham! and the intention was for Nomis to sell up and split the spoils. The only certainty in the affair was that George Michael had successfully extricated himself – and only himself – from the tangle and provided the ideal launching pad for his solo career.

Communication between George and Nomis changed

dramatically from personal calls to dealing through lawyers. On Friday, 21 February the statement was released by George Michael, but not Andrew Ridgeley, stating that Wham! was severing its links with Nomis. This way, even if Nomis had gone through with the Sun City deal, Wham! would be ideologically extricated. As it was, the deal would never be ratified without Wham!, Nomis's only real asset, and sure enough, as news filtered back to Kunick's office, the deal and £5 million soon evaporated.

As George slipped silently from the Nomis noose, Andrew was left hanging. Following George's announcement, the British press showed that their powers of detection were far superior to George's, swiftly tracking Andrew down to Room 6236 of the Loews Hotel in Monte Carlo. Andrew was not surprisingly belligerent when informed that his meal ticket had been withdrawn. 'Nobody told me anything. Why don't you fuck off. The whole business makes me sick,' was his own unofficial press statement.

Like Mark Dean, Napier-Bell and Summers, Ridgeley found himself jettisoned from George's game-plan with a handsome settlement. All that was left for them to do was smoothly wind up Wham!. Where this could be conceived at leisure, the public split with Nomis had occurred with painful alacrity. As Jazz Summers says, 'Literally overnight we lost the biggest band in the world.'

An interested party on the sidelines of the affair was Harvey Goldsmith, whose Allied Entertainments was part of the package. He perhaps lends credibility to the notion that the Kunick negotiations were carried out in complete ignorance of the Sun City connection. Goldsmith had impeccable political credentials which he would surely have been loath to lose. Over the years he had been instrumental in setting up a number of benefit concerts starting with the Rock For Kampuchea Benefit and culminating in Live Aid. As a trustee of Live Aid he seemed beyond reproach. Indeed, having pulled his burly frame from the jaws of the Kunick beast his unimpeachability helped him to become the promoter behind the ultimate anti-apartheid concert, celebrating Nelson Mandela's seventieth birthday at Wembley Stadium, not to mention restoring his good standing in George's eyes enough to be asked to organize the British leg of his 'Faith' tour in 1988.

10

Twilight of the Idols

The closing stages of George Michael's life with Wham!
saw a continued period of unabated success. Initially hoping
to bow out with an epochal concert and accompanying
album, a combination of pressure and apathy conspired
against his muse to shrink the final vinyl product down to
an EP. Working in Los Angeles, George was preoccupied
with planning for his new life. Away from the studio he
embarked on a relationship with Sino-American model
and make-up artist Kathy Jeung and mingled freely in
clubs where even superstars were given a chance to enjoy
themselves away from the glare of attention. Here he could
finally begin to put Wham! behind him and get down to the
serious business of, as he described it, 'growing up with
taste'.

The duo remained as popular as ever, recognition coming from the unlikeliest of corners. When former MP for
Derbyshire West Matthew Parris took over as presenter
of political current affairs programme Weekend World, he
came out of the closet in the *Mail on Sunday* and revealed
that he was a great fan of Wham!, even listening to their
music with Margaret Thatcher. Opinions on their split
were not proffered by the 'confirmed bachelor', nor did
he confess that he had been a fan since the dolebusting
'Wham! Rap'. That would have been intriguing; Parris had
once attempted to don the caring face of Thatcherism when
he accepted a challenge from another television programme
to live for a week on unemployment benefit. The dramatic

drop in income had come as something of a shock to his system and although he saw it through he ran out of electricity before time – and he was subscribing to a political party that had been consigning millions to live in such a parlous state for the foreseeable future.

From a business point of view, Napier-Bell condemned the split as financial suicide; Wham! could easily have milked their success for another couple of years. But George was more concerned with his art, his sanity and his credibility to bother himself with bank balances. Napier-Bell shirtily put the lost potential earnings at somewhere in the region of £50 million; but he was also quick to put right those who wrote off Ridgeley saying that they would be taught a lesson and that he would end up as the star. Napier-Bell's loyal hype was typical of his showbiz chutzpah; Andrew had yet to choose his own management for the future, so the sharp manipulator was still hoping to have a vested interest in the lesser half of Wham!. To the flamboyant fixer the split also hurt his pride as he rapidly saw his influence over George wane: the star assumed an increasingly independent drive, deigning to listen to the advice of others but insisting on making his own decisions.

While Napier-Bell's fulsome ego prevented him from admitting his faults with Wham!, Summers looks on their period in office as a wholly worthwhile experience that taught him more about management and entrepreneurialism than business school ever could: 'You can never be bigger than your artist. You could use all your ideas and determination to make an artist huge, but you can't do it unless they have talent and look great. Pop stars are human beings not soap powder. If you get the music right, the money will come after. If you just look for money it won't happen.'

George's second solo single 'A Different Corner', released in March, comfortably laid the foundations for his bona fide solo career, knocking pop's Peter Pan Cliff Richard and

comedians the Young Ones' remake of 'Livin' Doll' from
the top of the charts. 'A Different Corner' marked a changed
George Michael. It was neither a downbeat departure from
Wham!'s non-stop frivolity nor a genuine companion piece
to 'Careless Whisper'. 'A Different Corner' did away with
George's conventional ballad technique. In fact it threw
away any preconceived notions of the rock rubric. Almost
avant-garde by George's standards, 'A Different Corner'
eschewed all commercial considerations of melody, chorus,
hook line and rhythm. Yet as it effortlessly cruised to the
top of the charts George Michael proved the extent of his
Midas' touch.

Lyrically 'A Different Corner' was another of George's
pixilated *romans-à-clef*, this time the sound of a thwarted
man pouring his heart out. Clearly his professional Midas'
touch didn't extend to his private life. Years later it would
be the song he found most painful to listen to because of
its traumatic resonances. 'Careless Whisper' was deeply
personal, but its narrative had harked back to the carefree
days of youth. They were long gone now. As George
remarked about his first solo hit, 'It might as well be
someone else's record.' 'A Different Corner' launched an
introspective George. His ballad days were over, angst
was in. 'A Different Corner' was porcelain pop which
you felt would shatter if handled too roughly. Reeking of
painful sensitivity, the video echoed George's feelings of
vulnerability; clad in white and crouching in a corner as if
in sumptuous solitary confinement it was his most delicate
appearance in years. His hair was once more streaked
blonde and long extensions gave him an overpoweringly
feminine grace.

As ever it was a song inspired by personal experience, but
he was not giving anything away. Only in the aftermath of
Wham! would the catalyst for 'A Different Corner' become
apparent. By hiding his personal crisis, all it seemed to
signify was George's ever-increasing professional success,
making history as the first number one to be conceived,

written, arranged, produced, played and sung by the same person. Solo efforts did not come any more solo. Only George's private life needed someone else.

Fleet Street's latest role for George was as the Howard Hughes of pop. There he was with a fortune estimated at £28 million but still renting his flat, possessing little more than the clothes on his back, content to fly in an economy class seat. It was a largely false portrayal. The fortune was a conservative estimate; he did rent a flat in London but only because he had not had a chance to buy a home – and he did own some property around the world; the 'clothes on his back' was not a cheap battered old jacket but a £1000 Versace designer number; flying economy class was arrant nonsense.

On 6 April the *Sunday People* featured another of its more imaginative non-stories with an exposé of George's supposed teenage marriage. An exquisitely vague set of speculations suggested an arranged marriage had taken place with a fellow Greek Cypriot but that it had no legal status in Great Britain. It was another story that had no grounding in fact. The perpetrators of the tale were ex-members of one of the Executive's changing line-ups, Jamie Gould and Tony Bywaters, currently working for British Telecom and in 'rapidly rising band Ego'.

This was not enough, however, to scotch the highly prized gay slurs from rearing their heads again. As members of Wham!'s backing band became aware of their imminent redundancy there was a rather undignified scramble, with various members proffering their inside stories of the real George Michael. Loyalty, of a kind, seemed to be the order of the day. 'George the superstud' was the party line. Drummer Danny Cummings, for instance, scotched the myth with a knowing wink and discreet confirmation from his on-the-road escapades that George was 'straight as a die'.

According to trumpeter Colin Graham, George's favourite woman was his mum and the bashful bandleader had been as embarrassed as a 'blushing schoolboy' when the group had partaken of one of rock and roll's less upstanding traditions and presented him with a strippergram on his birthday. Building up a rapport with musicians with whom he had little in common in terms of lifestyle and experience was always a problem for George. One enterprising hack managed to track down black ex-girlfriend Pat Fernandes who had been jilted by George after being his constant companion for a long time and was now seeking solace as manageress of the Body Shop in Oman. She had been offered £50,000 for confirming the 'George is gay' rumours, but declined. For his pains, a few innocuous quotes were stapled together with some thinly veiled racism to make up something of a non-story.

Napier-Bell had not wound down his own PR machine in the light of Wham!'s departure. But contrary to popular belief emanating from Nomis, in the run-up to Wham!'s farewell Napier-Bell and Summer had ceased to be involved in the day-to-day running of affairs. George's feelings for Napier-Bell had been mixed at the best of times, and his ideological distaste for the South African involvement at least temporarily soured their relationship further. Organization of events leading up to 'The Final' was placed in the hands of George's seasoned tour manager, Jake Duncan.

Duncan, who had orchestrated much of the China Tour, was an excellent manager but his relationship with George was a strictly professional one; on one tour Duncan's girlfriend had a baby and George did not even know about it. In many respects, George resented having to take advice from these music industry veterans whom he felt he had little in common with. Having been deceived in the past George was wary of everyone, even his sisters, who continued to help him out with his costumes and hair. It was a professional paranoia that at times seemed to be getting out of hand. Yioda, his sister, had been a teacher before she started to help him out with his wardrobe. She doted on George, so much so that she had never seen him live, a combination of nerves and attention to duty confining her backstage during his shows.

But the combination of the professional sleight of hand and George's ongoing personal problems left him in a profound state of disillusionment. He was feeling increasingly cut off. He had once enjoyed going clubbing with the band, but as they bathed in the vicarious glow of George's celebrity, he hated all the attention; and whenever there was a crowd in tow the paparazzi seemed to follow, giving George the kind of star treatment he was coming to despise.

At the same time he found himself drifting away from his old employees. Where everyone had once been pulling in the same direction to make Wham! the biggest band in the world, George was now expressing a distaste for the methods that were, and continued to be, used. Fictional stories about his love life were pumped out to press contacts, which undermined George's business acumen and musical abilities. This was not the way he felt he could make the transition from scream star to serious artist.

As a result George began to pay even closer attention to the running of his career; but the structure of his semi-hands-on management threw up still more contradictions regarding his self-styled approach to socialism. Every aspect of the Wham! set-up operated on a strictly hierarchical basis. Inevitably the pay was poor and the hours long for those at the bottom, and a strict pecking order operated in the office. Affairs were overseen by Duncan, but George made it his business to come in at least once a week to go through Wham!'s activities, far more so than would be the norm for a pop star. As the organization worked towards the farewell concert there was tremendous pressure in the office. Even the road crew found themselves working under an unusually severe regime. Pay varied dramatically, some assistants getting as little as £100 per week and working from eleven in the morning to eleven in the evening. In the run-up to The Final anyone who was late faced dismissal, and even the crew were only allowed one free ticket each for the last Wham! concert.

The atmosphere in the office, above George's accountants, was riddled with petty jealousies and rivalries. There was not just a pecking order but also an intense air of snobbery. One applicant for the job there secured her position largely on the basis that when she contacted them she gave them a friend's Belgravia phone number as her own, suitably impressing her prospective employers. This was the juvenile legacy and obsession with status in their business that had prevented George and Andrew from establishing firm friendships with others; affairs were conducted on a distinctly superficial basis. One day Donia Fiorentino came into the office while Andrew was away and was hanging around when someone tactfully asked why she didn't go and see some of Andrew's friends. She replied that her paramour had hundreds of acquaintances but no friends. The ultimate party animal was inept, through no fault of his own, outside his hedonistic habitat. In the face of this kind of professional isolation, George battled grimly to hold on to the few friends he had from pre-Wham! days.

Difficulties in administration of the Wham! industry were exacerbated as the minutiae of the split with Nomis began to take shape. The reality of the pressure on the Nomis staff was revealed as assistants began to jump ship and announce that they were going to continue working for George. Siobhan Bailey, a long-time employee of Napier-Bell, had developed a close working relationship with George over the years. She was one of the few people whom he felt he could trust and who was interested in him as a person rather than a product.

Siobhan was one of the few people in the organization who was genuinely pleased for George each time he notched up a hit because she saw that that was what made him most happy. In recent months, her solicitous manner had elevated her to the position virtually of surrogate mother to George; she arranged his driving lessons, did his shopping and generally attended to his personal, domestic needs. She became the only person with a direct line to George; even Connie Filippello found herself having to pass messages on to him via Siobhan.

George would personally vet the new staff taken on to administer his business, from technicians down to office 'gophers' before they were employed. New help was brought in, but others were hived off from the old Nomis operation. George wanted to continue with the few people he knew he trusted.

While the tabloids were forced to steal quotes from other sources, the quality press was treated to pearls of wisdom in exclusive interviews. Somewhat prematurely George was the recipient of some surprisingly reverent obituaries. Journalist Julie Burchill played avenging agony aunt in *The Times*, seeing him moving on to a new phase in his life and a whole new set of problems, away from the teenage disco-angst of Wham! as the property of youth. George and Fleet Street's aspiring Queen Bitch candidly discussed Andrew's fate over the preceding four years like a couple of psychoanalytically-sussed wise owls: 'The fact that he didn't contribute anything must have been a terrible blow to his ego,' George admitted. His own position, on the other hand, was a dream come true: 'This must be the only business in the world where you can have so much money and no one to answer to . . . what better job can you have?' Yet between the copy-worthy lines there remained nagging doubts about his potential: 'I'm not what stars are made of. I'm not Prince and I'm not Madonna.'

Even without George's direct patronage, Fleet Street and the pop industry were living in cosy harmony; the continuing decline of the serious weekly music press was indicated when Wham!'s final date at Wembley Stadium on 28 June was announced to the newspapers first. Pop had finally taken up residence in the general public domain. It was no longer a passing phase for teenagers only. The rock fan demographic had aged over the years until the music had become an essential component of eighties lifestyle, not just for teens and pre-teens; as the original pop and rock audience aged, so the demographic aged and increased accordingly. It could no longer be consigned to a specialist press. And at the heart of this synthesis were Wham!. As George put it: 'We've transcended the idea of a pop group with this concert . . . become more like a tiny part of the fabric of society.'

George returned to London from Los Angeles at the beginning of June to take his driving test. Youth had raced by so fast that it was something he had never got round to doing, although in recent months people in the Wham! office had lost count of how many lessons he had had. During his early days as a learner he had driven straight into an unlit skip one night. Perched precariously inside an anonymous Ford Escort he passed, and borrowed his sister Melanie's X-registration Volkswagen until he could decide on the right car to buy – something with the right blend of sophistication and style and the minimum of flash. In the end he decided on a hardly discreet Mercedes Sports.

On 9 June 1986, exactly four years after their début single, Wham! released their final new record, a modest EP, which was followed soon afterwards by the Greatest Hits compilation. 'The Edge of Heaven' was backed by 'Where Did Our Love Go', 'Battlestations' and a remix of 'Wham! Rap', 'Wham! Rap '86' with Elton John joining in on piano. Not one of George's better compositions, 'The Edge Of Heaven' was at least a suitably rousing finale to Wham!'s recording career, summing up their music in its energetic, punchy chorus and incessant chanting of 'yeah, yeah, yeah'.

The video shoot for 'Edge Of Heaven' on 16 June gave George a chance to return to a past he had never had, filming in a mock-up of a sweaty rock club reminiscent of the Marquee in Wardour Street. In a perverse parody of the real rock life, George had actually been here before; the video for 'I'm Your Man' had actually been filmed at the Marquee in an attempt to effect some glitzy credibility for the group in its earlier life.

Three hundred students from Epsom College of Art and sundry smiling extras were bussed in to earn £30 for a day of enthusiastic dancing. Most of their time was spent hanging around waiting to be graced by the stars. The difference between George's and Andrew's behaviour was telling. While George remained aloof but professional, unavailable until he was called on stage, Andrew mingled with the extras outside.

Security was tight on the set with a total ban on the tabloids. One maverick paparazzo Dave Hogan spent four hours squatting in a broom cupboard to get his precious photo exclusive of the last Wham! video shoot. But out the back on the Twickenham film lot there were people going through an even more tedious routine for considerably less remuneration. The band's chauffeurs were instructed to wait in the cars for the duration of the shoot – a total of thirty-six hours.

The initial eagerness had waned before George appeared. The director Andy Morahan had to egg the residue of the cast on with pleas for 'lots of screaming, lots of screaming . . . and lots of arm-waving'. After four hours of muscle-aching waves George arrived, coming over all butch on stage in a mock live setting with Andrew and David Austin mugging up to the camera on guitars. Clips from previous videos were superimposed on a backdrop – their whole life flashed behind their eyes – while at the end the word 'Good-Bye' touchingly flashed onto the screen.

As George took himself more seriously by the minute, Andrew, cut free of any responsibility, became increasingly frivolous by similar degrees. While George soon became intent on making Wham! the biggest band in the world,

Andrew was just a distraction. George was enthusing about recording with soul legend Aretha Franklin in the PR push before The Final when *Number 1* journalist Peter Martin asked him how he would manage without Andrew. The two musketeers had stuck to the essential code of 'honour and friendship', but for George the strain of making this the most amicable split in pop history was beginning to show as he let slip a viperish aside: 'Well, it's not going to damage my musical output. Andrew knew he was there for a purpose.' The opportunity was snatched to rewrite pop history. A virulent dose of rampant revisionism saw George putting Wham!'s sun-kissed frivolity behind him: 'I regret that people have misconstrued my personality with that of the group. They couldn't understand that it was my trying to be the ultimate performer, reflecting what I saw as the ultimate pop song in the only way possible. I hated being the ultimate pin-up band around the time of "Go Go" and "Freedom".'

At the same time a humble George asserted that little had changed: 'All we ever wanted to do was be a pop band and we're the only people I can remember in the last five or six years that haven't really turned around and tried to be taken desperately seriously by changing our music . . . "The Edge Of Heaven" is as Wham! as "Go Go" was and that's two years later. We've come through all that flak and the public like us more than ever, because they appreciate honesty.' But beneath the glow of achievement and the modest recognition of the facts, George had changed irreconcilably: 'It's like I'm at one end of a tunnel, and I can't see the other end any more. And I couldn't see this end of the tunnel when I was at the beginning of it!'

In *Number 1* he revealed the private torment that was part of the baggage of stardom: 'I've never given anything personal away and I never will. There's so little that I have left to myself that I'm going to keep it to myself.' But at least the future held a few questions for

George which were yet to be answered: 'How can you end Wham! more perfectly than in front of 72,000 people, still good friends, with hopefully a number one record. I've almost done too much too young and it leaves me an awful long time to fill, but I think that's exciting. That's my new challenge.'

Events leading up to the last show were as fraught for George as they were dull for Andrew. Informed by insurers that he could not race in the run-up, he could only bide his time and ponder his future. In the run-up to The Final George joined in with the tenth anniversary celebrations of the Prince's Trust at Wembley Arena. Unlike Live Aid's choice of commercially appealing acts, this was the old guard aristocracy of pop and rock. Mick Jagger, Paul McCartney, David Bowie, Elton John, Rod Stewart, Eric Clapton, Phil Collins, Sting et al. pressed the flesh with the real royals. And there was George again making a surprise appearance, duetting with Paul Young on 'Every Time You Go Away'.

There were other more pressing engagements south of the Thames in the week before Wembley. Wham! played two secret warm-up concerts at Brixton's Academy Theatre, partly for the benefit of their long-suffering fan club, partly to raise money for the charity Help A London Child and partly to try out their act before Saturday's one-off show.

Saturday 28 June was a blisteringly hot day as 72,000 fans sweltered along Empire Way into the stadium. Four times that number had sent £13.50 each for tickets in vain; Wham! had resisted the temptation to milk the occasion by playing extra dates, in the process of making this a unique event.

As if to trowel irony upon irony, the great campaigner for racial equality found his farewell gig coinciding with a free anti-apartheid festival on Clapham Common in south London. That afternoon Clapham played host to 200,000 fans and a dazzling array of major stars from Sade to Big

Audio Dynamite and ubiquitous bleeding heart Sting. It was an event orchestrated by Artists Against Apartheid, the agitpop organization set up by Jerry Dammers, leader of the Specials, the group that had inspired George's initial flawed blueprint for stardom, the Executive.

Among the special guests in Clapham was a decidedly bedraggled Boy George, making his own solo début in the wake of Culture Club's acrimonious disintegration. Boy George had never been a classical Adonis but today he looked particularly haggard. The tabloids had recently been performing their familiar vulture act, circling around him for confirmation of his rumoured heroin addiction. In response he had come up with an intriguing tactic to thwart photographers: sporting a suit made from newspaper headlines (the irony probably fell on stony ground), especially conceived for the occasion, that said genuinely unprintable things like 'Fuck me stupid'. It was to be a brief respite from his descent. Soon afterwards his fall would appear every bit as thorough as his namesake's ascendance.

The set-up of The Final emphasizes Wham!'s domination of pop but the support bands who briefly relive their own glory days also reveal the transient essence of teen pop. At 4.03 Gary Glitter is trundled out to get the day underway. This anachronistic figure has some superficial similarities to George Michael – an enduring battle of the bulge and a penchant for pastiching earlier musical forms – but you could never really see this Bacofoil-clad figure conquering the globe. His breakthrough came when quality was in short supply and there was a lot of superfluous cash waiting to be spent on singles. Having tried as many different names as hairstyles, he seemed to have been around since time immemorial before he finally made the big time. Now he is permanently stuck in a self-parodying time-warp, a predicament that Boy George is heading for, a permanent pantomime clown much loved but doomed never to be taken seriously. Apart from this brief return to glory, an eternity of Freshers' Weeks stretches ahead of him. Today's show is good-humoured and politely received, the affable figure being presented not with a deserved pension book but a bunch of red roses which he camply distributes among the crowd.

Next up is ex-Haircut 100 heart-throb Nick Heyward. For a while what takes place is like a parallel universe. Imagine for a moment that Wham! had never happened and that Haircut 100 were still in favour in the hearts of a million schoolgirls. Once, this slightly goofy figure was also acclaimed as the man with the finest-turned pop sensibility in the business. He too had signed a lucrative publishing deal with Bryan Morrison and was championed as a new McCartney. Perhaps this explains his presence, another vain attempt by his publishers to relaunch his solo career.

Since Haircut 100's unhappy split Heyward's fortunes have been mixed; he has been a staple feature of the gossip columns but not the charts. Nor has his post-teenage phase garnered him any credibility – the same challenge faces George. But at least Wham! are going out on top. Recent events have seen a discreet and not altogether surprising reunion of Haircut 100. Onstage with him are fellow former crimpers, saxophonist Phil Smith and lanky bass guitarist Les Nemes – the Ridgeley to Heyward's Michael.

Slick and stylish, they win over the crowd with their greatest hits and his solo singles thrown in for good measure. An encore of 'Fantastic Day' from 1982 sums up the buoyant mood of the crowd who in a few years, concerned more with mortgages and children of their own, will wonder what all the fuss was about. For now the concert takes priority. Exam revision has been shelved, that first job application lies uncompleted on the sideboard and their biggest dilemma is whether to cut their souvenir posters in half before they stick them on their bedroom walls.

As water douses the seething mass on the turf, backstage there is an air of near surreal calm belying the significance of the day. Elton John mingles graciously with Simon Le Bon, Gary Kemp and ubiquitous lager liggers Frankie Goes To Hollywood. Their high jinks involve splashing people with the paddling pool water. George's sister Melanie is busy sculpting her younger brother's extravagant coiffure before his public appearance. The logistics of having Elton John there have proved more demanding than having both support acts. Not only does he always travel with an enormous entourage, not only does he come complete with a ludicrous amount of finery, but his white grand piano also has to be hauled onto the stage for his secret guest appearance.

Out front there is an extra 'treat' to make the day special: the video screens come alive at 6.18 for the first public screening of 'Foreign Skies: Wham! in China'. Their historic trip has evolved into a hi-tech upgrading of their early mid-show home movies. The high-gloss tourist snaps on the big screens capture the attention of the crowd for a few minutes before attention turns intermittently to packed lunches and tepid drinks.

Lindsay Anderson's distinctive editing ended up on a cutting room floor once he had been sacked from the project. He had not been involved in any disagreements with George; in fact George had not turned up for their proposed meeting before the final edit and remix. Regardless of his inexperience, George had simply decided to take over the project to be sure that it met with his approval. Lindsay Anderson had been paid off, but regretted the incident, not because of the blow to his ego – he had learnt enough about the conceit of George Michael not to let that get to him – but because: 'the film I made was rather good. They took it over and fucked it up. It was a lack of intelligence on George's part that he didn't learn from it. It ended up awful and badly edited. They had made an absurd amount of money and didn't seem bothered about wasting it. George even seemed pleased to hear that it had cost £1 million; he just shrugged his shoulders and said "So what?". Poor little rich girl.'

Instead Jazz Summers, video director Andy Morahan and Strathford Hamilton have put together a hagiographic glimpse of George at work and at play in the Far East. The crowd remain unmoved. They can see videos any time; today only flesh can satisfy them.

At 7.35 the mellifluous funk of 'Everything She Wants' wafts through the air to announce the real show. This could almost be George's solo show as the enormous curtains embossed with 'The Final' open to reveal his only companions to be two anonymous dancers. Dressed in black leather, his hair is shorn of its golden tresses and is back to its (almost) natural brown, matching his freshly acquired stubble. Teased from curl into wave, this is a sharp contrast to the manicured blow-waves of 'Foreign Skies'. Eventually George's supporting cast joins him on stage. Ridgeley enters, dispelling heinous thoughts of his premature ejection and graciously waits for Pepsi and Shirlie to relieve him of the usual frock coat before he is strapped into his guitar, an act that only compounds the view of his legendary laziness and lack of ability to do anything remotely musical.

The glitterati have taken their place in the royal box. Andrew's self-aggrandizing parents have been careful to invite the right friends, while George's mother and father have taken their son's unimaginable status in their stride. The once sceptical Jack has finally realized that Georgios is only doing all this to attain the same kind of financial security that he strived for twenty years earlier in different surroundings.

Among the self-styled pop royals are Yasmin Le Bon, Rod Stewart, Paula Yates, designer Jasper Conran and Patsy Kensit. In the audience the ubiquitous banners are unfurled possibly for the last time. One lovingly crafted sign reads 'Nob out George'. Inevitably tonight is to be a greatest hits package. In fact when you glance back over their brief career you suddenly realize that there is not very much apart from the greatest hits. Even the most casual listener to Radio 1 would know ninety-nine per cent of their material.

By the time 'Everything She Wants' is over, every seat has been filled, every corner of the stadium covered, necks craning and binoculars raised to catch sight of George and Andrew. Everything finally seems to fit; their tight black outfits make them look like real stars. Even as a dot on the horizon from the back of the stadium George cuts a dramatic dash against the azure skyline as he sprints across the stage. He may have his moments of lethargy in private but in public George betrays the fitness of an Olympic athlete. On the gargantuan video screens he even seems to have assumed the stature of an Olympian god.

The second number, 'Club Tropicana' is followed by George's brief introduction to his followers: 'This is obviously the most important gig we have ever played . . . we've got four years of thank you's to say this evening and I know we're going to enjoy saying them, so let's get started.' Overcome by the situation, Andy continually mumbles, 'You look good . . . you really do,' at the sheer numbers rather than the aesthetic splendour of the crowd.

Behind George, Pepsi and Shirlie are like pantomime foils, swapping outfits with the rapidity of a farce. Spray-on rubber dresses, then rockabilly cats with skyscraper beehives sending up rock, emphasizing how Wham! owe more to showbiz than traditional rock and roll.

The catalogue of hits that pours forth reiterates the sheer exuberance and simplicity of Wham!'s body of work. These are the songs that even Wham!'s most grudging fans will be dancing to in years to come. At Wembley even the police, drafted in to quell the hysteria if it steps beyond the bounds of good humour, have stripped to their shirt sleeves and smile as they dance along. George is very big on audience participation: for 'Heartbeat' he conducts everyone while they chant 'Woah woah'. 'Battlestations' from the current EP is a brisk Robert Palmer-ish upbeat song with an uncharacteristically downbeat narrative; his ballads have usually been the province of his reflective work. 'Battlestations' employs military metaphor to talk of passions rent asunder: 'Now we spend more time in battle than we ever did in bed.' As if to hint at some change in his outlook he tells the crowd that this is his favourite song on the record. 'Bad Boys' is all rock and roll parody before George pays some respect to one of his inspirations, the Isley Brothers, with a dutiful cover of 'If You Were There'.

After an hour of hits and the occasional filler from their albums, the white grand piano appears onstage to herald their special guest. The ultimate showman, Elton John is gaudy even by his own standards, decked out as Ronald McDonald, the hamburger clown. Like Gary Glitter, here is a man of the past who found his *métier* in camp over-indulgence; but Elton has penned enough classic songs to become an international institution. Like George, Elton was never physically perfect but triumphed in adversity by exaggerating his flaws. When hair transplants failed he took to wearing ludicrous wigs ranging from mohican styles to Mozartian bouffants. George simply combined will-power with blow-dryer to tame his Chico Marx locks. Elton has finally succumbed to middle-aged spread, while George works his body into physical perfection with athletic dance routines and stern self-discipline, curbing binges on seafood and mayonnaise and Galaxy bars. Of late he has even tried a vegetarian diet to keep his fat intake down.

Current number 1 'The Edge of Heaven' signals the return of former busking partner David Austin and a rigorous rehearsal of audience participation as a different third of the audience sings each 'yeah' of the chorus. For 'Candle In The Wind' Elton accompanies George's rather po-faced rendition of the song recounting the pitfalls and tragedy of stardom as experienced by Marilyn Monroe.

After some frantic sexual preening and audience-baiting, George slows things down to cool the crowd's ardour and catch his breath, dedicating 'A Different Corner' mysteriously to 'one special person . . . they know who they are', 'they' fudging the sexual identity of the person.

Things return to happier days with 'Wham! Rap' before George covers his abiding heroine Carly Simon's 'Why', reputedly the first single he ever bought. Next comes the unlikely cover version from the 'Edge of Heaven' EP. Was (Not Was)'s 'Where Did Your Heart Go?' is a mellow ballad that George could easily have composed the music for. The words, however, are a different matter. Was (Not Was)'s speciality is plastering irony upon irony upon a conventional musical backdrop. The Detroit songwriters Don and David Was (neither brothers nor really called Was) deal in surreal parodic pop that appeals to George's wit although he has yet to attempt a similar approach, preferring literal narrative grounded in personal experience. Besides, in 1986 the world is not ready for Was (Not Was). They have credibility and commercial success in inverse proportions to George, but will have to wait until 1988 for their first hit single, 'Walk the Dinosaur'; too clever by half, they are still small cheese by comparison with George.

Where Was (Not Was) invert Motown's narrative tradition, George's direct inspirational descendence from the golden era of sixties pop is reiterated with 'Freedom''s jangling refrain. And then Wham! leave the stage after two hours of the most relentless pop barrage of the eighties. But one rock cliché they are going to pay lip-service to is the not-so-spontaneous encore. Why else have three number one singles been omitted from the set?

On his return to eardrum-bursting cheers after the briefest of intervals it seems as if George Michael has decided to commence his solo career right here. 'Careless Whisper' manages to hush the audience a little but there is still the constant hum of hysteria, rising once more when the rest of the band join him for 'Young Guns (Go For It)'. As the evening hauls itself inexorably towards its climax, multicoloured fireworks strafe the summer sky, and a Mexican wave shudders around the stadium as the hitherto anonymous group are finally introduced one by one during an extended instrumental introduction to 'I'm Your Man'. Elton John returns, having abandoned his Big Mac outfit for a pink mohican and matching drape coat, while a cheerful Simon Le Bon joins George on vocals. Le Bon has good reason to smile; he knows that with Wham! gone, Duran Duran might reclaim the grail of teen supremacy.

But before the chubby twosome become too chummy, the real duo of the night are reunited as Andrew joins George on vocals at the front of the stage. Nobody can hear Ridgeley, but nobody ever has. All that matters is that the illusion of comradeship is maintained to the bitter end. It is an undeniably moving sight – the pair with their arms around each other, a combination of tears and sweat raining down their faces as they bid each other and 72,000 fans the most public of goodbyes.

At 10.17 p.m. the audience begins to stream out silently, a sudden sense of mourning overcoming the celebratory sense of occasion as the reality of the farewell begins to sink in. Many of the pasty faces shuffling disconsolately back down Empire Way will shed a few tears on their Wham! pillowcases tonight; sold by the *Sun* for £2.99, 50% cotton and 50% polyester, half fabricated, half natural, the cases are more like their heroes than the sleeping heads probably realize.

Behind the scenes champagne runs as freely as tears as the entourage heads for the farewell party at Peter Stringfellow's Hippodrome club in Leicester Square, where the exclusive goodbye has cost a princely £65,000. Significantly George heads directly for the West End. Eighteen months earlier when Wham! had played the Arena just around the corner, George had been driven the short distance north to Radlett to celebrate at home. Inside the club artificial snow has been sprinkled everywhere giving a surreal Yuletide flavour to the night as Wham!'s own Christmas hit reverberates endlessly around the plush surrounds. Wham!'s confirmation as part of the beau monde is marked as they dance away at the centre of attention with their respective stilettoed girlfriends. Diona Fiorentino for Ridgeley, the enigmatic Kathy Jeung for George.

In the days following, inflated stories of George's newly discovered romantic intrigue are only usurped in the tabloids by news of Wham! 2, featuring George and David Austin, following George's appearance in the studio with Austin. In reality George is attempting to apply his patent Midas' touch to his friend's latest destined-for-the-dumper solo single. Gilt by association was never to be. The success of Wham! could not be repeated so easily.

As for the famous duo, they had succeeded in weaving themselves into the very fabric of everybody's lives. Now George faced a new task: weaving himself out for a while.

11

Alone Again Unnaturally

Embarking on a solo career was George Michael's way of avoiding the 'pop trap'. He wanted to write songs that could be heard not just above the screaming but without the screaming. Much as he was gratified by his elevation to the ranks of sex symbol, he yearned for a mature audience that would appreciate his craft as well as his officially sexiest bottom. He had seen the sexual fix of pop coming a year earlier: 'If you make uplifting, euphoric, optimistic records and you also happen to be twenty-one and not ugly – even if you are just reasonable looking – you automatically get screamed at. You can't say fuck this, I don't want it.' Pop has been sold on sex since day one; charisma was just a drawing room euphemism for sex appeal. But the style-stifling eighties had forced the look into the foreground at the expense of the song.

Your sex appeal rather than your music would make you a star. The apotheosis of this was Samantha Fox, who led a succession of topless models out of the photographic studios and into recording studios, to be followed closely by a flock of television soap stars. Rather than a vocation, pop was becoming another string to a careerist bow in an entertainment industry that could reap vast financial rewards from the media tie-up of music and television. Videos only accelerated the process of creating flash-in-the-pan icons; you could hardly appear unattractive in a clip that was created for the sole purpose of your promotion. And of course the Fleet Street tabloids were complicit in the illusion, putting the travails of the rich and famous on their front pages to the exclusion of real hard news.

Fleet Street had effectively made the pneumatic Ms Fox, first as a soft-porn pin-up and now as a pop star, and it would break Boy George in the weeks after The Final as it relentlessly stalked him down until he was eventually revealed as a heroin addict by his own brother. Fleet Street was a vicious beast that George Michael had managed to learn to live with over the years better than any of his contemporaries, largely by virtue of the fact that he did so little out of the ordinary.

George wanted to hold onto his fans as they settled down into adult life. As they started taking life seriously they would begin to take him seriously rather than camp outside his office and hold competitions to see who could get his photograph the most times. So far George's professional life had been faultless, but in the summer of 1986 his personal life was reaching crisis point.

Wham!'s bombastic, epochal farewell gave George Michael a chance to step out of the spotlight for a while. There was no reason to dive straight into a solo career; in fact he needed a break to escape from his past, just as long as he did not leave it too long. For a while at least he could wallow in the freedom that wealth had presented him with: 'Who wants to drive a beautiful car if you have to drive it to work each day?'

But as he slipped from sight there was no hint of the emotional turmoil that had beset him in the preceding months. Prior to the disintegration of Wham! George had been the victim of rejection himself, and he had taken it extremely badly. For the first time someone had not wanted the star. Success had made forming relationships and impressing people easier, but he had finally encountered someone who was not interested in him. It was the first time that he had not been the one to do the rejecting and, inevitably, the lack of interest only fanned the flames of George's desire further. The elation of his public life contrasted painfully with the agonies of his private life. Since his doting parents had always lavished gifts, comfort and love on their only son, to him not getting one's way was something that happened to other people.

The ongoing trauma of 1986 was a period that he was not prepared to open up about then and remains confused, uneasy and secretive about even today: 'I don't know if I'd classify it as true love any more. I think it's the first time I was infatuated and rejected. Just because it's the strongest feeling does not mean it was love. Somehow you always assume that the worst you could possibly feel must mean you were the most in love . . . I don't know.' As ever, he was coy about the sexual identity of the person that had thwarted him. His vague pronouncements recalled the probing analysis of Dr Guy Fielding, Lecturer in Communcation Studies at Sheffield Polytechnic, who deconstructed the lyrical content of 'I'm Your Man': 'The song seems to be the work of a schizophrenic . . . it reveals someone who has insides like jelly and a soft centre. It's almost as if the song was written by a woman.' If George supposedly based his material on his own experiences, it appears he was selling himself short in adhering to the brilliantly sterile soul of later Wham!; he must have left a lot bubbling under the surface. Did the rejection come from his long-term companion Pat Fernandes? It would appear not – he 'jilted' her after he passed his driving test and no longer needed her chauffeur service, implied one tabloid. Was it the collapse of his relationship with Andrew? Was it someone else?

The temporary retirement following The Final only brought things into sharper focus. With time on his hands to take stock he did not like what he saw, and worse still, a self-pitying streak emerged. In *Time Out* he said: 'I used that depression to look at myself as this trapped individual – that I created this Wham! monster.' After four frantic years the one thing he found he could not handle was the emptiness. While preparing for The Final the rejection had been hidden at the back of his mind, and his new companion Kathy Jeung had temporarily allayed his gloom, but now he had no other thoughts to preoccupy him. Freed from the shackles of work he went more than a little bit wild, and things began to slip.

England was the last place he wanted to be. Apart from being hounded by the press, he did not want his family to see him in his current state. During the days of Wham! George must have been one of the few superstars who rang his mother regularly every day for a chat. Where so many stars strive for fame because of a lack of stability in childhood, George's unbroken run of youthful happiness had helped to make him one of the most well-adjusted pop stars until now.

In America that summer he found a laid-back attitude to fame that allowed stars a certain amount of leeway. In Los Angeles and New York he renewed his acquaintance with clubs – and alcohol. Wham!'s early days had raced by in a haze of white wine, but more recently most excessive drinking had been banished so that he could concentrate on his career. Now George and the flagon returned with a vengeance. Much of the remaining half of 1986 consisted of forgotten nights and hangovers that would have made even Andrew Ridgeley at his most bibulous wince.

The fact that he did his wallowing in some of the most glamorous watering holes of the world failed to ease the pain. Standing back from Wham! and trying to get the last four years into perspective came as a revelation to George. The fact was that his pop life had forced him to change not just his name but his personality. Where Prince and Madonna were quite content to be Prince and Madonna twenty-four hours a day, Georgios Panayiotou was not the George Michael that entered into everyone's life via the media. The intensity of his work had made him forget that; in his current state he could not escape the truth. Stardom as big as his was unreal enough to knock anyone's sanity for six, let alone someone barely out of their teens.

Before Wham! he and Andrew had been two archetypal lads. George had needed alcohol to become as lecherous as his self-confident partner; sober he was as well-behaved as a choirboy. While Wham! were public property he found that he was in demand from both sexes; after a brief phase of promiscuity he had seen the error of his ways and had felt compelled to suppress this sleazier part of his personality. It was a confusing time which he tried to make sense of in Q magazine: 'I became this harmless, feminine-looking David Cassidy figure who all the little girls could take home without any fear of my putting my hand up their skirt. It was a strange situation because before that I wasn't the type of guy who could walk into a room and pull any bird, and suddenly, at nineteen, I could.'

During his early forays into America he had realized the powerful attraction of stardom when he discovered that his position gave him the opportunity to sleep with almost anyone. Although he and Andrew had originally wound up the press with their imaginary sexual exploits, there was a reality to their fables as well. George took great delight in exercising his newly discovered droit de seigneur. Everything he wanted was his – until his rejection: 'My problem was that I had no problem; what I really needed was a kick in the arse.'

In his more lucid moments that summer he attempted to untangle the mess of his public and private life, but to no avail. Could he blame his career for ruining the one relationship he had wanted to succeed? Would he have had the chance of that relationship without his career? It was an impossible conundrum to crack. His conclusions only served to make things look blacker than ever and drive him further off the rails: 'I thought – I have finally woken up. I have sussed it out and it is all a pile of shit.'

By all accounts it was a twisted, strange period even by pop's larger than life standards, as he recalled in Q magazine: 'I got into fist-fights with friends, threw photographers against walls, acted very macho.' His worst behaviour

172

was all the more disturbing in that it occurred when he had not been drinking. 'I'd go completely out of character. My voice would drop about an octave and I'd start talking with this incredibly heavy slang.'

Had this period of intense paranoia occurred in the past, it would always have been nipped in the bud by Andrew whose droll abuse would have dragged George back to reality, reminding him who he really was and what they had been through together. And if that did not work Andrew was not averse to literally giving him that much needed kick in the arse. Without his childhood friend to bounce against, George was heading for an inevitable fall. The same force that drove George on to greater heights of success could just as easily drive him further off the rails. Andrew was necessary to protect George, the insatiable spoilt child who would always want more, however much he had: 'I have a very strong tendency to go for people that I know I can't ever fully have. And that tendency became a full-blown fact once I could have anyone, basically, that I wanted. It became totally unattractive to me to have anyone and everyone I wanted because for a while I did. I mucked about a lot for about eight months to a year, really. And then you realize that you are a bigger mug than they are, because you're the one that gets talked about in their office the next day.' Racked with self-doubt after his rejection, the decision to finish Wham! slotted neatly into his plan to start all over again. But that summer he found that he needed redemption more than ever.

Help came in part from his new companion Kathy Jeung, with whom he headed to St Tropez in August. Another compulsive party animal, who at various times had been a DJ, a make-up artist and a model, their relationship bloomed after a few faltering meetings when both their passions were fired by ostensible mutual disinterest. George found her indifference compelling. Her residency in Los Angeles allowed a natural distance between them giving George the best of both worlds: a stable relationship combined with room to breathe. Her own career negated any possibility of their setting up home in London together, but this also suggested that her involvement with George was merely professional, a smoke screen to help deflect irritating questions about George's sexuality. There was much talk of their nights out when they would go through the motions for the paparazzi at nightclub doors only to separate once inside. With the Atlantic Ocean frequently dividing them, it certainly seemed a very convenient relationship.

Kathy was not sycophantic towards George as so many acquaintances were. She had worked with enough famous people not to be fazed by stardom. Coming into his life when he was about to enter a trough, she filled the void left by rejection: 'I believe that if you are sleeping with a lot of girls you don't develop much as a person. My relationship with Kathy has changed me a lot. I've developed, I've become more directed and positive. I can concentrate more on my career and the things that are important to me without having the distraction of looking for something.' George's promiscuous days were over. He had a quarter share in a Soho bachelor pad in case he met someone at a club that he wanted to take back, but he had never used it. Privacy was far more attractive: 'I've never lived with a girl. I need to be on my own. I need to be able to shut myself off from everyone.' There was no doubting that it was lonely at the top for George Michael.

In the south of France George was only a stone's throw from Andrew Ridgeley's new base, Monte Carlo, but unlike his friend, George's residency was distinctly temporary. Ensconced in the Hotel Byblos that August, he swam, topped up his tan and attemped to recoup his energies in Mediterranean style. He flew back to London, not for a trim this time but to check on the opposition, Prince, at Wembley Arena. Beneath the superficially innocuous bouts of hedonism he continued to drink heavily. First of all he drank from the bottle but eventually the bottle began to drink out of him, draining him emotionally and spiritually. Fighting to keep depression at bay he tried his best to be philosophical about his position when probed by *You* magazine: 'I'm glad I've grown up quickly because it means I can enjoy the rest of my life more. Growing up's not very enjoyable.'

With time on his hands George became unsettled. He lived out a travelogue, attempting to keep one step ahead of the storm clouds. There was Portugal, Los Angeles, even Australia. Anywhere but London. Things seemed so bleak he felt he could not even turn to his ever-supportive family. Occasionally he would rendezvous with Kathy but more often than not he was alone. It gave him an opportunity to take a close look at his life and wonder whether he 'wanted to come back into this again'.

It was an unlikely figure, one who had been on good terms with the inside of a bottle himself, who put George back on the right track again. Andrew Ridgeley invited George out for a drink one night in Los Angeles and was greeted by a sorry figure. The split had been a greater relief to Andrew, allowing him to pursue a life outside the imposing shadow of George. He never thought he would be called upon to fulfil the role of fellow barfly, counsellor and father confessor all rolled into one. But at the same time it seemed so natural. Andrew still knew George's predicament better than anyone, dubbing him TLTI – 'the legend that is'. Jokingly he referred to his younger companion as Geoff Michaels – but even in jest it was enough to give anyone an identity crisis. Deep into the night George spilt his troubles out to his old friend. Drink lubricated the encounter and for a while it recalled happier, more innocent days when a drunken George had poured out his insecurities and the contents of his stomach in front of his friend.

The aftermath of this second confession saw a renewed George Michael. As the singer returned from the slough of despond he talked about how that night seemed 'like an exorcism'. Had he been the kind of pop star that read Nietzsche he would probably have talked about that which does not kill us making us stronger. George realized that there was only one life open to him. Like some old Broadway trouper he got his own show back on the road: 'I gave myself a quick kick and said, "You know there's not really anything else you would want to do." I decided just to come back and do it again, but maybe on different terms.'

Georgios Panayiotou could now be put back in the box for a while longer.

This black period was George's biggest set-back to date. It was the one time the personal impinged upon the professional to negative effect. In his past he had been able to turn negative experiences in on themselves and even into hits. Both solo singles had been inspired by real incidents. It even seemed for a while as if 'A Different Corner', originally entitled 'Stephen', had been triggered by this particular rejection (although in a typical bout of media muddling, he also suggested it was about a recently bereaved friend). But in his own way, he was able to turn even this set-back to the most important advantage yet. Even as he was coming through the experience he was taking on board the maturity to produce the reflective adult solo album that would prove his mettle. Even in his darkest hour George Michael was stirring up the ingredients of his next hit record.

If Wham! had forced him to age prematurely, the post-Wham! era had accelerated the process. Later on he said himself that 'I talk like I'm fifty'. Growing up in public had made him grow up fast, but growing up in private made it happen even faster.

By the autumn of 1986 it seemed as if, as far as Fleet Street was concerned, George had used up his quota of nice stories. On Monday, 13 October, the *Sun* ran a front

page 'exclusive' – 'Wham!'s George In Booze Shame',
claimed that a drunken George had been throwing his
weight around at the Limelight club in London. Having
gatecrashed a private party to mark the launch of the
'Phantom of the Opera', George had behaved in a manner
that would have done his ex-partner proud, reducing his
'pretty blonde date to tears by puking all over her low-cut
evening dress and shoes'. Typically for Rupert Murdoch's
newspaper this was considered an item of such international
impact that it relegated news of the summit between
Reagan and Gorbachev to the inside pages.

George was furious. The story tried to paint him as
an ungracious yob. George may have had moments of
obnoxiousness during his recent spate of misdemeanours,
but even in his drunkest hour he had avoided the most
public of clubs, and denied the story tartly: 'I pride myself
on having steered away from that kind of public image.'
He went on an immediate offensive, giving an interview
to London's LBC Radio to deny the allegations. Conscious
of what the tabloids had done to Andrew, embroidering
the bad times until people believed them, George was
determined to nip a potential vendetta in the bud. The
awkward détente between the press and George Michael
that had been halted after the Chinese tour was to be well
and truly severed.

Legal action was threatened before events overtook liti-
gations. Before George had a chance to institute proceedings against the *Sun* he issued a writ against *Time Out*
for not putting him on the cover, thus 'costing him the
opportunity to enhance his reputation'. *Time Out* placated
George's wrath by settling out of court; the lesson was
learnt and George's determination to keep control of his
coverage was acknowledged; it was an exercise in media
manipulation that Simon Napier-Bell would have been
proud of.

The press did, however, finally squeeze some reluctant
confessions from George's old flame Pat Fernandes, who

revealed that November that she soon realized that their relationship was on the rocks when certain portents of doom manifested themselves even in their moments of leisure. A game of Trivial Pursuit was all it took to trigger off her volatile friend: 'He just got so angry when he could not answer a question or got it wrong. We even had a bust-up over the name of Andy Pandy's girlfriend.'

Christmas without a concert seemed unnatural for George. As the festive season approached, his muse had to be satisfied. After giving the matter some thought he came up with an appropriate solution. With about thirty friends he donned a lank hippy wig and toured the local pubs singing carols. Not daring to risk recognition by singing his own compositions, the incognito superstar discovered that Beatles songs went down best, enabling his group to raise the modest sum of £7.50.

24 January 1987 marked the launch, of sorts, of George Michael's solo career. 'I Knew You Were Waiting' saw him appearing as half of a duo again, but his new partner Aretha Franklin could lay claim to rather more musical credibility than Andrew Ridgeley. Approached by Aretha's record company, Arista, George was under no illusion that he was chosen as the 'acceptable honky' to help the Queen of Soul expand her following, but George, undoubtedly flattered by the approach, was well aware that he could make the record work for his career and credibility as well. The track, written by Simon Climie (later to step in front of the cameras as half of the unashamedly Wham!-inspired duo Climie Fisher) and Dennis Morgan, had been recorded during the death throes of Wham! and was finally released to coincide with the soul diva's latest album.

For once George had to comply with somebody else's demands: the video was filmed the previous November in Detroit, due to Aretha Franklin's virtual agoraphobia. Director Andy Morahan, who had been the aspiring Eisenstein whipping the crowds into a frenzy on 'Edge Of

Heaven', used the Diamond Vision video screen, last seen at Live Aid and The Final, to imbue the performers with a larger-than-life stature, pushing the cost of the two-day shoot up to £150,000.

'I Knew You Were Waiting' was actually more of a historic achievement for Aretha Franklin. For George it was just another number one (which incidentally kept his former employees Pepsi and Shirlie at number two with their neo-Wham!-y début single, 'Heartache'), but for the soul legend it was her first in nearly two decades. The two voices worked well together in a doggedly uptempo rock/soul arrangement, a rather more 'pop' treatment than the young R&B aspirant would have liked. Crossover was the name of the game here, and this was indicative of the kind of material being recorded by black artists at the time in an attempt to embrace a wider audience in the wake of Michael Jackson and Prince's successive forays into rock territories. in the 1980s, virtually the exclusive domain of white artists, where Michael Jackson employed heavy metal guitarist Eddie Van Halen to contribute to his single 'Beat It'. Ms Franklin got her pop exposure from George while the new rock audience was drawn in by Keith Richards grinding his axe on her version of 'Jumpin' Jack Flash'.

The collaboration was clearly an idea concocted in a boardroom rather than Aretha's mind; unaware of George's *oeuvre* she reputedly later said she would never sing with him again because his songs were dirty. George had played the part of the acceptable honky admirably, in return garnering respect from authentic black circles which would help him break out of the pop ghetto in America and into the more refined stratosphere of the predominantly black R&B charts.

With Aretha, George laid the foundations of the startling American success of the *Faith* album. At last the people buying his records were not the people who bought them as an alternative to Culture Club and Duran Duran; they were the people who bought them as an alternative to Prince and

Michael Jackson, that all-important adult market that had been so difficult for other British exports to breach.

'I Knew You Were Waiting''s success came at a time when soul was undergoing a revival courtesy of some grateful old pretenders. Ben E. King had a number one hit with 'Stand By Me' twenty-six years after its original release, thanks to the eponymous American rites of passage movie and more particularly its inclusion in the advertising campaign for Levi 501s. Percy Sledge's 'When A Man Loves A Woman' also made a late entry at the top of the charts on the back of a pair of old jeans. It was an unwitting irony that these were the kind of svelte performers who wouldn't ever have been seen dead in jeans, but no matter, such is the illusion of pop.

Even among her peers Aretha Franklin has remained an enigma. A child-star from the ubiquitous gospel background, recent years had seen her less willing to travel outside Detroit. There was little point in asking her to join the promotional gravy train. Recently she had been inducted into the rock and roll hall of fame, established to honour the greatest performers in musical history (no one with less than twenty-five years' service in the industry is eligible), and was the only living inductee not present at the New York ceremony.

Persistent rumours suggested that another collaboration was in the pipeline, this time with Michael Jackson. It was a fascinating concept, the biggest black star in the world and the fastest rising white counterpart singing a duet together. An extra *frisson* was added when it was revealed that the project that had been discussed was an anti-apartheid single. George had indeed had a meeting with Michael, but it appeared that the ensuing publicity, which turned a mumbled possibility into a definite by the time the *Sun* reported it, stymied the precariously poised project. The last thing either wanted to be involved in was a squalid publicity stunt. Michael Jackson certainly did not need it, and the upward inclination of George's career suggested that he could get along fine without it too. George was making a name for himself as a session man to the stars after Elton and Aretha, but all this time he appeared to be procrastinating over his own solo career.

It took pop music's recognition of AIDS as a global issue to motivate George Michael into launching a bona fide solo career. Unlike fashion and theatre, pop had an awkward, ambivalent attitude to AIDS. In the West, a high proportion of AIDS fatalities had been gay men, and even though music is an industry that has drawn in many members of the gay community, it was slow to lend its support to increasing awareness and helping to fund research into a cure for the virus. As the disease spread in the early eighties, figures in the pop world were fatally stricken, among them disco star Sylvester and his producer, Patrick Cowley, who died of AIDS in 1983. Ironically Cowley had been responsible for the remix of Donna Summer's 'I Feel Love' which was a hit after his death. A favourite on the gay disco scene, Summer had become a born-again Christian in 1984 and in a moralistic huff denounced AIDS as a punishment sent from God. Her large gay following swiftly abandoned her, holding a public burning of her records.

As a result of the moral backlash building up in America and the growth of concern following the death of Rock Hudson in October 1985, the music industry started to raise money for AIDS research. Dionne Warwick, Gladys Knight, Stevie Wonder and Elton John recorded 'That's What Friends Are For', which topped the US charts for three weeks at the beginning of 1986, picking up on the lesson Band Aid had taught that pop had a purpose and a potential beyond mere entertainment.

1987 saw a massive Government campaign to increase awareness of AIDS in the UK. TV adverts and poster campaigns alerted the population to the need for safe sex while leaflets were widely distributed. Since it influenced the impressionable young and because its post-Live Aid conscience was now well known, the music industry was expected to back the campaign. An alarming amount of indifference and ignorance was uncovered. Simply Red's Mick Hucknall said he couldn't use a condom because it would make him feel like cattle while overnight pop sensation Curiosity Killed the Cat revealed a combination of stupidity and incipient homophobia by declaring that they were safe because they were heterosexual. There were, however, openly gay groups who refused to ignore the issue. Frankie Goes to Hollywood revived their slogan T-shirt with 'Frankie Say Use Condoms'. Boy George, newly sanctified now that he had recovered from heroin addiction, lent his support to the campaign, and Scot Jimmy Somerville put his band the Communards up for any future fund-raising AIDS concert. Some were slower to take up the gauntlet. The Pet Shop Boys' sound and image was drawn directly from the heavy gay discos of New York and Europe; at the time they refused to make their sexuality public, but in June 1988 they made partial amends by playing their first ever live concert at a show to campaign against the potentially draconian Clause 28, which threatened to remove any works of art that 'promoted homosexuality' as a pretended family relationship from local authority-funded schools and institutions.

Other gay figures steadfastly failed to face up to their responsibilities and remained in the closet. With the growing hysteria over AIDS many feared a McCarthyite witch-hunt for the so-called corrupters of youth. Indeed a homophobic backlash seemed to strengthen the resolve of the tabloids to get that gay angle on George. In 1987 the *Sun* pounced on a story about Elton John enjoying the favours of rent boys, but it looked as if the press had finally overstepped the mark. There was soon discreet discussion among various stars on whom the tabloids reputedly 'had a contract out' about pooling their financial resources and suing anyone who printed specious stories. Indeed, Elton himself issued a number of writs against the *Sun* and in late 1988 the stories were proved untrue and he won a record £1 million in damages.

In a two-pronged assault on the world's consciousness and conscience 1 April 1987 was declared International AIDS Day. A series of concerts was planned to tie in with a wider campaign which would culminate in a mass rally at Wembley Arena, dubbed 'The Party'. The organizers approached every big name in pop and got an impressive response. Stars named for the concert spanned every age, style and sexual preference: Meatloaf, Kim Wilde, the Communards, Andy Summers, Boy George, Bob Geldof, Holly Johnson, Aswad, Sandie Shaw, Elton John – who defied doctors' orders and made his first live appearance since his throat operation in Australia in January – and George Michael.

The event marked another sea-change in eighties pop. Boy George was making his public return after being dragged through both the courts and the tabloids, who took an unsightly relish in crucifying him for his addiction. Culture Club had finally fragmented amid bitterness and recriminations, and Boy George was also making his official solo début. And although Frankie Goes to Hollywood had collectively supported the campaign, lead singer Holly Johnson's solo appearance signified their imminent demise too. With George also scheduled to perform alone, the golden age of New Pop seemed officially over, the most talented remnants trying to salvage their own respective careers. Each artist vied to be viewed in a new light, appealing to adults as well as screaming prepubescents. Ever the impeccable careerist, George had made the cleanest break from his past – at his peak rather than after it – and was destined to win the day. The event was notable for the diversity of the acts. Rather than a roll call of the rent-a-cause cast, the unlikeliest names had lent their support. Cynics pointed to the PR value, but the event would hardly have the global impact of Live Aid;

plans to sell the concert to British TV were tentative and it was eventually broadcast late at night.

The theme of the concert was sex. There was definitely sex in the air; a flotilla of condoms bobbed around the arena as the stage was occupied by successive acts. The atmosphere backstage was as frantic as out the front by the time Paula Yates introduced George in a way which was hyperbolic even for the helium-filled ex-convent girl: 'He's so georgeous, so talented, so wicked, everyone here is going to want to bonk him . . . but not without a Durex.' The familiar sinuous strains of 'Everything She Wants' begged the question of whether George would really be solo. And indeed, out from the wings soon emerged special guest Andrew Ridgeley. Sensibly the reunion was short-lived, and an unusually dignified Ridgeley soon retired to the wings, allowing perennial bassist Deon Estus to join George at the front for Len Barry's old pop standard, '1,2,3'. Closing, George chose appropriately a cover of Stevie Wonder's 'Love's In Need Of Love Today', with its apt line, 'We must all take precautionary measures.'

As events ran late the stage was hurriedly prepared for further acts while co-host DJ John Sachs auctioned off a signed programme, giving one horrendously ostentatious punter the opportunity to display how much more compassionate he was than the rest by handing over a cool £6500 for the booklet. Elton John's bravura performance showed that it was possible to be bisexual and still have a successful pop career whatever the press tried to do to destroy you. But then his appeal lay in his eccentricity and his gayness was not seen as anything more deviant than that, and thus tolerable. Amid stiff competition from Boy George, Elton John had assumed the mantle of the Liberace of pop.

As a shambolic massed choir of superstars, led by the unlikely figures of the Who's John Entwhistle and super-annuated Policeman Andy Summers, drew the evening to a close with 'Stand By Me', the show was declared a success.

At a hefty £25 a ticket the evening had succeeded in raising £120,000 for the Terrence Higgins Trust. And more importantly, on a personal note for George Michael, he had not just lent his support to another worthy cause, but amid the furore had successfully negotiated that all-important solo début.

12

Sex

On 3 June 1987 George Michael blessed the world with a preview of his forthcoming LP, provisionally titled *Kissing A Fool*. Three different versions of the single 'I Want Your Sex' made their way into the world's record shops to be greeted by a storm of controversy. In a prudish display of media disgust not seen since the furore over Frankie Goes To Hollywood's 'Relax' in 1984, George was to find himself garnering a lot more publicity but a lot less airplay for his first post-Wham! solo single than he had ever expected.

A sticky advance on the primordial pop of Wham!, 'I Want Your Sex' revealed that George had indeed been mugging up on Prince following that flying visit to Wembley Arena the previous August. Like the diminutive diva, who had hewn his lurid reputation out of thinly veiled metaphorical treatises such as 'Little Red Corvette', George had addressed himself to the issue of sex. Like Prince he had also utilized the technique of altering the speed of his vocals to reproduce his voice at different pitches, wrapping some distinctly tumescent tonsils around an otherwise standard slab of synthesized soul. The process extended his range and rendered it in places neither masculine nor feminine but eerily other-worldly.

George explained the trio of variations on the theme in rather demagogical fashion as 'Impatience, trying to explain what you want, then resignation. Where "Different Corner" had been about a brief encounter, "I Want Your

Sex

Sex" was originally about a hopeless conquest but changed
to accommodate Kathy.' He had originally written the
song, calling it 'Johnny Sex', in another attempt to kickstart
David Austin's solo career, but had reclaimed his composition suspecting that it would somehow be more *risqué* and
less likely to get airplay if recorded by an unknown singer.
With its Princely posturing, this hi-tech blue-eyed soul was
clearly intended as a stab at the American market, but for
all the wrong reasons it was rapidly becoming the talk of
Great Britain.

The storm blew up because the release coincided with
the full-frontal assault of the Government's Aids Awareness Campaign; in the midst of re-educating people about
their sexual behaviour, 'I Want Your Sex' appeared to be
advocating promiscuity. In the light of George's recent
appearance at the AIDS concert his fans knew the arrant
nonsense of this theory. Indeed, in the current climate it
would have been naïve, if not commercial suicide, to be
so irresponsible.

And if that was not enough, George's critics could
always have listened more attentively to the lyrics. Rather
than address himself to womanhood as a whole, as the more
cocksure heavy rock fraternity might have done, George
was clearly aiming the song at an individual. 'I Want Your
Sex' was a priapic paean to passion combined with the
intensity of monogamous love: 'Sex is natural – sex is
good/Not everybody does it/But everybody should/Sex
is natural – sex is fun/Sex is best when it's . . . one
on one.' Masters and Johnson would have been proud
of George.

George was not ashamed to admit that he had been
through a promiscuous phase (in fact he mentions it so
often you begin to wonder if he is in retrospect rather
proud of it), but it was all behind him now and the song was
a testament to a new stability, both sexual and emotional.
Yet, strangely for a celebration of love, the catalogue
number was 'Lust 1'. George was still having considerable

difficulties reconciling his trenchant hedonism with his new mantle of responsibility. 'I Want Your Sex' was his attempt to bridge the gap between the Apollonian and Dionysian sides of his personality. A line towards the end popped the question: 'What do you consider pornography?' Probed for an answer in an interview, George replied with a libertine boldness, 'Sex detached from feeling. People fucking for the sake of fucking is fine. People fucking for the sake of other people is pornography. In terms of casual sex there are great lovers and lousy lovers. I think I'm pretty good, probably.'

What raised hackles at the BBC was that the word 'sex' appeared in the title. In the current climate, George's biggest sin was bad timing. Suddenly the controller of Radio 1, Johnny Beerling, announced that they would not be playing the single before nine o'clock in the evening because of the sexually explicit nature of the lyrics, which was the same as the watershed applied on TV, after which 'adult viewing' could be screened. But on Radio 1 at the time there were only DJs Janice Long and John Peel after nine; both harboured defiantly 'alternative' stances, championing non-chart acts, while Radio 2 was the stiff-jointed middle-aged option that wouldn't have played the record anyway. Neither seemed likely to give any airtime to the record, so the single was effectively presented with a blanket ban by default.

George could bathe in the Antichrist-like kudos of being a pop star censored by the media, but on the other hand his adult aspirations were dealt a critical body blow when he realized that the reason his single was banned was because the BBC considered that the majority of his fans were still impressionable children. None the less, people could always buy his record. With only a handful of plays in seven weeks on Radio 1 the record swiftly climbed, sound unheard, to number three.

With feelings already running high the video was destined to exacerbate matters. In the clip, directed by George and Andy Morahan, Kathy Jeung appears as a typical male fantasy figure, strutting in disembodied suspenders and corsage around George ('I think high heels are the best invention ever'), perched in his bare boudoir. George's video concept was no more original than Wham!'s post-Motown fluff. In one scene, familiar to anyone that had seen the recent 'erotic' movie *9½ Weeks* with Mickey Rourke and Kim Basinger, a scantily clad George (later revealed as double Chris Beedie) blindfolds his amour before embarking on a series of hackneyed sexual antics involving water, silk sheets and an acreage of naked flesh.

It was the provocatively witty visual punchline, however, that both fuelled the call for a ban and was proffered by George as ample evidence of a responsible morality. In the final scene George writes the words 'Explore Monogamy' in lipstick on his girlfriend's back. Basically he was preaching a sensible, downright fogeyish sexual sermon – 'enjoy sex but within a stable relationship'; the ever-endearing iconaclastic *Smash Hits* euphemistically explained the meaning of monogamy as 'Going out with just one person.' Morality did not come any more responsible than this. George indignantly denied that he had personally engineered the affair to elicit the maximum of publicity. The problem was in the mind of the media, not in the music.

It was not the first time that a record had been banned and it would certainly not be the last. The BBC was under particular pressure to tighten its moral reins amid the recent departure of Director General Alasdair Milne that February, and the bringing in of a new Government-appointed chairman, Marmaduke Hussey; everyone was being extra-cautious. In the past, explicitly erotic releases such as Marvin Gaye's 'Sexual Healing' had passed with little fuss, but suddenly there seemed to be a big chill in the light of AIDS and Margaret Thatcher's espousal of Victorian values and championing of the family unit.

The ban said more about the sexual mores of Great Britain than those of George Michael.

In the wake of the daytime radio ban George instructed his record company not to send any more copies to the BBC. Yet while the inestimable Mr Beerling was codedly voicing fears that the song might be the catalyst to spark an AIDS epidemic because George was listened to by a lot of impressionable young girls, the Play Safe Aids Campaign, clearly paying closer attention to the lyrics, actively praised the record's sentiments. And as if to close the lid on the Great British Absurdity of the case, it later transpired that on the more enlightened Continent, Belgian TV was using a translated version with the video to teach sex education to Flemish children.

The flurry of activity over something that in all honesty was hardly likely to change anyone's sexual behaviour for better or worse reflected a new puritanism sweeping through the British media. Apart from the Frankie fuss and the lurid coverage of Boy George's heroin addiction which Fleet Street had succeeded in both condemning and sensationalizing to boost circulations, DJ Mike Smith had managed to get the Jesus and Mary Chain's 'Some Candy Talking' banned by suggesting it was about drugs. It appeared that a select band of radio DJs and producers was effectively setting the agenda for the pop-obsessed press who pounced on any hint of scandal in the music world. The mass hysteria of Britain's self-appointed moral majority was almost tangible.

Ironically, many items far more offensive than 'I Want Your Sex' had passed by the critical ears of the careerist DJs who basked in the cult of personality and chose to pass ill-advised judgements on issues well outside their juris-diction. Frankie's 'Relax' had been performed on *Top of the Pops* before Mike Read twigged the sexual connotations and in high dudgeon took it upon himself not to slip the disc onto his turntable (though today the record is being used, with hardly an eyebrow raised, to advertise sun-tan oil). And latest pop sensation Transvision Vamp celebrated their first Top Ten hit last year with a single, 'I Want Your Love', which has gone out on children's TV and daytime radio with the line 'I want your fucking love' changed to 'I want your funky love' which still sounded uncannily similar.

In America the Parents' Music Resource Centre was gaining ground each day, getting records and magazines withdrawn from shops and stamping its jackboot on the morality of a nation. But the PMRC was busy venting its spleen on devil-worshipping heavy metal acts and 'I Want Your Sex' was met with a rather saner response than at home, though even without the association of a national *cause célèbre* it scaled the pop charts. MTV welcomed the promo, and the advocacy of sexual fidelity was more than acceptable to American ears. Curiouser still, 'I Want Your Sex' was banned from an Oregon radio station on religious rather than moral grounds, because of the supposedly sacrilegious line 'I don't need no bible, just look in my eyes.' It was the first time a record had been banned from American Catholic radio stations since the Singing Nun had been taken off the air. A few righteous stations did remove 'I Want Your Sex' from their playlists because of its lyrics while one, WZGC, cannily edited out the offending three-letter word and spliced in the world 'love' from elsewhere in the lyrics. George's American label swiftly latched on to the unnecessarily sanitized substitution and distributed this edition to the more moralistic stations.

Although 'I Want Your Sex' made number one in various US charts, it only reached the runner-up's spot in the authoritative Billboard Chart, because their positions were based on a collation of sales and airplay, and George's limited but unbanned exposure adversely affected the latter poll. It was given an added boost, though, by its appearance on the soundtrack of the Eddie Murphy vehicle, *Beverly Hills Cop II*. George was not averse to this kind of media tie-in; his earliest assaults on the American consciousness were helped when 'Wham! Rap' was featured heavily on the soundtrack of *Perfect*, which starred his idol John Travolta as the roving *Rolling Stone* hack uncovering the aerobics phenomenon. None the less, 'I Want Your Sex''s American success confirmed that while he was still shaking off an image as some kind of bastard offspring of Donny Osmond in England, he was beginning to be taken much more seriously across the Atlantic.

Being banned was probably the last vestige of rock and roll rebellion that George could aspire to. The blanket ban on the video gave George the opportunity to become benevolent pop progenitor and rebel rolled into one when he personally underwrote the costs of the video so that it could be sold – certificate 15 – for little more than the price of the twelve-inch single.

During the 'sex' controversy, George revealed that his attitude to relationships had undergone a considerable reassessment since 1985. Just before his twenty-second birthday that year he had spoken frankly to Tony Parsons in *The Face*, saying what most twenty-one-year-olds would say, particularly before AIDS broke through: 'My honest view is that if you can actually find someone who you can be faithful with then you're a lucky bastard . . . I don't believe that fidelity is all it's cracked up to be. I think if your girlfriend or husband or wife or whatever is screwing other people on the odd occasion throughout a marriage or a relationship they get into a situation where somebody's throwing themselves at them. If they're sleeping with that person because they are not getting what they want from you then you've got problems. If they are just sleeping with that person because they're curious sexually and they can't control it – or not that they can't control it but that they don't want to control it – then I don't think there is any big problem.' Two years on, AIDS had dramatically altered the traditional recreational habits of pop stars. Groupies were *persona non grata* even for those that, like George, had been rather less discriminating about their sexual partners in the past. If nothing else, George Michael is a superb pragmatist.

After five years of the media game George was the first to realize that its power could be harnessed to his own advantage. Having seen 'Relax''s explicit sexual directive help to make it one of the biggest selling singles in history in 1984, George now could not resist playing up to the media rather than trying to calm the storm. The last thing he wanted now was to be ignored. 'I Want Your Sex''s rakish undertones stirred up interest in George's sexual preferences. He spoke relatively freely about why he had never denied being gay. Firstly he reminded readers that he had taken a leaf out of Bowie and Jagger's book and claimed to be playing around with the idea of sexual ambiguity to maintain people's curiosity, once again emphasizing the appeal of media manipulation. His second reason was more pertinent to the current pop climate. Why should anyone have to prove their sexuality one way or another once they get into a position of public renown? He closed his pronouncements fatalistically: 'Besides, what's the point of denying it? If people want to believe it they will. Sexuality is a totally private thing and it should always stay that way.' In any event, his videos continued to portray and unconsciously sanction traditional heterosexual relationships in a decidedly reactionary fashion.

The controversy over 'I Want Your Sex' smacked of hypocrisy run riot that perhaps could only be understood by grasping the sociopolitical mood of the day. Only in a country where the Government of the day was canvassing for a return to Victorian values could something as simple as a pop record ignite such a steamy heap of disgust. As the *Independent* was swift to remind us, the BBC as ever was run by tittering ex-public schoolboys with nothing better to think about than smut. The reaction to 'I Want Your Sex' echoed absurd notions about class and morality in Britain in the 1980s that were riddled with double-think. Besides, in the light of recent political scandals involving MPs Cecil Parkinson and Harvey Proctor, it appeared that the cupboards in the corridors of Westminster concealed more skeletons than pop could ever aspire to.

With a General Election fixed for 11 June the upper classes appeared to have been forgiven their indiscretions as the Conservative Party returned for a third term in power. Lobbied by the press on his political preferences, George was well aware that slogans carried more weight than policies, and had reduced his support for the Labour Party to the one simple issue that had captured his vote four years earlier: 'Because of their promise to unilaterally disarm nuclear weapons.' It seemed to be the only belief he had retained from the Wham! years.

When the dust settled around his own battles, George came out a clear victor, sustaining a socially observant profile where he managed to advocate sex but condemn casual sex. The lines between good and bad had been clearly drawn: 'Sex is not the enemy, promiscuity is.'

In tandem with his solo career, George was still collaborating with others. Having helped to revive Elton John and David Cassidy's careers by singing on their records, his attention turned to Andros Gorgiou, whose band Boogie Box High released their version of the Bee Gees' classic disco strut, 'Jive Talking' in July.

Although it was strenuously denied, it did not need Sherlock Holmes to work out who had supplied the tight-trousered vibrato vocals in the background. The clues, strategically leaked to the press like the contents of some Government White Paper, soon added up. The perpetrator of the single, Andros, was George's club-running cousin. George's father is Andros' godfather. Guitarist on the record was Nick Heyward, last sighted supporting Wham! at Wembley, and also signed to publisher Bryan Morrison. But confirmation must have been in the choice of song;

after Elton and Cassidy it looked as if George's childhood heroes were all returning to haunt him. *Saturday Night Fever* clearly still burned bright in George's memory. Uncannily, when the Bee Gees returned to the charts later that year with 'You Win Again' it was vocalist Barry Gibb, sporting wavy brown hair on his head and chest and a neatly trimmed beard, who looked as if he had modelled himself on George.

During the Top Ten success of 'Jive Talking', George awoke one morning to read that 'George Flees Mrs Rocky'. To his consternation he had refused a date with Brigitte Nielsen, Sylvester Stallone's estranged cantilevered wife who was reputed to have expressed an interest in the entire line-up of Boogie Box High that was not strictly musical. The tabloids were still a double-edged sword for George. He did not shy away from the publicity which maintained his profile, but was acutely aware of the lengths they would go to concoct a story out of less than nothing. But George was not going to let the press run his social life, and turned up for the Limelight club's first birthday party on 15 July. His supposedly oafish behaviour at the deconsecrated church earlier in the year appeared to be forgotten as he made his entrance, complete with entourage, late in the evening. This was no longer the George Michael discreetly frequenting one of his favoured haunts, but George Michael bathing in the glow of fame. He could only hope that in time the less attractive media obsessions would run their course.

By the end of July he had succumbed to the ultimate lure of superstardom, reputedly paying out £1.43 million – in cash – for the obligatory mansion close to his parents in Hertfordshire. The Howard Hughes of pop still kept tabs on his outgoings. A £25,000 home gym meant there was no necessity for public flexing of his well-tanned biceps at the health club, but pride of place went to his very own solarium, purchased at a snip in the Harrods sale. In the competitive world of luxury goods it was reassuring to know that decadence could still be bought at a knock-down price.

According to the *Sun*, George had now notched up six house purchases (as well as a seven-seated Cessna Citation worth £3 million). There was his £500,000 apartment overlooking Harrods in Knightsbridge, a £350,000 mews house in St Johns Wood, a beach-front pad valued at £350,000 in Newport Beach near Los Angeles, a Soho love-nest for £80,000 and a place on the Portuguese coast, also costing £350,000, as well as his Hertfordshire pile. There was a grain of truth in this story. It could be safely assumed that George was no longer living with his family.

On the eve of the solo album début came 'Faith' the single in October. The accompanying image that stretched from record sleeve to press shot to video marked the unveiling of George's new look; his youthful gaiety was replaced by his distinctly adult concept of what a star should look like. From his broad-shouldered customized leather jacket and sunglasses down to his silver-tipped black leather pointed cowboy boots he looked as if he had walked into Johnsons outfitters in the King's Road and said, 'Make me look like a rock star'. The chic shrink-wrapped strutting cliché complete with rebel pout on permanent loan from James Dean was not altogether successful; George looked like a well-preserved forty-four-year-old trying to dress like a twenty-four-year-old rock star. George had never been the best of dressers in the past – although his fondness for billowing white shirts and cummerbunds was finally behind him – but now there was an air of tackiness that no amount of expenditure could halt. This was a young man suffering from a severe case of delusions of adulthood. A deep tan and rictus pout made him look as if he was in pain; perhaps his *Top Gun* aviator shades were riveted to his ears.

But George was back in the public consciousness all over

again. The look was a ludicrous collage of camp – one which echoed the mock rock of the song – yet high streets everywhere seemed to be sprouting pallid imitations of this figure, complete with solarium shine, pompadour quiff and wiry stubble.

That month *The Face* carried an in-depth interview with George Michael. Turn to page 43 of the same edition and you do a double-take: '5,874–0 in 60 seconds,' screams the stylish advertisement beside a picture of a neatly trimmed stubbled face. Rather than plugging a speedy sports car this was promoting another essential accoutrement of the designer age, the electric razor. And on closer inspection the chin belongs not to George but an anonymous model. Phrases like 'designer grip' and 'contoured rib' make something as simple as the Braun electric razor sound like some yuppie contraceptive essential for the smooth running of your sex life, while 'high performance . . . cruise' alludes to the traditional ad analogies between cars and women. Fast cars/fast women have now been joined as essential adjuncts to the glamorous life by fast razors. With one of these you too could be mistaken briefly for George Michael. Weekend stubble was all the rage, the kind of casual off-duty look removable for the office. The difference for the public face of George was that he had to keep his on full-time, it was a part of the image that earned him his living every bit as much as any songwriting talent.

For this reconstructed rock and roller, it was not surprising that the single was devised as a rockabilly pastiche, pilfering a Bo Diddley acoustic guitar riff and the basic feel of Elvis Presley's Sun sessions. Although 'Faith' reached number two in England (and eventually number one on the Billboard charts) the edifice seemed so unnatural and out of time that the sum total ended up coming across as an out-take of popcorn rock revivalist Shakin' Stevens. Perhaps the album would make amends.

The release of *Faith* the album in November 1987 signified

George's graduation party as it jostled for attention that week with emotional outpourings from other distinctly adult performers bracing themselves for the Christmas push. Pop was rapidly turning into a business of grown-ups making music for grown-ups. Professional lounge lizard Bryan Ferry returned to the fray with 'Bête Noire'; ex-Beatle George Harrison's refreshingly upbeat 'Cloud Nine' was his first recording for a number of years. The band that Jazz Summers had wanted to take under his wing, the Eurythmics, seemed to be faring pretty well without him, promoting the eclectic 'Savage', while guitar virtuoso Ry Cooder catered for all discerning rock connoisseurs with 'Get Rhythm'. Rising to the challenge, *Faith* demonstrated George's ability to dabble in studio boffinry with the best of them, playing around with his vocals and using the latest technology. At the same time he came across as a traditional dyed-in-the-wool songwriter, with a soupçon of cynicism, sounding in places like a graduate of business school rather than rock and roll's school of hard knocks. It was a shrewd mix of playing brilliantly safe and market-crossing diversification that helped the LP beat down the opposition and enter the UK charts in pole position. *Faith*'s reign at the top of the UK charts was a brief one, but in America it was a different story. Reaching number one across the Atlantic in January 1988 it loitered around the top spot, returning to it twice, in the process achieving the longest ever period at the top by a British solo artist.

Faith opens ominously with a brief glimpse of the past seen through contemporary mores. Before the opening title track a fleeting funereal coda of 'Freedom' can be heard, this time played on a cathedral organ; no wonder critics pondered erroneously the idea of the protagonist as a born-again Christian. In fact 'Freedom' sounds like nothing more than the 'Wedding March'. Would *Faith* mark a premature slip into middle-aged cosy monogamous stability for George?

There is certainly a refreshing blast of adult intent in his tackling of serious issues for the first time. Occasionally he even seems to be psychic. 'Hand To Mouth' reportedly attacks Margaret Thatcher for 'turning the UK into little America', showing how Britain is becoming as violent and uncaring as the US. Not only does the song inadvertently refer to October's Stock Market crash which happened after the recording was finished, but also to an American murderer, commenting on the growth of indiscriminate violence and lax gun laws. That August, two weeks after the song had been completed, an incident much closer to home in the town of Hungerford stamped its macabre identity on the song in Britain. The opening lines 'Jimmy Got Nothing made himself a name/with a gun that he polished for a rainy day/a smile and a quote from a vigilante movie/our boy Jimmy just blew them all away', took on a whole new frame of reference. *Faith* was bursting with messages. If not necessarily proselytizing, George had certainly shifted from the hard-bitten hothouse of hedonism of old. But more than anything else, *Faith* was undeniably aimed at an American market.

As the title suggests, *Faith* is stained with religious imagery, leading commentators to the lazy conclusion that George had got God, his ever-present crucifix earring only serving to compound erroneous comparisons with evangelical evergreen Cliff Richard. On the contrary, George was using religion and the idea of *Faith* in a considerably more abstract and ambitious fashion. *Faith* represented 'hope and optimism', his mood of the time – he remarked that the songs were a result of the last two years of his life. They charted his cleansed, refreshed and recharged outlook following his darkest hour. Its diversity of style certainly reveals it as the work of a man with catholic tastes. He had turned against the provisional title of 'Kissing A Fool' in favour of something that echoed his discovery of the strength of the opposing forces of good and evil that had battled out within him. The track of the same name survived, however, as a shuffling piece of supper club fake jazz that stands up only in terms of its parodic appeal. The weakest track is the sloppy rock-out 'Look At Your Hands', co-penned by George's faithful spear-carrier, David Austin.

In many respects *Faith* is as much a curriculum vitae as a manifesto; it shows what George is capable of across the board, but in terms of pop appeal he seemed to be underselling himself; there is simply nothing as celebratory and carefree as Wham!'s finest moments; typical of his solo career, George was taking himself far too seriously in an effort to escape his irresponsible upbeat roots. He could be a smooth balladeer, a soulful libertarian, a recidivist rocker, but he seemed to have lost his sense of fun as well as his sense of funk. This was a world away from Wham!'s candyfloss confection of pastiche. In an attempt to shake off the past he had perhaps strayed from his most natural proclivities. Above all, *Faith* is an album of public and private examination (the latter most surreally exemplified by the cover which features a broody George in leather jacket apparently sniffing his right armpit).

The only thing *Faith* has in common with his past canon is the criticism of similarity which he once more defended as the accidental by-product of his listening habits. If this was the case he had certainly broadened his tastes since his youth. Apart from the bubblegum rock of the title track, George had riffled through the stylistic directory of, among others, Prince, Stax-era soul and jazz. George Michael certainly stamped his own indelible print on top of each tonal template. At the end of the day, the best thing one could say about *Faith* was that it was recorded in the style of George Michael.

Stylistically George had followed the simple dictum of divide and rule. He had learnt from Michael Jackson and more particularly Prince that jumping between the polarities of pop not only helped one to cross over to different demographics but it also provided a moving target to keep him one step ahead of his critics. It was the right time to diversify; now more than ever before rock and pop was fragmenting. As cultures clashed, collided and interbred the global village was taking shape. Hip-hop and reggae were cross-fertilizing, as was rock and disco. Even George's once-beloved soul-boys were divided between the lush balladry of the successors to Marvin and Smokey, Luther Vandross and former Prince sidekick Alexander O'Neal, and the harsh raps of Run DMC and the Beastie Boys. Pop was crying out for someone who could pull all the strands together again and George's splintered soul was his attempt to accommodate that.

A side effect of *Faith*'s release was that Andrew Ridgeley's first solo single 'Show Me' had to be delayed. More than ever Andrew Ridgeley was becoming a sideshow in a pop world dominated by George Michael.

The real test was America. Wham! had only really had one hit album there and a historic but short stadium tour. *Faith* would tell George if the Americans wanted more than just a consolidation of Wham!'s success. George wasn't interested in maintaining his position, he wanted more. In America George had to breach that adult pop market, so jealously guarded by the cartel of Springsteen, Madonna, Jackson and Prince. But at least in America he did not have to enter into battle with the tabloids; with success almost worshipped as a religion, there was no credibility gap to be plugged; even Wham!'s success had been essentially on their musical merits after the fuss over their early MTV showings had died down. *Faith* was George's bid to match Michael Jackson's epochal *Thriller* album and spawned an endless stream of hit singles. He was soon to be challenged in a pre-Christmas head-to-head battle with Jackson's long-awaited follow-up, *Bad*. The least worried people were Epic Records, responsible for the release of both of them. Convinced of the adult tenor of *Faith*, George made the ultimate challenge to his detractors in *Rolling Stone*: 'If you can listen to this album and not like anything on it, then you do not like pop music.'

George put the case for the much-derided pop as an art form in itself, trying to revive a golden era in the sixties when Motown and the Beatles ruled the charts *and* retained their critical credibility: 'People have this perception that if all you write is pop music, as opposed to something that reveals a far deeper character, it's because that's all you can do. Not because it's all you choose to do, and not because it's the area you love. Somewhere along the way pop lost its respect. And I think I kind of stubbornly stick up for all of that.'

The launch party for *Faith* eclipsed even Wham!'s bacchanalian soirées. The usual catalogue of stars turned up at the Savoy Hotel on Hallowe'en for a bash liberally estimated to have cost Epic £100,000. Latest mediacrat to bathe in the cult of personality was Jonathan Ross; even television presenters have an aura of pop stardom about them these days. In a survey in the *Sunday Mirror*, George and the suave, streetwise Ross were proclaimed to be the two main symbols of appeal in an article about male bimbos – himbos – men 'able to melt a girl at a single glance' with their flashing teeth and tans. Past masters, including Rod Stewart and Omar Sharif were, according to the report, past it. Perhaps the fact that Ross was the latest client of publicist Gary Farrow had something to do with his and George's mutually extensive exposure.

Faith did more than anything before to pigeonhole George as the yuppie of pop. Much to his chagrin, the right of centre *Daily Mail* championed George as the role model of 'Thatcher's Youth'. Putting the establishment jackboot into the idealistic hippy movement, it informed its readers that these days kids want style and material goods and are going for it: 'Free love and communal poverty are out.' George was the symbol for everyone to aspire to. To journalist Gill Hudson he tried to play down his role as golden guru: 'I honestly don't think I'm a fascinating person.' A nation remained unconvinced. In *Blitz* he confessed that normality was the secret of his success: 'People think I'm going to be such an arsehole it's not difficult to give them a real surprise. I just have to be myself.'

Meanwhile, back at the party, Elton John arrived with wife Renata, while other guests on the rent-a-celebrity circuit included homely brothel-keeper now star 'Madame Cyn', Cynthia Payne, TV AM presenter and duchess of dullness, Anne Diamond, the ubiquitous Bob Geldof and Paula Yates and *EastEnders* soap star Anita Dobson. Inside various alcoves jazz and classical bands provided live music, while one never had to strain one's ears too hard to hear *Faith* forever floating around the catacombs.

Christmas approached for George amid a reputed mael-strom of excess. The *Sun* reported with glee how he had spent £6,257,000 on presents for family and close friends that year. In contrast Tommy Eyre, musical director on the China Tour, had been given just a souvenir programme and £3 T-shirt as a memento. He had even had to pay for his own gold disc for playing on *Fantastic*. George bought sister Melanie a BMW 320i for £14,000, duplicating the one he had given his mother the year before. His father was presented with a Rolls-Royce while Kathy Jeung was honoured with a £17,000 Toyota Celica. If reports were to be given any credence he could afford it. Eighties money madness was summed up when *Money Magazine* published a league table of the two hundred richest people in Great Britain. The Queen came top with a fortune of £3,340m; Bowie had a mere £13m ahead of George. But George knew his money was still pouring in; Bowie had peaked. George confidently predicted that by the end of 1988 he would have overtaken the *passé* Bowie, but he was swift to emphasize that it was not his main objective: 'I wanted to become a star to satisfy my ego, not so I could buy flash furniture.'

On 29 December the third single was drawn from the

Faith album. Perhaps George had learnt his lesson well following 'I Want Your Sex'. 'Father Figure' saw him swallowed up by more controversy over the video when the steamy bedroom gymnastics had to be cut for *Top of the Pops*; commercial television's short-lived response *The Roxy* chose to show an oblique one-minute excerpt of director Tony Scott's pocket-sized epic. In the post-Yuletide vacuum the single stalled at number 11 in Great Britain but George could console himself with the fact that the accompanying LP was padding out Christmas stockings up and down the land. And more significantly, it was by now rapidly climbing the American Billboard charts.

In spring 1988 the BPI Awards once more confirmed George as Best Male Vocalist. By now he was the last remnant of new pop's old guard. Frankie, Duran Duran and Boy George were fading fast; George's new rivals Jackson and Madonna were not eligible for the British awards. Instead there was a new flock feverishly trying to follow in his footsteps. Scottish soul pretenders Wet Wet Wet were declared Best Newcomers, while the Pet Shop Boys graciously received the award as Best Group. But these were acts firmly rooted in teen pop and presented no real challenge to George now. The only act that looked like a threat was the American Terence Trent D'Arby, the lithe Anglophile who collected the best International Newcomer Award – the only award open to all comers – who had shrewdly taken an amalgam of Michael Jackson, Prince and James Brown as his role models. A more typical recipient of the teenypop beanfeast was the insignificant Rick Astley, the teenager who had gone from being production wizards Stock, Aitken and Waterman's teaboy to their latest puppet protégé in twelve months. His single 'Never Gonna Give You Up' was honoured as Best Single of the Year but as he walked on to collect it, the live broadcast cut to The Who, reformed yet again just for this orgy of industry backslapping. They had apparently stipulated that they had to do three songs on air or they would do none at all. In a frenzy of confusion the end of the show was a shambles, leaving Astley bewildered in the middle of the arena, but notching up useful publicity for Pete Townshend and Co.

But England was becoming less rewarding for George. There seemed to be little left to challenge him in what resembled a shabby seaside resort populated by fading bit-parters. Rather than bother himself here for so little respect his eyes were set across the Atlantic, where his talents would be more warmly welcomed. Unwittingly he echoed his early mentor Mark Dean, whose sights were also set on the opportunistic paradise across the Atlantic. He had identified the fundamental difference between the two nations when he realized how positive the American philosophy was: 'In England I'm known as the man who lost Wham!. In America I'm known as the man who discovered Wham!.'

13

Faith

Is George Michael really Mr Clean?

In an age where success breeds excess and stockbrokers are cocaine fiends, frequenting toilets euphemistically dubbed powder rooms, can George Michael really be so pure? Admitting to a promiscuous past during the first flushes of success he has shown that he too was prone to the temptations of his occupation. Sexual impropriety however is clearly consigned to the past. George now chooses his friends carefully and his sexual partners with considerably greater caution.

Cocaine and Ecstacy are the only vices he admits to trying. Coke was not to his liking: 'I got a bit ill and a bit depressed.' Recoiling from the experience he said he would never indulge in it on a regular basis because he valued the shape of his nose too much. Back in the last days of Wham! cocaine was sometimes used by some of his entourage, employed by them as an extremely decadent aid to slimming to help maintain that essential wasted rock and roll physique. George would rather work with drug-free people but it is a damning indictment of the music business that many of the best exponents are habitual drug-users; profits invariably disappear up nearby noses. Having started out as a star virtually straightaway, George has tried to buck the system and keep an inner circle that eschews use of drugs. This puritanical streak, and the fact that he did not serve an 'apprenticeship', has led to George's isolation. But if there is one thing George fears more than commercial failure it is a real scandal breaking. It might not damage his sales but it would damage his soul; and the bigger he has become the more distrustful and paranoid he has become. At times it has seemed as if every time a friend needed their roof repaired they would sell a titbit on George. Why not? the moral argument runs, the paper would make up a story anyway. But the result is that George has turned further inwards, tightening the knot on the close-knit group of friends that he feels he can trust.

Most press encounters over the last five years have been gentle preambles before the question about the 'obligatory homosexual experience'. As a result George can handle the question better than most of the interviewers. At best they have been known to lull him into a false sense of security; one reporter smuggled the question in so casually that, he recalls, George was 'clearly embarrassed' by it. But generally he is too assured, too cautious today actually to let anything slip about anything that he has not decided to divulge in advance. Because of its elusiveness (probably because it is non-existent) that gay angle haunts the press more than it haunts George himself. For a while there was a reputed £50,000 'contract' out on getting a story on George's sex life. The precise payment supposedly varied on a sliding scale depending on the numbers and sexual permutations of his partners. The fact that there have been no takers reaffirms the care with which George selects his partners.

There have certainly been plenty of coded clues laid along the way to give the press food for thought ever since he first appeared in archetypal gay clone leather and Levi's and talked of 'choosing to cruise' in 1982. By then, of course, gay culture had infiltrated general street fashion through the rise of disco; camp as he was, and still is, George's sartorial influences were derived from the West End club scene rather than the underground culture.

Pat Fernandes appears to be a grey figure in George's sexual past. Where Kathy Jeung has been described as

George's new love (albeit a strangely long-distance one), Pat Fernandes tended to be captioned as his companion when she was snapped with George, an unusually restrained description in a press that was eager to trap George in any kind of sexual imbroglio, used primarily so that the right-wing press were not seen to condone a multiracial relationship. But Fernandes had been a long-time platonic friend of Boy George, in homosexual parlance a 'fag hag'. Very early on in George's rise she switched allegiance, hanging around with him when Wham! were little more than the Bushey gang getting legless at Steve Strange's Club For Heroes. Swiftly inveigling herself into his inner circle, Fernandes spent a great deal of time at the Panayiotou residence, striking up a close friendship with George's mother and going on lavish shopping sprees with his sisters. She was a cause of much early friction between George and Andrew, the latter never really enjoying her company.

It has become a regular pastime to speculate on the sexuality of people in the public eye, from pop stars to ultra-macho heavyweight boxing champion Mike Tyson. It seems that the least likely the personality, the more the press wants to point the finger. Public figures make so many appearances in our homes via the television, for instance, that we want to know everything about them. After all, we don't want complete strangers coming into our house every evening, do we?

One can get obsessed by the questions and start to look for answers that fit the desired solution. What was the real reason behind his fierce loyalty towards Andrew? Is his overtly macho image in *Faith* designed to suppress his feminine side? One can indulge in cod-psychology until the cows come home: what effect did the fact that his mother dominated his early years while his father worked all hours have on him? What about his virtual suffocation by his two over-indulgent elder sisters? Was there any significance in the fact that one of his first girlfriends was

Lesley Bywaters, who shared the same first name as his adoring mother? Oedipus would have a field day, but the questions remain tantalizingly inconclusive. Speculation sells papers, and George has not failed to notice that papers sell pop.

Why should George worry about disclosures regarding his sexuality? His remarks that he wanted to play on his sexuality like Bowie and Jagger were merely flannel, a way of parrying awkward questions. Being gay has not harmed his friends Elton John and Freddie Mercury, either commercially or artistically. But times have changed since the tolerant seventies. The chill factor of the homophobic backlash has yet to be felt. Clause 28 has now become law and has yet to produce a test case but its principle of banning anything that might promote homosexuality could feasibly be stretched to cover records by openly gay performers. Where others have come out in protest against this potentially draconian measure, George seems quite content to be portrayed by the media as profoundly heterosexual. His legs-and-lingerie-draped videos have hardly served the cause of feminism well. George does have a deeply reactionary view when it comes to the representation of women, an issue he does not seem prepared to grapple with; it is something that he does not even seem to see as political. He would rather equate politics with simple, emotive issues such as nuclear war.

This kind of vote-winning sloganeering has been indicative of one of the dichotomies of George Michael's decade. Live Aid demonstrated that pop has finally come of age and accepted adult responsibilities, but the benefit concert has now become another marketing tool. The second AIDS show in 1988 was cancelled due to lack of support, seemingly because its star pulling power was undermined by the globally broadcast Mandela Day Concert scheduled a few weeks later. It seems that anyone is prepared to support any cause as long as the TV rights have been sold. It is not just a matter of supporting a cause but being seen to be doing it by consumers, and the more the better.

Having projected a suitably acceptable image onto the public psyche, George now wanted to prove himself as a performer; one on a par with Jagger, Jackson and the Beatles, people whose legendary status had been established long before the advent of video. The Faith Tour was to be the safari that would leave George Michael's imprimatur on the world, and make Wham!'s achievements look positively second division. Planning the itinerary George's attentions focused on one territory in particular: 'I've been building up to this for five years. My ego needed to prove that I could do in America what I've done in England.'

The 150-date tour kicked off in February 1988 on the other side of the world; Japan was a sensible place to start. George knew he had a mandate there when *Faith* was voted Album of 1987. He also knew that Japanese audiences were some of the most well-mannered in the world. The show at the 11,000-seater Budokan Theatre would have to be an unmitigated disaster for them to respond negatively.

In many respects Japan lagged behind the West in its grasp of rock and roll. Their belated economic boom had created their own swinging sixties twenty years on and the population was still experiencing its first liberating rush of exhilaration from Western pop acts, and did not seem that fussy about authenticity. Mick Jagger had been able to take an anonymous line-up of session musicians there and rake in the yen by running through old Rolling Stones hits simply because the audience had never had the chance to hear them live before.

For George, the tour was both the best and the worst part of his job. He described performing as the second-best experience one can ever have, but the numbing horror of daily life on the road was another matter entirely. George still wanted some time to be Georgios Panayiotou; for the duration of the tour he had to be George Michael twenty-four hours a day. Needing close, trusted friends around to feel comfortable and to help him relax, whenever possible he would fly home between dates.

Touring became a prison. He was surrounded by an entourage that at the end of the day were not even workmates but employees reliant on him for their livelihood. There was little rapport between George and the band, who expressed a distaste for his hidebound moral uprightness. Professionally they had little contact and offstage they had little in common; the band's ideas of fun centred on the rock and roll antics that George had come to despise.

Realizing the magnitude of the tour, George had finally succumbed to bringing in a high-powered management team, the formidable American duo of Michael Lippman and Rob Kahane. The Sunset Boulevard based company's best-known clients to date were producers rather than artists, ranging from composer Giorgio Moroder to the man largely credited with discovering Madonna, pop star *manqué* Jellybean Benitez. Lippman and Kahane's typically American forthrightness made Simon Napier-Bell look quaint by comparison. They swiftly began to give their new client the archetypal superstar treatment which George resented but was convinced was a neccessity. The key to their treatment was distancing George. Even Connie Filippello discovered the tightening of the lattice-work of bureaucracy that had to be negotiated before she could gain access to the star. Only his personal assistant Siobhan retained the hotline to George.

Security was a necessary measure now as George prepared for the big time. Even during Wham!'s heyday George had had some nervous moments with uninvited guests. In America, once, a fan managed to talk her way into his room with a story about her father having died. George reacted sympathetically and tried to be hospitable, but while she was chatting she referred to her father and it became apparent that he was very much alive. George politely but firmly threw her out.

Another time in Adam and Eve Mews he had answered the door's videophone not realizing that he had pressed the entry button. Moments later he came in from the kitchen with some toast to find a six-foot-two girl in his lounge. The shock of the meeting suddenly hit her and she passed out. George managed to wake her but it was too much for the awestruck fan; all she kept mumbling was 'You're real, you're George Michael . . . you're real,' while touching his arm to confirm her suspicions. George did his best to put her at her ease, making her tea and sitting with her for a while, but as soon as he could he eased her gently back into the reality of the street.

Death threats were one of stardom's occupational hazards in the decade ushered in by Lennon's assassination. As more and more people wanted a piece of George Michael, his management was not prepared to let him take foolish chances (as much for the protection of their own positions as their client), and on tour he was now constantly in the company of fearsome man-mountain minders. Even at the height of Wham!'s success George would go to the Wag Club in London for a night out unmanned; now that was out of the question.

George's dreams during nights of fitful sleep on tour offered snapshots of his perennial insecurities. His rest would be punctuated by visions where he would hear himself being announced onstage while he was in the bar and he would not be able to find the way onstage. By the time he had negotiated the labyrinthine corridors of the nameless theatre he would arrive on the stage to find the audience leaving. On other nights his dreams would consist of turning up unprepared for what he expected to be a rehearsal only to find that it was the actual gig and that he did not know what he should be playing or how to play it. It seemed that there was a burning guilt about his position, as if he knew he had not worked hard enough to deserve it and one day he would be found out. Perhaps the pop gods were paying him back for not paying his dues. He started to have more premonitions of his own mortality and an early death. Scrape away the greasepaint and prise off the dark glasses and George was not a wholly happy man. His constant fears of the press discovering some non-existent career-shattering scandal did not help matters; they had brought down Boy George, would he be their next target?

A George Michael Tour would not be complete without the British press tagging along. In Japan they soon found something to get into a self-righteous lather about when they saw George's show. Apparently the Japanese authorities had deemed it 'too sexy' and had instructed George to cut out the more explicit moves. The *Sun*'s Rick Sky had little difficulty filing this story – it was identical to the story he had filed during his service with the *Daily Star* when Wham! played in China. The press reported that the Japanese feared he would trigger off an AIDS epidemic. Rather than good old rock rebels causing riots in the streets one man and his hips would cause a collapse of sexual restraint. In fact the tabloids displayed a singular ignorance of Japanese sexual morality. Although there was an air of squeaky cleanness, Japanese attitudes to sex were far more complex than first met the eye. Violent pornography was rife; there was even a heroic comic character called Rapeman who punished criminals of all sexes by raping them: sex was an issue far more complicated than the press were prepared to confront. The *Sun* was keener to indulge in their favourite pastime of Communist-bashing by 'reporting' that George had refused an offer of a Russian tour because he could not be guaranteed a constant supply of solariums to top up his tan.

The audience had little grasp of English but loved George. Sold on his conventional sexy rebel rocker image as a direct contrast to Boy George's camp eccentricity they embraced his larger-than-life pop caricature. His off-the-peg Western classicism combined with his quintessential crotch-thrusting might have seemed ripe for a Las Vegas cabaret season to the trained European eye, but here they could not get enough of it. Backstage George's personal travelling chef (George has travelling chefs and trainers like ordinary mortals have travelling clocks) prepared his roast potatoes, chicken and salad while his personal trainer relaxed with the thought that so much running about on stage would mean fewer work-outs during the days. Although the weight problem still haunted George, he certainly looked slimmer and better toned up than during the latter days of Wham! when he had taken to wearing elevators in his shoes onstage to help him look taller and better proportioned.

'Exclusive' took on a new meaning in Tokyo when the *Daily Star*'s woman on tour Annette Witheridge told her loyal readers how poor George was suffering because the 'shallow pop scene is just tearing him apart'. In yet another 'exclusive' she catalogued the circumstances that were causing George so much heartache. 'He hates the shallow showbiz circle that he's been catapulted into. He has never enjoyed going on the road. On tour he is tense, tetchy and miserable. He no longer enjoys writing songs and working in the recording studio. *And* [their italics] he is furious about a spate of totally untrue stories that have found their way into newspapers.' George as usual had given no interviews to the tabloids, but Ms Witheridge went on to inform her constituency that various stories had come her way; that George was forsaking pop for films but had turned down the role in *Madame Butterfly* because it was too sexy, and that girlfriend Kathy Jeung gave up a £250,000 Hollywood career to tour with George.

She may have been rather economical with the truth in her reportage but it was quite possible that these stories were emanating from an official source. George's PR person, Connie Filippello, happily admitted to making up stories about another client, singer Sinitta, to bolster her public profile, and under Nomis's guidance, similar tactics had originally been used for Wham!. The *Star*'s reporter claimed she had been fed stories about George weeping on his opening night because Andrew was not there, how he had found himself in the middle of an earthquake when going up in a lift to his hotel suite . . . the mind had never been so boggled. Clearly George's refusal to talk to the tabloids since the China tour had not stopped him from being a regular feature of their news pages. But George's press officer was not totally to blame; there was a regular bounty for any stories leaked out of the George Michael camp and his team were tempted to pump out fictions for cash.

The scale of the tour began to take its toll on George. In the arid climate of Australia he started to suffer from throat problems and he recuperated in Hawaii, meeting up with Elton John and Andrew Ridgeley. And if his throat was not the problem it was his back. What appeared to be a congenital problem forced him to suspend tennis for the tour, one of his few pleasurable recreations. His back had plagued him sporadically since his youth (uncharitable critics might have said that carrying Andrew for four years did not help it) and he had exacerbated the situation during one of Wham!'s drunken nights when in spirit of adolescent high-jinks he had injured himself by hoisting a friend onto his shoulders. His hectic lifestyle prevented the spine from hardening, and healing up properly.

The Faith Roadshow's media blitz had reached saturation point by 12 April when George opened the European leg of the tour with a press conference in Rotterdam. In the converted aircraft hangar above the Ahoy Stadium where he was due to play six hours later, he reluctantly faced his critics.

Typically, George was not giving much away to the two hundred members of the press, nor to MTV and the satellite stations who had dutifully turned up to cover the occasion. That unwitting parody of the archetypal elusive star in leather motorcycle jacket, ubiquitous shades in the bright spring afternoon shielded his eyes. An explanation for the sunglasses was offered as he mixed his metaphors in a cryptic opening gambit: 'If you saw my eyes you'd know I was lying through my teeth.' One was reminded that in an earlier revealing aside he had actually said that he could not even remember what it was like to be honest.

The conference was laid on for the Continental press but the organizers did not allow for the herdlike instincts of the gentlefolk of the UK press, who were soon sighted barging their uncouth way to the front. There was little point barring them since they would cover the tour anyway. Eternally optimistic if fetchingly naïve, George thought that they might just write something decent, honest and truthful for a change if they had some direct quotes.

George set out the parameters of the meeting with his tints firmly fixed on the Anglo-Saxon contingent: 'What I'm not here to do is make a series of denials into speculations about my private life.' As superficial chatter ensued he appeared to have evaded any serious probing. The Continental press seemed to combine the docility of lapdogs and a command of English matched only by their command of forelock-tugging sycophancy as they hung on George's every pronouncement as if it was carved in stone.

As the final question was invited, the *Daily Mirror*'s Gill Pringle asked George with as much insouciant charm as the unctuous blonde reporter could muster if he had had an AIDS test. Caught off guard, George replied no. While the Continental press passed over the titbit, George awoke the next morning to find himself starring as the lead item in the tabloids, each one managing to devise an uncannily similar story about how the superstar millionaire would not have a test because he lived in fear of AIDS. All from one word.

The Ahoy was the first venue big enough to accommodate the onstage cage especially designed to contain the group before opening up dramatically for the duration of the show. Meticulous planning had mapped out the show like a military manoeuvre, but as soon as George stepped onto the stage he realized that preparations had been too thorough. The floor had been so efficiently polished that he had to curb his fleet-footed routines to avoid sliding over. The star's precarious stance apart, the packed arena was seduced by the note-perfect performance.

Playing to a packed house dominated by vocal teenaged females (but with a respectable adult contingent too, of both sexes – even with Wham! they had been a not insubstantial silent minority), he fought a losing battle to be heard above the constant cry of 'We love you George'. His solution was to encourage the noisy crowd to sing along at other points in the hope of silence during the ballads. 'Faith' became a near-a cappella number with the audience providing the deafening chorus before George closed the proceedings with a defiantly raunchy encore of Labelle's 'Lady Marmalade', grinding his pelvis into the small of co-vocalist Lyn Mabry's back.

The sound of the band was good and tight. Too good and tight in fact. Behind the scenes a Synclavier computer, programmed to reproduce some of the bass and drum sounds from the album, had been employed, allowing the musicians to concentrate on affecting their favourite rock poses. Symptomatic of the artifice of eighties pop, the ultimate in live shows turned out not to be a live show. At least George was singing for real. This was all a long way from the humiliating ill-conceived miming of the Miners' Benefit of yesteryear. As for those early disco PAs, they seemed like somebody else's life to George.

Relations with his band were limited by now to a forced jollity. Behind his back they called their glorious leader the Bubble with the Stubble (as in bubble and squeak, rhyming slang for Greek) and Stavros (after comedian

Harry Enfield's all-conquering kebab-owner). Neither was intended as affectionate, the musicians making sure the epithets were not employed in George's presence. Strained relationships had made for a regular turnover of employees over the years. But with lucrative salaries, personal chauffeurs and as many groupies as their post-AIDS conscience would allow them the team tried to be on their best behaviour. In return George did his best to turn a blind eye to their chemical indiscretions.

George's distanced predicament as employer is one shared by all stars, but as a solo performer he now had no close professional friends; Andrew Ridgeley had at least cosmetically dissipated some of the power balance. His closest companions now were his ever present Strepsils throat lozenges. Occasionally he would pay for an old pre-stardom friend to fly out for a few days, but he stuck to the same close friends. Acquaintances from Bushey Meads had been difficult to retain. It was the old paradox of the star returning to his local pub; if you buy a round of drinks you're a flash bastard, if you don't buy a round you're a tight bastard. Except that George's predicament was magnified to the nth degree.

At the same time, George was intent on maintaining a clean-cut public image, making it publicly known that he had sold off his shares in a company when he heard that they were involved in selling arms to the Contras in Nicaragua. Less publicized was his discreet support for a sit-in protesting against education cuts at Middlesex Polytechnic. But he continued to invest his money for the best returns when he could have approached brokers who deal on the market for ideologically sound organizations such as Greenpeace which deal exclusively in politically credible commodities. As a walking billboard George was constantly assailed with offers of sponsorship and he eventually inked a lucrative deal with Sony to endorse their brand name.

The European leg of the tour coincided with the release of

another single from *Faith*. 'One More Try' was the funereal ballad that echoed George's pleading, confessional mood of 'Careless Whisper'. In England interest in George's records seemed to be waning. Any fans had the album by now, and with the B-side 'Look At Your Hands' also drawn from *Faith* they had little incentive to buy the single. Indeed, it only reached number eight, poor by Wham!'s standards.

In America, however, George's inexorable rise was signalled by 'One More Try' 's pursuit of its predecessors, as it reached the top of the Billboard Charts. It also marked George's arrival as a bona fide soul star when it reached the top of the black R&B charts too.

On 29 April, as the tour edged ever nearer to its England dates, the *Sun* soared way past even its own sleazy, cancerous credos with a histrionic headline 'The Poofs Of Pop'. This was one piece Connie Filippello presumably had not initiated. In a barely held back hysteria of homophobic bile Rick Sky and Kevin O'Sullivan regaled their readers with a top ten of records by gay artists or bands including gays, accompanied by a prominent picture of George in rapt conversation with Boy George. The list, based on sales figures, included Frankie's 'Relax', 'Two Tribes', 'Bohemian Rhapsody' (Queen's Freddie Mercury had been the subject of recent gay slurs following a friend's death from AIDS), Culture Club's 'Do You Really Want To Hurt Me', David Bowie's 'Space Oddity', Soft Cell's 'Tainted Love', Bronski Beat's 'Smalltown Boy', Elton John's 'Rocket Man', The Village People's 'YMCA' and Culture Club's 'Karma Chameleon'. Judging by the calibre of the acts the piece ought to have been giving thanks to the gay contribution to pop but instead used the chart to vilify the homosexual community. Despite the prominent photograph of George, he did not feature in the chart.

In an attempt at some kind of justification for the piece, and as a spurious demonstration of their insight, they used this current glut of gay stars (ignoring the fact that 'YMCA', 'Space Oddity', 'Bohemian Rhapsody' and 'Rocket Man' were all virtually antediluvian hits) as the explanation for the recent profusion of female vocalists, such as Tiffany, Debbie Gibson and Kylie Minogue. There were not enough red-blooded male singers for young girls to lust after so instead they were buying records by females, whom they could at least model themselves on. In a flagrant piece of quote-pilfering George was reported as saying, 'It doesn't benefit anyone listening to my music to know if I was in bed with a man, woman or dog last night.' For once George's trenchant refusal to comment on the issue was justified amid the *Sun*'s anti-gay propaganda.

More health problems forced German dates to be cancelled and prompted rumours of drug-taking in the George Michael camp. Categorically denying any pill-popping, give or take the odd Strepsil, George abruptly flew to a Harley Street specialist in early May to check his health and to allay press paranoia about throat cancer each time he coughed. Inevitably the problem turned out to be pop's equivalent of athlete's foot, nodules. Everyone seemed to get them, from Siouxsie Sioux to Annie Lennox to Elton John, because of the strain of touring on an untrained voice. In the past, George had had a few singing lessons to discipline his voice but he had given them up, bracing himself instead for the inevitable strains. In the past he would go offstage for what were ostensibly costume changes, but in fact he would be breathing pure oxygen from a cylinder to revitalize his voice.

For a while the tour was in jeopardy but George was determined to see it through to the end in America in November, vowing however that he would never embark on something so ambitious again. He knew that having proved his Olympian stature like this he would hardly need to.

As the tour rolled relentlessly on, George left a trail of broken records behind him. In May *Faith* became the first album by a white solo artist to reach number one on the American Black Albums chart. Since the seventies disco era there had always been a few pale-skinned crossover acts but he was the most successful to date, even surpassing the achievement of his idols the Bee Gees, the group which had topped the black charts with *Saturday Night Fever* a decade earlier. In America, his record company Columbia chose to release a remix of 'Monkey' as the next single. This was particularly aimed at the same urban black audience, being remixed by Jimmy Jam and Terry Lewis, ex-members of Prince's backing band the Time, who as producers had since guided and gilded the soulful careers of, among others, Janet Jackson, the Human League and Alexander O'Neal.

Even though 'Monkey' was released to coincide with his Earls Court dates – and the inevitable onslaught of media half-truths – it only managed a semi-dignified scramble to number thirteen. Despite its driving, vivid funk backdrop, 'Monkey' was a lyrically insipid exercise for George. The dons of the Bodleian Library were hardly likely to analyse George's lyrical output at the best of times, but with glib lines like 'Why can't you set your monkey free?' he was plumbing depths of triteness not visited since the days of 'Wake Me Up Before You Go-Go'. In America, none the less, it was a different story; the febrile remix helped George to top Billboard's Hot 100 yet again.

That June there were more things going on in England than just pop. The country seemed to be awash with designer-labelled vandals breaching the peace of suburban beauty spots at pub-closing time each evening. Christened lager louts by the press their standard-bearer appeared to be comic creation Loadsamoney, the character developed alongside Stavros by comedian Harry Enfield. What was intended as a diatribe against hollow consumerism had turned into a Thatcherite totem itself – the sickest joke of all. Loadsamoney the plasterer seemed to have no redeeming features at all; no interest in culture except for its cost, he was only interested in money for money's sake. It was an attitude echoed by Fleet Street as it slavishly catalogued the lifestyles of the rich and famous – George's presents to his family, his gifts for friends, a breakdown of the cost of each car he purchased and emphasizing the value of each house he snapped up.

Of George's five sell-out London dates at Earls Court, Saturday 11 June is a special occasion. Throughout the day there has been a different kind of concert going on at Wembley Stadium; pop's interface with politics has come into sharp relief with the celebration of the seventieth birthday of jailed black South African leader Nelson Mandela. The audience – like George's – seem to be there more for the spectacle, the music and the social occasion than any deeper message. At Wembley, as each group takes the stage, their respective fans battle to the front to catch a closer gimpse of their idols. Dire Straits flags comfortably outnumber anti-apartheid banners. In England the BBC broadcasts the event with as little focus on the anti-apartheid banners as possible so as to remain apolitical and the artists have been asked not to mention the cause while in America the show is broadcast as the Freedom Festival and sponsored by Coca Cola; any residual political content – the show's very *raison d'être* – is edited out with a comprehensiveness that Goebbels would have envied.

Having played its part in the closing of one chapter in George's life when Wham!'s farewell concert coincided with the anti-apartheid concert on Clapham Common, apartheid has become an issue close to his heart and a happy coincidence in his tour schedule has enabled him to sing at the Mandela gig in the afternoon before heading the few miles south to Earls Court.

11 June 1988 was a day that summed up the decade. After the naïve idealism of Live Aid this was the day that career promotion and conspicuous compassion went hand in hand. Following Sting, George was the second

star to appear. Decked out in sombre black and shades, George chose to pay homage to his influences rather than plug *Faith*. Greeted by ear-splitting applause he performed Marvin Gaye's 'Sexual Healing' and Stevie Wonder's 'Village Ghetto Land', two choices which served to place him within a compelling maelstrom of horny intent and social concern. The day rolled on with the likes of the Eurythmics, Whitney and Cissy Houston and Dire Straits and some real soul from a supergroup of Freddie Jackson, Joe Cocker, Ashford and Simpson, Natalie Cole and the legendary Al Green. Where George Michael had been applauded and cheered on, the saintly Reverend Green was barely recognized by the youthful pop-saturated British crowd. Considering the motivation behind the event, it was a distasteful but not altogether surprising irony that a white soul singer was virtually deified by the crowd while one of the black guiding lights of soul remained virtually anonymous.

The Nelson Mandela Concert showed that in the late 1980s pop may be grown up but it has also grown safe. In the same way that rebellion in society is the purely cosmetic insurgency inspired by beer and bravado, so there is no room for rebellion in the charts today. For the first time since the war, there is no manifestation of the real seeds of rebellion among the disenchanted, who have been ground into submission under nearly ten years of Thatcherism. Instead conspicuous consumption has become a way of life. What better symbol of this decade of decadence than George Michael? A single-minded individualist; a champion of self-motivation. As touted by the merchandising stalls outside the arena, posters of George capture his sun-kissed rockin' James Dean look.

This evening massed Tannoys herd everyone into the Earls Court hangar as George's lean, loyal bassist Deon Estus shamelessly attempts to launch his own solo career by providing the supporting slot for his employer.

While Estus grinds through some mild-mannered funk the Campari and lager concessions do a roaring trade and toilet queues increase accordingly. The crowd is an amorphous mass, a school assembly on the scale of the Nuremberg Rally. There are a few George Michael clones but no real identifying style except a kind of pasty pastel eighties summer High Street look, all pink vests, court shoes, cheap gold, bleach and denim. The occasional Janet Jackson lookalike poured into circulation-cutting jeans turns heads, but the general mood is more downbeat and dull. These are the legions of lonely suburbanites that once briefly counted George Michael among their ranks. Eventually the glow of the green lasers turns into the five symbols on the album sleeve which signify the five most important things in George's life: music ('I'd rather write a song about my private life than talk about it'), money, love, faith and religion.

On the stage the big cage begins to open. Its crisp, simple white lines certainly beat David Bowie's corny and colossal Glass Spider of 1987. Opening up, out pops George Michael, furiously running across the stage and up the side ramps as 'I Want Your Sex' opens the show. His daily four-hour work-outs with his trainer are about to be severely put to the test. For someone who considers himself an adult performer there is going to be some serious bum-wiggling tonight.

It isn't long before he puts in a political word about the afternoon's events: 'This country's stand on South Africa is a fucking disgrace,' giving the tabloid contingent the four-letter outrage story that is enough to guarantee him a front page tomorrow as long as a royal birth, death, marriage or sneeze does not occur.

At the side of the auditorium one young girl has indulged in her own special George fantasy. With her Walkman headphones and £5 souvenir programme she has improvised an *ad hoc* pair of blinkers. As she faces the stage and follows the frantic figure racing across it, everything else is blocked out. For just one evening, she has her own private audience with her dream date George Michael.

Repeating the Amsterdam formula, George works through an alternating pattern of slow and fast numbers. Employing a smattering of Wham! songs to bulk out his slim solo catalogue, 'Faith' is performed a cappella with the audience invited to join in. His voice is in excellent form, but his dancing strikes an alarming dissonant note. Far more than ever before he seems to be trying really hard to be sexy. Too hard. For instance, during 'Monkey' he takes his jacket off and does a gawky disco strut. There is plenty of effort, plenty of sweating and running, but one can't help feeling that beneath all that perspiration there is an ambitious young man grunting away and trying to be Michael Jackson or Prince. Instead his gymnastics make the show reek of hackneyed cabaret. George may indeed have a potent white soul voice but in his presentation he rather over-reaches himself. There is little of Michael Jackson's extra-terrestrial uniqueness. None of Prince's metaphysical exposition of James Brown's finest steps. The bulk of the audience appear to have left their critical faculties at the door, granting him as many cheers for his bottom, pointed in their direction during 'Hand To Mouth', as for his well-mannered vocals during 'One More Try'. Taking his jacket off gets as many screams as his songs while rubbing his groin destroys a few thousand larynxes. In England at least George Michael is a sex symbol first and a songsmith second.

As important as George's British dates were to him, he now faced the biggest challenge of all. If his career so far had all been leading up to this tour, then this tour had all been leading up to America. Before the crucial 46-date American leg he managed to take some time off to rest his voice. Over the months it had taken a considerable pounding; that combined with performing an identical set every night was beginning to take its toll on George and he needed a break from performance, however brief, before he made the final ascent.

If George's post-Wham! record sales reflect a downturn in his popularity in the UK, the American leg and ensuing hysteria that followed the Faith tour tells a different story. Towards the end of Wham!, success became just a blur of figures – thirty-eight million in record sales, a hundred worldwide number ones, a place in the Top Twenty in *Forbes* magazine's chart of highest American earners – but in the second half of 1988 George Michael has experienced the kind of success in America that has eclipsed everything he has done so far. Today George is every bit as popular as Michael Jackson, and effectively on the strength of one album. Wham! clearly laid the groundwork in the United States, but nothing could have prepared George for the success of *Faith*. When George talked about his forthcoming solo LP he spoke in alarmingly self-confident terms about an album that would have ten hit singles and outsell Michael Jackson's *Thriller*. In England George's singles have fared relatively badly; in America *Faith* has spawned five consecutive Billboard number one singles (six but for 'I Want Your Sex' not getting comprehensive airplay), a record matched only by Michael Jackson. If in Britain George is suffering from growing pains and currently facing that difficult limbo between scream star and adult superstar, America has had no such qualms about taking George seriously. *Faith* has already notched up sales of fourteen million.

George is ripe for American success. Selling bleached soul back to the country it originated in, he is the right colour, the right sex, he has created an image that is every bit as identifiable as Springsteen's blue-collar rocker's jeans and checked shirts. The Americans still have a residual love for British pop, which George can churn out in abundance, but he can also deliver a more sophisticated form of adult funk. In England his music falls between two stools, being a bit too adult for the mass teenage market but not authentic enough for the serious soul merchants. Here he is having a certain amount of difficulty plugging a credibility gap that doesn't even exist in America.

George could end 1988 a happy man. Mark Dean's portrait of him is as fitting a tribute as anyone can provide: 'George is a very focused individual. He predicts where he wants to be in a year's time and he is always able to make it. Fame is the drug which drives him on to be the biggest star in the world.'

But still only twenty-five, how does he view his future? He appears to have reached the point of no return; the point where the likes of Madonna and Prince cease to be real people and become myth. George, however, seems too human to succumb to that fate. George's solo success in America has been his major achievement. He has effectively wiped the memory of Wham! out of the public consciousness. He still has a little way to go in England. It was George Orwell who said: 'He who destroys the past controls the future.'

The inevitable film offers have already flooded in. So far he has resisted them all. Inside that taut frame there still lurks the chubby teenager worried about his appearance. George knows that behind that exquisitely tended beard are the full cheeks he can never quite shed. If he offers himself up to a director he knows they will want more than his good side. Of all the late eighties stars George keeps the strictest control of his image. Of late he has even taken to directing and editing his own videos in an attempt to gain complete control. As few photographs are released as possible. Fifteen months on from the release of the *Faith* album the dutiful Connie Filippello was still sending out pictures from the same photographic session.

So far George has made himself synonymous with the eighties. Success for its own sake drives George on. He shuns the idea that he does it for money. He is happy to accommodate those trappings – the Mercedes, the artillery of Armani, collecting houses like others collect stamps – into his public persona. He happily waxes lyrical over the constant upgrading of his hi-fi system. Deny it as he might, he has a need for material security as much as his once-poor father; the manifestations of his wealth are merely his way of reminding himself of what he has achieved. Consumption has become an expression of his identity: 'I'm not a possession-orientated person, but I swear if I lost every penny tomorrow I'd be rich again within two years. Even if I couldn't do it for myself. Writing songs is my bank.' But what George has tried to do is avoid the airs and graces that surround the music industry. While the band made sure that their contracts assured that they had personal chauffeurs and Bentleys and Jaguars on call, George drives himself to video shoots, albeit in his Mercedes. If he is by common consent considered incredibly astute for a pop star, it says as much about the lack of intelligence in the business as it does about George.

This swirl of fame has certainly made George grow up fast. At twenty-five, he has the undeniable air of the young fogey about him. From the start his precocious production and arranging abilities set him apart from his contemporaries. Inevitably he felt more at home with established artists such as Elton John. And his disdain for rock and roll is one of his more endearing facets. But despite his ostensible self-assurance, insecurities still linger. Here is a man with the nerve and confidence to pull six singles from an album, yet when he drives around town he still pays attention to what releases record shops are advertising in their windows. These are the contradictions that continue to intrigue.

George Michael is the first superstar of the decade to make the leap from teen idol to adult star. Many have tried; few have succeeded: Adam Ant, Boy George, Duran Duran, Curiosity Killed the Cat. Bob Geldof got a knighthood more easily than another hit record. The list is endless. Bros tried to cross this particular Rubicon, and despite looking to the George Michael method for their rubric they failed miserably. No British pop act has achieved success on the scale of George Michael. The Nineties loom in the distance. Will George have a place there? What place does he want?

Epilogue to the paperback edition

Extreme Prejudice

If nothing else is true in the illusory world of pop, it's a fact
that dreams can come true. George Michael knows this.
As Christmas 1990 approached the ugliest boy in Bushey
spent his time with the five most beautiful women in the
world. George Michael was making the video for his single
'Freedom 90' and, tired of seeing his own mug plugging
his records, he decided to get some models in for some
hi-tech mummery.

Among the cast were Richard Gere's girlfriend Cindy
Crawford, who could be seen luxuriating in a bath, Naomi
Campbell, 'the black Bardot', Linda Evangelista, Tatjana
Patitz and Christy Turlington. Their combined fees for the
shoot came to an estimated £300,000, more than the single
would be likely to make. In a snappily edited sequence,
the cast lip-synched to the jaunty, house music style track,
while George was nowhere to be seen.

Once more, George became embroiled in a censorship
row à la 'I Want Your Sex'. At one point in the clip, Cindy
Crawford's nipples peeked out from her folded arms. For
a nanosecond. MTV asked for the offending protrusion to
be edited out, though in Britain, despite tabloid tittle-tattle
to the contrary, broadcasting watchdogs at the IBA did not
ask for any amputations. Also contrary to the impression
left by the papers, George was not solely responsible for
the video. It had been directed over five days in a warehouse
in Morden, Surrey by David Fincher, who in the past had
made Madonna's promos and was about to start shooting

the feature-length *Aliens III*. For once, however, George's thunder was stolen by Madonna. Her clip for 'Justify My Love', complete with lesbianism, kinky voyeurism and raunchy rumpy pumpy was also cut, but by the time the offending articles had been excised there was only about a second of videotape left. Both videos were saucy, but if Madonna's was *Last Tango In Paris*, George's was *Carry On At Your Convenience*. All that condensation suggested not so much heated passions as the fact that George had spent so much money on his cast that he could not afford a decent plumber.

1989 had been a quiet year for George; spent recuperating from the Faith Tour, recharging his neurons and ganglions for another bout of recording, and going for long walks on Hampstead Heath with his Labrador, Hippy. He lived in his north London hideaway which his mother came to clean for him. In America his lifestyle was similar, quietly living in Encino, California. It was also a year of squash and self-assessment, as he embarked on an autobiography, working in cahoots with famed angry young journalist of punk Tony Parsons. Like the indulged child he had once been, George was getting what he wanted, untold stardom, well-publicized riches, but still he wasn't satisfied.

George spent much of the time beneath the parapets, occasionally surfacing to scotch rumours about his growing Garboesque agoraphobia and about his ongoing trysts with Pentagon blonde, Fawn Hall, last heard of helping out action man Oliver North. He made an advert for Diet Coke, directed by filmmaker Stephen Frears, which topped up his coffers to the tune of a reputed £3 million. The ad, which gave George plenty of acreage but barely mentioned the gluggable product, was only shown in the USA. He was originally scheduled to appear at the Knebworth Charity Show, where he would have been the token twenty-something among a line-up of Collins, Clapton, Robert Plant and various assorted veterans, but recording commitments forced him to withdraw.

In fact, in the early part of 1990, Andrew Ridgeley was actually more visible than George. After withdrawing gracefully from his motor racing career, Ridgeley was back in England. He had two things to say to the world. The first was that he had a solo record out. It was called 'Shake' and it was awful, a neanderthal slab of raunchy heavy metal that Bad Company might have knocked out on a dark day in the mid-seventies. It flopped. He was also announcing the launch of his restaurant in Rickmansworth. Ridgeley was heading the way of other deposed champs, John Conteh, Bobby Moore, Geno Washington, and going into the leisure industry in a modest way. It was certainly a more sensible option after the panning that his album received.

George's Love Me Love My Dog lip-buttoned period soon ended with the release of *Listen Without Prejudice Volume 1* in September. The title itself immediately screamed two things: that George wanted to be judged on musical merits and not on his past catalogue of press clippings, and that this was just a first instalment. The follow-up to *Faith* had been through numerous rumoured incarnations. George was initially said to be playing every instrument on it. A double album. A single album of smoochy tracks followed by a single album of dance tracks. Two versions had already been scrapped. The possibility of a jazz album. Maybe a session of gaelic ceilidhs would be leaked out at some point? The two-album theory was the most likely and also presented a neat analysis of George's divided soul: the twin pulls of commercialism and art, the intellectual versus the hedonist, part Rodin's Thinker, part Emma 'wild child' Ridley party animal. Back in the Wham! days the schizophrenia was solved by Andrew Ridgeley taking on the characteristics George wanted to suppress but in Andrew's absence the crisis was at its most acute. The end product (with a second half slated for '91) was a more conventional two-sided album presenting the many moods of Michael. The main thing that symbolically set this record apart from *Faith* was that George's familiar profile was nowhere to be seen on the front. Instead the cover featured a classic black and white shot of an amorphous 1940s summer crowd having fun in the sun.

Apart from the singles to date, 'Praying For Time', 'Waiting For That Day' and 'Freedom 90', the album was full of ups and downs. A haunting version of Stevie Wonder's 'They Won't Go When I Go' was serious music *in extremis*, the stark setting echoing the spine-shivering effect of Billie Holliday singing 'Strange Fruit'. The lighter 'Cowboys and Angels' had a sixties film soundtrack feel to make sure that his fans didn't OD on despair. Similarly 'Heal The Pain' had a honeyed vocal to sugar the angst-in-the-stonewashed-pants approach. A great album that grew on you, it was a marked improvement on *Faith*, and it sold by the truckload. Released on 3 September, the record caused a stir but nothing like the impact of George's statement that he was going to stop doing interviews or videos. George was becoming precious in his endeavours to be taken seriously – and he also seemed to be developing that strange habit that superstars have of talking about themselves in the third person. 'If I can step outside the promotion and marketing of George Michael then that's the only chance I have of surviving as a successful musician.' The papers were pissed that he wasn't going to do interviews (lord knows why, they'd got on fine without him speaking to them in the past), and his record company were cheesed off by the absence of promos, particularly as their contribution to promotion costs amounted to an unusually high £1 per unit, in the form of £300,000 worth of TV, press and poster campaigns.

There were also less official forms of promotion. George's autobiography *Bare* garnered some advance publicity when a copy was obtained from Tony Parsons' agents by deception. This was particularly irksome to the *Daily Mail*, who had shelled out £250,000 for the exclusive serialization rights. The culprits were never apprehended and rumours were rife, with so many interested parties wanting to get a look at what George had to say. (In fact there was little in the book that hadn't been said before, just George reminiscing on stardom and its trappings, the hits, holidays and heterosexual close encounters.)

The first single off the album, 'Praying For Time', came out with little of the usual promotional paraphernalia. The lack of a video gave it little chance of being screened on ITV's influential *Chart Show*, and, unless George was prepared to hightail it to White City, a snowball's chance in hell of getting onto *Top Of The Pops*. In the circumstances there must have been a collective sigh of relief around Soho Square's Epic Records office when the record reached the Top Five on airplay alone. 'Praying For Time' was an unlikely first single off an album. For a start it was a slow song. So slow in fact that one initially wondered whether it was playing at the right speed. This was George, the son of a preacher man, the rich kid trying to come to terms with his own material success when so many in the world had so little. It was 'Let It Be', Band Aid, a party political broadcast on behalf of the George Party and 'Away In A Manger' all rolled into one great big hummable hymn. Just as Saint Bob Geldof was trashing his millstone by singing 'The Great Song Of Indifference', George was putting down his marker and claiming a halo. He even printed the lyrics on the sleeve, as if to say: "These are my beliefs and they are worth listening to." Unfortunately the wrong people listened. One of the downsides of the pacifist sermon was that the single was adopted by troops in the Gulf. Great for PR but war was not the kind of thing George wanted to be associated with. There would be no tours of the Middle East in the foreseeable future.

George might have been keeping mum but there were still plenty of outlets to see that he wasn't completely ignored. Most importantly there was a South Bank Show profile of George to tie in with the album and autobiography. London Weekend Television's prestigious arts flagship had chosen George as the subject of the first programme in a new series because, as presenter Melvyn Bragg nasally intoned at the beginning of the programme, George Michael was "the most successful pop artist of the decade". The aim of the programme was to assess him as a serious songwriter, skimming over the scandals of the past and focusing on George in baseball cap and Nike trainers in the studio and arranging the album. The programme failed to find any chinks in George's armour and instead made him seem like some puritanical hybrid of wunderkind Mozart and Benjamin Britten. George and Melvyn chitted and chatted but nothing of any great substance that hadn't been said before was revealed. Those still in favour in the George camp paid homage. Simon Napier-Bell (who refused to be interviewed for this book because it didn't have George's consent) was the most vocal but the most absent was Andrew Ridgeley: This was the rewriting of George Michael's history that the singer had been waiting for. Ridgeley was finally expunged from the past. This once-great arts programme seemed to have lost its teeth. It had never been known for baring them too harshly but in an effort to present George as worthy of such coverage Melvyn had to hang on George's every strained pronouncement. The problem was not so much that George was not a worthwhile subject, but that by kowtowing to George's requests that the programme should concentrate on his writing – and thus become the televisual wing of his latest bit of growing up in public – The South Bank Show completely missed the point. George may be a great writer but he is no Dickens (who was the following week's subject) and he may be a great singer, but the story of George Michael is really a story about pop music in the 1980s, its hype, hope, horror and happiness, and with unerring ease director Alan Benson seemed to miss the point. As if the exercise wasn't a cynical enough piece of television anyone who missed the programme could purchase it when it became commercially available on video at Christmas. You can rest assured this was done for George Michael fans rather than South Bank Show acolytes.

George's spurious anti-personality cult posturing found critics in high places. Frank Sinatra was simply astounded by George's approach and wrote an open letter to the *Los Angeles Times* telling him so. One of the all-time greats – both as singer and publicity manipulator – acknowledged George's gift and urged him to untense those shoulders and, in a belated attempt to squeeze into *Private Eye*'s Pseud's Corner, 'Dust off those gossamer wings and fly yourself to the moon.' The critical crooner continued, "Talent must not be wasted. Those who have it must hug it, embrace it, nurture it and share it lest it be taken away from you as fast as it was loaned to you . . . Come on, George. Loosen up. Swing, man."

The second single off the album was 'Waiting For That Day', released on 15 October. Here George showed he was not afraid to rock, liberally quoting from the Rolling Stones' 'You Can't Always Get What You Want' and probably referring to his own personal and professional frustrations too. As promised there was no accompanying video. What it coincided with, however, was an advert for the album, made by George but not featuring George that went out on TV. A man and a woman listened to *Listen Without Prejudice* and then took their clothes off and got ready for bed. You didn't need to be Freud to realize the implicit message here – listen to George Michael and you'll be raring for sex. Either that or after you'd heard this you'll be dying for a good long nap. This was from the man who wanted to be taken seriously? Slimline George wanted to have his cake and eat it. Par for the course the ad had to be cut when the IBA said you could see too much of the couple's bottoms.

By the end of 1990 George reneged on his plans to withdraw from 'dehumanizing' tours. The Cover to Cover tour was nothing like the global blanketing of Faith, concentrating on some big dates in America,

Canada and the UK but it was still the sound of an artist hawking his wares. There was even a one off – honestly – reunion of Wham! in Rio. There was also much talk of George having to buckle down and accept that even he had to go out and promote his product or the public would forget about him, but this didn't seem to bother George. Then again, it's hard to tell whether you've got a hunted look in your eyes when it seems as if you have a pair of Raybans spot-welded to your face. One can only extrapolate on past history to map out George's future. If that is any guide, he'll get everything he wants. The only problem is, like the spoilt child who got his tape recorder, drum kit, contact lenses and whims indulged by his parents, he'll then find out he wants something else.

Postscript

It's the Friday before Christmas as I'm finishing off this book. Over the road the local government building is having their office party. The music is so loud that it is difficult to work. By about 11.00pm I'm beginning to wonder when the non-stop disco frolics are going to end. Then a familiar record begins to reverberate. It's a sure sign that smooch time has begun and the party is winding down. Sure enough it turns out to be the last record. It is, of course, 'Careless Whisper'. Inside that building teenagers and fifty-year-olds are dancing to George Michael and making trysts and promises that they may later regret. When the recent singles had failed to top the charts I began to wonder if George Michael would last after all. I only had to hear 'Careless Whisper' once to have those fears allayed.

Discography

Wham!
Singles

'Wham! Rap (Enjoy What You Do)'/'Wham! Rap (Enjoy
What You Do)' (Club Mix)
Innervision IVLA 2442. June 1982.

'Young Guns (Go For It)'/'Going For It'
Innervision IVLA 2766. September 1982.

'Bad Boys'/'Bad Boys' (Instrumental)
Innervision IVLA 3134. May 1983.

'Club Tropicana'/'Blue (Armed With Love)'
Innervision IVLA 3613. July 1983.

'Club Fantastic Megamix'/'A Ray Of Sunshine' (Instrumental)
Innervision IVLA 3586. November 1983.

'Wake Me Up Before You Go Go'/'Wake Me Up Before
You Go Go' (Instrumental)
Epic A 4440. May 1984.

'Freedom'/'Freedom' (Instrumental)
Epic A 4743. October 1984.

'Last Christmas'/'Everything She Wants'
Epic GA 4949. December 1984.

'Everything She Wants' (Remix)/'Last Christmas'
Epic QA 4949. January 1985.

'I'm Your Man'/'Do It Right' (Instrumental)
Epic A 6716. November 1985.

'Last Christmas'/'Blue (Armed With Love)' (Live)
Epic Wham! 1. December 1985.

'The Edge Of Heaven'/'Battlestations'/'Where Did Your
Heart Go?'/'Wham! Rap '86'
Epic Fin 1. June 1986.

'Last Christmas' (Pudding Mix)'/'Where Did Your Heart
Go?'
Epic 650 2697. December 1986.

Albums

Fantastic (*July 1983*)
'Bad Boys'; 'A Ray Of Sunshine'; 'Love Machine'; 'Wham!
Rap (Enjoy What You Do)'; 'Club Tropicana'; 'Nothing
Looks The Same In The Light'; 'Come On'; 'Young Guns
(Go For It)'.
(*Innervision IVL 25328*)

Make It Big (*November 1984*)
'Wake Me Up Before You Go-Go'; 'Everything She
Wants'; 'Heartbeat'; 'Like A Baby'; 'Freedom'; 'If You
Were There'; 'Credit Card Baby'; 'Careless Whisper'.
(*Epic EPC 86311*)

The Final (*July 1986*)
'Wham! Rap (Enjoy What You Do)' (12 inch); 'Young Guns
(Go For It)' (12 inch); 'Bad Boys' (12 inch); 'Club Tropicana';
'Wake Me Up Before You Go-Go'; 'Careless Whisper' (12
inch); 'Freedom'; 'Last Christmas' (12 inch); 'Everything
She Wants' (12 inch); 'I'm Your Man' (Extended Stimula-
tion); 'Blue (Armed With Love)'; 'A Different Corner';
'Battlestations'; 'Where Did Your Heart Go?'; 'The Edge of
Heaven'.
(*Simultaneously released on gold disc in collector's box, with
T-shirt, notebook, pencil, calendar and numbered certificate.*)
(*Epic Wham 2*)

Solo
Singles

'Careless Whisper'/'Careless Whisper' (Instrumental)
Epic A 4603. August 1984

'A Different Corner'/'A Different Corner' (Instrumental)
Epic A 7033. March 1986.

'I Want Your Sex'/'I Want Your Sex' (Instrumental)
Epic Lust 1. June 1987

'Faith'/'Hand To Mouth'
Epic EMU 3. October 1987.

'Father Figure'/'Love's In Need Of Love Today'
Epic EMU 4. December 1987.

'One More Try'/'Look At Your Hands'
Epic EMU 5. April 1988.

'Monkey'/'Monkey' (version)
Epic EMU 6. June 1988.

'Kissing A Fool'
Epic EMU 7. November 1988.

'Praying For Time'
Epic GEO 1. August 1990

'Waiting For That Day'
Epic GEO 2. October 1990

'Freedom 90'
Epic GEO 3. December 1990

Collaborations

With Elton John
'Wrap Her Up'/'Restless'
Rocket EJS 10. November 1985.

With Aretha Franklin
'I Knew You Were Waiting For Me'/'I Knew You Were
Waiting For Me' (Instrumental)
Epic Duet 2. January 1987.

George Michael also contributed to Elton John's 'Nikita',
David Cassidy's 'The Last Kiss', Boogie Box High's 'Jive
Talking' and Deon Estus' solo album, *Spell*

Albums

Faith (*November 1987*)
'Faith'; 'Father Figure'; 'I Want Your Sex'; 'One More Try';
'Hard Day'; 'Hand To Mouth'; 'Look At Your Hands';
'Monkey'; 'Kissing A Fool'.
(*Epic 631 5221*)

Listen Without Prejudice (*September 1990*)
'Praying For Time'; 'Freedom 90'; 'They Won't Go When I Go'; 'Something to Save'; 'Cowboys and Angels'; 'Waiting for That Day'; 'Mother's Pride'; 'Heal The Pain'; 'Soul Free'; 'Waiting' (reprise).
(*Epic 467 2952*)

All singles were also released on 12 inch format. All albums are also available on compact disc and cassette.

All Pan books are available at your local bookshop or newsagent, or can be ordered direct from the publisher. Indicate the number of copies required and fill in the form below.

Send to: **CS Department, Pan Books Ltd., P.O. Box 40,**
             Basingstoke, Hants.   RG21 2YT.

or phone: 0256 469551 (Ansaphone), quoting title, author
             and Credit Card number.

Please enclose a remittance* to the value of the cover price plus: 60p for the first book plus 30p per copy for each additional book ordered to a maximum charge of £2.40 to cover postage and packing.

*Payment may be made in sterling by UK personal cheque, postal order, sterling draft or international money order, made payable to Pan Books Ltd.

Alternatively by Barclaycard/Access:

Card No. | | | | | | | | | | | | | | | | | | |

Signature:

Applicable only in the UK and Republic of Ireland.

While every effort is made to keep prices low, it is sometimes necessary to increase prices at short notice. Pan Books reserve the right to show on covers and charge new retail prices which may differ from those advertised in the text or elsewhere.

NAME AND ADDRESS IN BLOCK LETTERS PLEASE:

....

Name ————————————————————————————

Address ——————————————————————————

————————————————————————————————

————————————————————————————————

————————————————————————————————

3/87